MW01253345

The nascent field of Memory Studies emerges from contemporary trends that include a shift from concern with historical knowledge of events to that of memory, from 'what we know' to 'how we remember it'; changes in generational memory; the rapid advance of technologies of memory; panics over declining powers of memory, which mirror our fascination with the possibilities of memory enhancement; and the development of trauma narratives in reshaping the past.

These factors have contributed to an intensification of public discourses on our past over the last thirty years. Technological, political, interpersonal, social and cultural shifts affect what, how and why people and societies remember and forget. This groundbreaking series tackles questions such as: What is 'memory' under these conditions? What are its prospects, and also the prospects for its interdisciplinary and systematic study? What are the conceptual, theoretical and methodological tools for its investigation and illumination?

Jason James
PRESERVATION AND NATIONAL BELONGING IN EASTERN GERMANY
Heritage Fetishism and Redeeming Germanness

Emily Keightley and Michael Pickering
THE MNEMONIC IMAGINATION
Remembering as Creative Practice

Mikyoung Kim and Barry Schwartz (editors)
NORTHEAST ASIA'S DIFFICULT PAST
Essays in Collective Memory

Philip Lee and Pradip Ninan Thomas (editors)
PUBLIC MEMORY, PUBLIC MEDIA AND THE POLITICS OF JUSTICE

Erica Lehrer, Cynthia E. Milton and Monica Eileen Patterson (editors)
CURATING DIFFICULT KNOWLEDGE
Violent Pasts in Public Places

Motti Neiger, Oren Meyers and Eyal Zandberg (editors)
ON MEDIA MEMORY
Collective Memory in a New Media Age

Anna Saunders and Debbie Pinfold (editors)
REMEMBERING AND RETHINKING THE GDR
Multiple Perspectives and Plural Authenticities

V. Seidler
REMEMBERING DIANA
Cultural Memory and the Reinvention of Authority

Evelyn B. Tribble and Nicholas Keene
COGNITIVE ECOLOGIES AND THE HISTORY OF REMEMBERING
Religion, Education and Memory in Early Modern England

Forthcoming titles:

Owain Jones and Joanne Garde-Hansen (editors)
GEOGRAPHY AND MEMORY
Exploring Identity, Place and Becoming

Palgrave Macmillan Memory Studies
Series Standing Order ISBN 978–0–230–23851–0 (hardback)
978–0–230–23852–7 (paperback)
(*outside North America only*)

You can receive future titles in this series as they are published by placing a standing order. Please contact your bookseller or, in case of difficulty, write to us at the address below with your name and address, the title of the series and the ISBN quoted above.

Customer Services Department, Macmillan Distribution Ltd, Houndmills, Basingstoke, Hampshire RG21 6XS, England

Mediation at the Holocaust Memorial in Berlin

Irit Dekel
Postdoctoral Fellow, Humboldt University, Berlin

palgrave
macmillan

First published 2013 by
PALGRAVE MACMILLAN

Palgrave Macmillan in the UK is an imprint of Macmillan Publishers Limited, registered in England, company number 785998, of Houndmills, Basingstoke, Hampshire RG21 6XS.

Palgrave Macmillan in the US is a division of St Martin's Press LLC, 175 Fifth Avenue, New York, NY 10010.

Palgrave Macmillan is the global academic imprint of the above companies and has companies and representatives throughout the world.

Palgrave® and Macmillan® are registered trademarks in the United States, the United Kingdom, Europe and other countries.

ISBN 978–0–230–36330–4

This book is printed on paper suitable for recycling and made from fully managed and sustained forest sources. Logging, pulping and manufacturing processes are expected to conform to the environmental regulations of the country of origin.

A catalogue record for this book is available from the British Library.

A catalog record for this book is available from the Library of Congress.

Typeset by MPS Limited, Chennai, India.

In memory of my grandparents Shmuel and Rivka Weintraub

Contents

List of Figures

Acknowledgments

This book was written over the course of five years. The list of individuals and institutions that supported the research and writing is long for this temporal reason as well as for the many encounters, conversations, discussions and events that an ethnographic research entails. My first thanks are dedicated to my dissertation committee members at the New School for Social Research, who advised the research from which this project developed, and provided my intellectual growth with endless support, creativity and precision: Vera Zolberg, Jeffrey Goldfarb and Oz Frankel. Klaus Eder from Humboldt University in Berlin guided my early research and writing in Berlin, first as the DAAD host, and then my work on the book since. His theoretical clarity and sophistication, close reading and institutional support were invaluable both for writing the book and for my intellectual and professional development.

This book is based on a dialogue I was most fortunate to take part in around the opening, work, institutionalization and changes of the Holocaust Memorial in Berlin. I would like to thank Wofgang Benz, chair of the Center for Anti-Semitism Research in the Technical University in Berlin, and Wolfgang Kaschuba, chair of the European Ethnology Institute at Humboldt University in Berlin, for hosting me during my research in 2005–6. Memorial Foundation guides and workers were most generous and open in providing me with information, illuminating issues at the core of the site's work and discussing every topic I found interesting. Stefan Bamberg, my first and best guide to Berlin, has offered numerous conversations, materials and thoughts about the memorial, memory politics and guiding groups in it. Memorial Foundation director Uwe Neumaerker and Foundation pedagogue Barbara Koester were most helpful with any request and interest I presented to them and for that I am grateful. Foundation workers Daniel Baranowski, Anne Bobzin, Ulrich Bumann, Florian Kemmelmeier, Adam Kerpel-Fronius, Doron Oberhand, Daniel Ratner, Petra Schmidt-Dreiblatt and Gabriele Zuern have shared their perspective and readings, doubts and concerns, which helped me form questions and understandings of the site. Conversations, walks, correspondence wandering with them were fascinating encounters between persons, the city, their memories and mediations.

Many colleagues and teachers read and discussed book chapters and presentations with me. I would like to name a few but extend my gratitude to other readers, listeners and discussants in the three continents in which the research and writing took place: Nadine Blumer, Y. Michal Bodemann, Peter Carrier, Carola Dietze, Amos Goldberg, Don Handelman, Elke Heckner, Haim Hazan, Jackie Feldman, Yifat Gutman, Tamar Katriel, Shaul Kelner, Michalis Kontopodis, Anja Peleikins, Thomas Scheffer, Pnina Steinberg, Ilana Szobel, Heidemarie Uhl, Christiane Wilke and Gökce Yurdakul.

The research and write up of the project were supported by institutions and foundations in Berlin, the United States and Israel. The DAAD research fellowship supported the fieldwork in 2005–6. The New School for Social Research Dissertation Fellowship and the Memorial Foundation for Jewish Culture supported the dissertation write up in 2007–8. The Hebrew University of Jerusalem, Center for German Studies' individual research grant in 2009 allowed the development of my work on media in the site. The Minerva Short Term Research Grant in Berlin in winter 2010 and the DAAD returning Scientists Program in the fall of 2010 enabled the setting up of follow-up research, and the Fritz Thyssen Foundation Research Stipend in 2010–11 enabled its completion.

An earlier version of Chapter 1, 'Navigating Experience', has been published in 'Pan-topia: Exposing the Palimpsest of Meanings at the Holocaust Memorial, Berlin,' *History and Theory: The Protocols Bezalel Academy of Design* 14. I am grateful to the Bezalel Academy of Arts and Design, Jerusalem for their permission to use this work.

An earlier version of Chapter 4, 'Mediation at the Holocaust Memorial', has been published in 'Mediated Space, Mediated Memory: New Archives at the Holocaust Memorial, Berlin,' in M. Neiger, O. Meyers and E. Zandberg, eds, *On Media Memory*, New York: Palgrave Macmillan. I am grateful to Palgrave Macmillan Press for their permission to use this work.

As a post-doctoral fellow at the Sociology and Anthropology department and the Center for German Studies at the Hebrew University, I would like to thank Nachman Ben-Yehuda and Vered Vinitzky-Seroussi for their support. In the last phase of writing, as a postdoctoral fellow at the Humboldt Center for Social and Political Research, I was fortunate to discuss my work both with scholars from the Social Science Institute and with the memory and civil society colloquium, as well as fellows and scholars from the Center for Jewish Studies. A special thanks to Felicity Plester and the Palgrave Macmillan Memory Studies series editors for their support and belief in this project, open-mindedness and help in its publication process. I warmly thank Penny Simmons whose brightness and kindness made the book clearer and this last phase enriching as well as a pleasure.

I am grateful to my family, which grew in the years between dissertation completion and the book, and endured days and nights of writing and editing: to Ido who asked whether I had finished writing my book so that we could play more together, and Rona who was born just before the manuscript was completed. They both gave writing and thinking a deeper and more rewarding structure, for which I am grateful. To my partner, closest friend, first and last reader, Michael Weinman, thanks for the infinite support, theoretical discussions and humorous reflections, which made the writing at every stage a worthwhile pursuit. I thank my parents David and Leah Dekel, who stand perplexed in the site, fascinated as well as burdened by its shape and the shape of action in it; but while I take sole responsibility for the analysis it presents and hope that its discussions enrich our understanding of memory work and mediation I will not be able to tell them, any more than the readers of this book, whether this is the right way to remember the Holocaust.

Introduction

This book explores action in a newly erected site of Holocaust memory in the center of Berlin called the Memorial to the Murdered Jews of Europe. It examines the political implications of memory work in and around the site, and asks in what ways and to what extent the discourse on remembering the Holocaust in Germany affects action at the memorial, and how this action, in turn, recasts old and new discursive modes about the past and present politics in contemporary Germany. As the first ethnographic monograph written on the memorial, it offers an analysis of the tension between the experience of, and action in, the site, its aesthetics and the discussions around it.

The book articulates a shift away from traditional and established approaches to memorial sites in general and to this one in particular. Whereas studies of the memorial tend to focus analytically on the debates concerning its construction and operation, and its various proposed designs with their aesthetic, moral and historical implications from a postmodern philosophical and historical perspective, this book reads their accounts as building blocks to understand the memory discourse yielding action in the memorial, and is innovative in its focus on visitors and group experience along with that of guides and memorial workers. The novelty and importance of the central claim here goes beyond the originality of the research subject matter. It rests more substantially on the new theoretical approach to the interrelations between the site, its experience, aesthetics, and processes of mediation. Namely, moving away from the models of post-trauma, post-memory and secondary witnessing as the prevalent forms of memory transmission for those who did not witness the events of the Holocaust, this book introduces a new and more flexible model of performance, and thus a fresh approach to memory work. This model does not aim to homogenize the memorial experience within the pedagogical touristic setting that refers to the Holocaust as the original source of experience and moral authority. Instead, the focus on various performances is open to the precariousness and variations of memory work in the memorial, and asks how visitors actually engage with the *act* of remembrance rather than with the *object* of remembrance. Furthermore, this engagement is mainly with the ways others engage with the site and the codes of 'remembering' shaped in and by this and other sites of Holocaust remembrance in Germany and Europe.

This approach thus offers a move away from the question of witnessing with the survivors, into the realm of civic engagement. Participation in memory work is thus cast as an act of citizenship, defined both through the lens of the particular German experience of the site, but no less importantly, in cosmopolitan terms as well. By exploring these different forms of participation at the memorial, I shed light on and theorize the performed moral career of visitors. I thus do not assume positive or negative ethics in the act of memory. However, visitors and I could of course speak of right and wrong in going about the site, and this is precisely what is performed there: the judgment of moral and immoral remembrance. In place of this binary normative model of assessment, I have here developed a more nuanced sense of the process of memory work and of self-understanding, as performed in the act of remembrance and the reflection on that act.

I present and analyze the memorial as a touristy site, a kind of open museum, and as such analyze it as a social, economic and political institution, the experience of which stands in relation to memory work done in different sites, media and times by different groups. The memorial was opened in May 2005. It was built in the New Berlin (Till 2005), into a memory culture that had already discussed its own voids, victories and failures, and decided that abstractness suits it best (Young 2003). Since the memorial's concept was intended to complement other, so-called authentic, sites of Holocaust memory, it was decided that the Holocaust Memorial's focus would be limited to telling the story of Jewish persecution, 'from the victims' perspective.'[1] The site is experienced by individuals in and outside its confines in time and place. This is true of other memorials whose experience always exceeds their physical boundaries and the temporal confines of the visit. Unlike other such memorials, this one is abstract, invented and located not in a site of persecution, but instead on a large plot in the center of Berlin between the Brandenburg Gate and Potsdamer Platz (see Figure 0.1). This new characteristic of a Holocaust Memorial frames its disorienting

Figure 0.1 The *Stelenfeld*: Holocaust Memorial with the Reichstag building and Brandenburg Gate
Photo: Irit Dekel 2006.

and reorienting experience, which stands in contrast to 'authentic' memorial sites that are bound to a specific history which took place on its premises and in which, it is presumed, some approximation of the victim's voice can be represented (DeKoven Ezrahi 2004). Additionally, as opposed to other Holocaust Memorial sites, this is a 'place with no things' that bear direct relation to authentic artifacts, either in the form of holding and exhibiting them, or discussing their absence through remnants and documents. Like other Holocaust memorial sites, entrance to the site is free of charge. Educational programs are offered at reasonable prices and will be discussed in the first chapter.

Above ground, the *Stelenfeld* is a field of slabs on a 20,000 square meter plot, designed by architect Peter Eisenman of New York.

Underground, beneath the Stelenfeld, there is a small 'Information Center', or literally the 'place of information', built to clarify and complement the memorial above. It has four rooms telling the story of the Nazi persecution of Jews and was designed by designer and artist Dagmar von Wilcken. The installation focuses on individual fates and on the European dimension of the destruction of Jewish life. Its aesthetic concept, as introduced to me and as presented on the Memorial Foundation's website, is meant to complement and reflect the site above ground, which is achieved by a reverse reflection of the stones above ground in the Information Center. The relationship between the open 'field' above ground and bounded 'place' underground will be delineated throughout the book.

The Memorial Foundation uses materials in the Information Center which were taken from other Holocaust memorial museums like Yad Vashem and Lochamei Hagetaot in Israel, major and smaller memorials and documentation centers in Europe and the US Holocaust Memorial Museum. These materials have been reworked for presentation in the Information Center, and often new research was conducted by the foundation's historians. For instance, names from Yad Vashem's database of pages of testimonies were researched and more information was added about the lives and fates of individual victims for the reading of names and personal information in the 'Room of Names.'

The Memorial Foundation employs hosts, positioned by the Information Center's entrance, whose role is to assist in clarifying the memorial to visitors' and monitor order at the site. There is a security company which guards the site both above and underground with the aid of security cameras – the majority of which are located in the Information Center. The Foundation employs around 25 guides who give guided tours of the site above ground, hold discussion tours and lead workshops in two dozen languages. The guides usually have an advanced university degree in history, social sciences or pedagogy.

The majority of guided tours are held in German. According to the Foundation's statistics for 2010, 2087 educational programs were booked in German and 320 in English. The third most popular language in which educational programs were booked was French (79), while Italian and Hebrew each had around 20 booked tours or workshops that year. A survey commissioned by the Memorial Foundation, and conducted in the Information Center between 2009 and 2012, listed the following reasons for visiting the memorial: one-third of visitors to the Information Center stated the reason for their visit as being part of a group or class. About 20 percent came spontaneously (with or without a tour) and about 12 percent came 'to commemorate the victims.' The same number, about 12 percent, came out of personal interest in learning more about the Holocaust. About 40 percent came for 'other reasons.'

I conducted fieldwork in the memorial between fall 2005 and summer 2006, and returned to the site in the fall of 2010 for follow-up research which lasted about a year and included participation in guided tours and workshops, interviews with Memorial Foundation workers and with visitors. Additionally, my return to the site with the simple question 'how has it changed?' revealed new and developed forms of representation in postcards, booklets and posters. My analysis is based on my participant observations in guided tours, articles about the memorial in German newspapers and magazines, academic and popular literature on the memorial, and materials provided by the Memorial Foundation, such as educational plans and instructions, curatorship meeting protocols, statistical information about the Information Center visitor numbers and countries of origin, as well as the report of a commissioned survey of the Information Center between 2009 and 2011. In addition, I analyzed visitors' book entries between 2005 and 2010, interviewed visitors in German, English and Hebrew in and outside of guided tours, as well as all the permanent workers in the Memorial Foundation in 2006 and partially again in 2011. Interviews were recorded and transcribed. In the very few cases that the interviewee preferred not to be recorded or the background noise in the *Stelenfeld* made it impossible, I wrote the answers and do not cite them directly.

What I found interesting in the memorial comes from my critical position as a sociologist, US-trained, born and raised in Israel. I understood the memorial as a site that invites all forms of actions, interpretations and engagements that are new to memorials and thus also shift what one can do with interpreting the relations between memory and politics today. In 2005–6, I saw the memorial as a site for exploration, not culmination, of identity; be it national or international, and as such shared by its workers and visitors alike (Dekel 2008, 2009a,b). However, and as guides also confirmed, the main change I observed in the ways visitors engage with the memorial between its opening and five years later is how much less likely visitors are to express doubt about how memory work should be done at the site and whether this is 'the right place' for such work, and how much more likely it is to assess the site and its practices as a fact.

The book focuses on the exploration of German identity in relation to the past not only since Germans constitute the majority of visitors to the site, but more importantly because it was discussed and erected as a 'German' site of Holocaust memory and visitors from other countries as well as those coming from Germany understood it as such. At the same time, the memorial is a 'tourist magnet' and portal to other memorials such as the Memorial to Homosexuals persecuted under the National Socialist Regime and the Memorial to Sinti and Roma. As stated in the Bundestag resolution to build it in June 1999, the site's goal is to complement other memorials. As such, the site invites reflection by visitors not interested solely in the persecution of the Jews, and many come from countries other than Germany, which clearly affects the interpretation of and engagement with the site. Its location, physical openness, newness and abstractness, besides its sheer size, make it a fascinating location for the staging, and performance of memory work, as well as study thereof.

The book's title directs our attention to actors, institutions and agency at the memorial. The Holocaust, when mentioned by visitors and guides, acts as a reference point to the present discussion of individual and public dealings with the past. Mediation also means that action at the memorial is facilitated by the imagination of other sites and media, a fact that is true for the analysis of contemporary museums but is more relevant to this one, since mediation is performed and reflected on by visitors, the institution and the media both in writing about the site, in photographing it and in its descriptions through metaphors that allude to emotional engagement. Through the focus on mediation, I develop an approach to memory work that moves away from restrictive notions of the Holocaust sublime toward speakability through the performance of memory.

The book focuses on visitors and their various interactions and experiences at the site, especially with the memorial guides. The visitors are often seen by the guides and workers as tools for mediation between meanings of Holocaust remembrance and the site. This mediating role makes them not only integral to the site but, as visitors and educators see it, also offers a formative, individual experience connecting and representing the link between individual and collective remembrance (Erll 2011). The photograph below (Figure 0.2) is taken from the brochure that each visitor receives or can pick up at the entrance to the Information Center.[2] We see six portraits of Jewish victims looking directly at the camera, which are being observed by three young-looking women seen from the back. Observing the victims as humans is presented by the Memorial Foundation as a reciprocal activity and becomes exemplary of a multi-directional mediation in which: (a) visitors look at victims looking back; (b) a photographer documents this act in the Information Center; and (c) a collective space of observation is framed in the Holocaust Memorial (Dekel 2009a).

In my analysis of engagement in and with the site, I do not suggest that this is a positive way to engage with Holocaust memory in a normative sense, but that it opened up new possibilities for engagement,

Figure 0.2   Entrance to exhibition in the Information Center
Photo: Marko Priske, 2011 © Memorial Foundation.

some more meaningful than others, and that this phenomenon on its own is worth studying, because it is affected by action in a plurality of memory practices and sites, and by mediation inspired by other mediation and socializing forms such as reality TV, social media, play and global tourism.

My analysis draws on guided tours for two main reasons: (1) The relative lack of literature about the roles of guides and the interaction between guides and visitors in touristy sites (Feldman 2007, Katriel 1997,

Macdonald 2009); (2) Interactions between visitors and their engagement with the memorial was best presented in and around the time of the tour. In other words, conversations with visitors, as well as following their discussions of the site, availed me with much more materials and insights than personal interviews above ground or conversations independent of tours underground, which tended to be short and not focused. This later feature of how reflection at the site is managed through its different imaginaries as a site for piety and learning, a recreational site or a site for the performance of emotion such as grief, joy, anger and indifference will be analyzed throughout the book.

However central guided tours are to my analysis, it is important to recognize that the Holocaust Memorial can be, and is, mostly engaged with by visitors without the mediation of tour guides or of guided tours, not booked through the Memorial Foundation into which I had access only through the result of the commissioned survey in the Information Center between 2009 and 2012. I here use some of the results from 2009–11. I interviewed guides and visitors who participate in such tours, most of whom did not have the time to enter the Information Center, but nevertheless heard an introduction to the history of the memorial. Many school groups had their own educational plan to which I had little and random access.

From Berlin city tourist information, shared with me in an interview with a Memorial Foundation worker who was responsible for relations with tourist agencies in 2010, it is estimated that about 12 percent of the visitors to the memorial actually enter the Information Center. About 50 percent of visitors to the Information Center engage in a tour or a workshop, according to the Foundation's commissioned survey. My 'sample' of participating in about 60 guided tours, workshops and discussions of all the kinds offered and booked at the time of the research gave me access to a large variety of the positions visitors took in the memorial, in and outside of guided tours. In other words, in interviews at the *Stelenfeld*, visitors had similar reactions to the memorial to their counterparts in guided tours. This brings us to the interesting and understudied role of the guide. I see the guides as mediators, facilitating knowledge and directing interests and experience, agents that are very much in contact with their fellow guides and affected by conversations with them and with Foundation workers, but also have, and take, the freedom to offer their own perspective on memory and politics in Germany outside of those confines.

In her analysis of heritage tours to the Nazi Rally Ground in Nuremberg, Macdonald (2009) recognizes that the audience participates in a media production, where history workers try to encode a preferred reading as part of a wider process of mediation. The process of 'encoding' is negotiated and shaped by: (1) convention and restriction of the medium and the genre (guided tour in a site of atrocity); (2) the materialities of the tour context (graffiti, open space and imposing architecture); and (3) audience – real and imagined. In our case, the conventions allude to those of sites of atrocity, but then make a point of literally playing with them. The materiality of the tour or the visit is of an open space which is accessible at all times to visitors coming from various countries with different levels of knowledge and interest above ground, and underground of visitors who chose to enter a thematic installation.

I have argued (Dekel 2008, 2009a) and will substantiate this argument in what follows, that visitors come to the memorial and expect some kind of transformation. I do not, however, assume that all visitors, or a majority of them, seek to ask themselves who they are or actually engage in identity search. Instead, I believe it best to take the performance of self-search through the metaphoric talk of getting lost in the maze of the memorial literally, as a performed entry to the site. Inspired by Aleida Assmann's (2007: 32) concept of a 'historical index' that is shared and is embodied by members of a certain generation in relation to how they experience history, and corresponding to the concept of habitus coined by Bourdieu, I will delineate the 'symbolic index' with which members of different age groups construct metaphors to describe their experience of the site. I will argue in Chapters 2 and 3 that the younger the visitors are (coming from Germany), the more inclined they are to describe their experience solely in metaphorical terms without any reference to history, and very much anchored in an embodied search, getting lost and being moved.

Fyfe and Ross (1996) describe class formation and identity construction in museums. They claim that museum visiting is a practice or a strategy by which some people acquire social capital and others do not. This is very much true of the memorial visit in which the (German) visitor is expected to have some former knowledge, preferably acquired in the media or from family and friends about the memorial and specifically the Information Center (as formed in the first question to visitors in the Information Center by the Foundation-commissioned survey mentioned earlier). This social capital should then be put to work in the acquisition of more knowledge and experience at the site, whereas when people lack this background, the expectation is lowered to the mere display of feelings. We will follow this process in Chapter 3.

Fyfe and Ross (1996) work with Douglas's structural concept of 'grid and group' to convey the relation between identity and structure. In 'group' there is a focus on boundaries, and identity is articulated through rituals and symbols. 'Grid' is the extent to which the social is nuanced as rules ordering relationship between individuals through time and space. Through this structure, I suggest that the grid is not accessible to tourists coming from outside of Germany (or to a lesser extent if they are Jewish and are then told that the visit to the Information Center 'is not for them'). It is also not accessible to visitors from the working class, who often find the site infuriating when met with a strong performance of the 'group' feature, or the boundaries of the legitimate utterances and activities at the site. Class is a cultural process which entails the organization of bodily habits and capacities. It organizes the gaze and makes it the means by which to set priorities within one's social milieu. As we could see in Figure 0.2, the visitor's gaze in the memorial is literally directed by all the Foundation's publications for visitors. As such, it was the central form of reflecting on the site in the German media: one is directed to look at others looking at other visitors above ground, and victims, as well as fellow visitors, underground. We will see that these identities (that of the visitor, the victims and the perpetrator) are not fixed and can be played with in the site, especially by visitors from the former East Germany and visitors who are Muslim migrants in Germany, as we will see in the analysis of their guided tours in Chapter 3.

Memorial with no things

The Information Center holds two kinds of material objects: remnants (*Spuren*), which are presented as authentic, such as letters and notes left behind by victims and presented in the first room at the Information Center; and things (*Dinge*), which can be locally produced, reworked and either allude to the past or to the present, such as the memorials portal which is accessible at the last foyer in the Information Center and accessible online on the Foundation Memorial's website. Both have an 'aura' of the real (Benjamin 1968), and potentially produce binding relations to the past or the present they encapsulate. The 'things' that the memorial produces are based on documents from the 1930s and 1940s – the largest and most central one composed of the photos of six individuals, Jews who perished in the Holocaust, looking directly at the camera before they became victims (see Figure 0.2) which are sold singly as postcards and posters at the memorial's bookstore. But the site does not rely only on the aura of reworked evidence to operate as aesthetic triggers of emotional engagement.

Given this distance in time and place from the Holocaust and its 'authentic' sites, it has been important for guided tours of the memorial to present its ground as replete with contaminated reminders of the Holocaust, such as Hitler's bunker, which is then taken over, above and underground, by the memorial. As Uhl (2008) argues, dealing with this possibly eruptive past that could surface at any time in the actual Information Center is an inherent part of creating this dialectic between authentic remnants and reminders of the Holocaust and the abstract field of stones, which together represent opposition-in-unity. The memorial thus creates a literal, affective and effective embodiment of Hegelian dialectics, which defined reason as negative, insofar as it resolves the determinations of understanding into literally nothing; and positive because it generates the universal and comprehends the particular therein. Quite literally, if we follow the 'self-cancelling' nature of reason, interpretation work in the memorial was preconditioned on an empty space, so that it reaches its determination. However, and as read and reiterated in the debate surrounding the memorial's erection (Cullen 1999), since the Holocaust should not be understood and its memory mastered, the site lends itself as the ultimate place for the dialectics – where the absence of things can actually be owned by many in their universality and particularity.

The meaning of ruins and voids and negating them is played with in the memorial's ground design and presentation in the Foundation's earlier brochures, which described the location of the memorial as adjacent to Hitler's bunker as well as to the Brandenburg Gate and old/new central sites such as the American Embassy, Hotel Adlon and Potsdamer Platz. Interestingly, brochures in 2012 focus on the history of the memorial's initiative and realization, and omit the history of the ground itself, which was quite central to the presentation of the site in their first versions.

Guided tours as well as popular depictions of the site in photography refer to the timelessness of vast monumental buildings from the Nazi time. As the memorial is filled with 'stelae' (another reference to timeless, Greek tombstones), its emptiness is of a new order that cannot be compared to a marching or a rally ground, allowing only one person to go between the stelae at a time. That this person can also be sitting in a wheelchair was a figurative fact which I heard in reference to the reduction of the number of stelae from about 4000 in the original Serra/Eisenman design, in order to enable handicapped access, and as a counter monument to ones who do not, or historical periods in which handicapped people were murdered. In the new historic and symbolic playground of the memorial, and as seen in its depiction in the local media, educational programs and visitors' reactions, past and present are presented in the form of historical buildings, new and old monuments: renovated, reconstructed or destroyed.

Second, a place without things gives the site the resonance of self-abdication that Eisenman (2005) was keen on making possible when saying that it stands for 'reason gone mad'. Lastly, and reflecting how well Eisenman understood and acted upon memory politics in Germany, a place with no 'things' can more easily present the universal (in our case 'The Murdered Jews of Europe') within which there are many particulars or various victim groups. This is central to the Foundation role in also facilitating visits to and educational programs at the Memorial to Homosexuals Persecuted under the National Socialist Regime and the Memorial to the Sinti and Roma Murdered under the National Socialist Regime.

It is thus important for the memorial professionals as well as for visitors to declare 'the Holocaust did not happen here.' Far from being any sort of suggestion that there are grounds to deny the Holocaust, this is done to differentiate the new work of memory on this particular site. A site that is a palimpsest of many different histories, since it is both the actual place where political decisions were made (in the Imperial and Nazi eras) and was later empty land adjacent to the wall. Hence the memorial's site can represent a different perspective, which is called by the Memorial Foundation 'the victim's perspective.' The Memorial Foundation (as a manifestation of the long discussions that preceded its realization) tries to speak in their voice, while also including them spatially in the history of Berlin in taking over this most sought after land, in bringing in the archives with their names from Israel and the United States, and projecting those names and biographies in the 'room of names.'

This allegedly victim's perspective putatively binds the disparate parts of the memorial experience in a Hegelian dialectic. Above ground there is the silent and unwritten thesis: Jews were murdered. This, the wandering visitors have to discover. Through this discovery, they alter the thesis as the thesis alters them emotionally in the self-search for meaning – a process which will be delineated in the second chapter. They thus explore ways to understand the site as a metaphor for understanding the Holocaust. This quest is bound with their moral career as citizens engaged in memory work there and in other authentic sites, to which it is crucial to show various ties. To illustrate this point, German visitors often reflect on how people act in the memorial – whether it is respectful to eat or play tag in it and whether they experience self-alteration as they walk in the *Stelenfeld*. The binding of site experience and the visitors' moral career will be analyzed in the third chapter.

Underground, there is knowledge: Jews were persecuted and murdered. This, the visitors must absorb as antithetical to the emotional activity above ground. For instance, when asked in a personal interview what they thought about the memorial, two women in their twenties from northern Germany said: 'It is nice. Well done. The people go in, look, but not with this background.' I asked: 'Which background, that of history?' They answered: 'Yes.' In the first and second chapters, interviews with individual visitors will be analyzed together with the themes of metaphorical emotional talk and transformative experience.

At the end of the visit in the Information Center visitors are expected (by guides and Memorial Foundation workers) to report on what most moved them there. In this light, visitors usually talk about the 'room of dimensions,' where the last notes of victims are shown on the ground, and the numbers of persecuted Jewish victims from each occupied land are written on the walls by the ceiling (see Figure 0.3). Finally, the visitors ascend from the Information Center, walk in the memorial again, and realize the synthesis of both parts of the victim's perspective, which are now one.

When I talk about the victim's perspective I do not mean that there actually is one perspective that does or could belong to victims, shared by them, or by survivors, or expressed in their name. I consider rather the projection and construction of such a perspective to be a social process that involves years of discussions on shame and guilt, and later on the responsibility to remember the Jewish victims that gets reproduced and performed in the Holocaust Memorial, then put to work on and by other victim groups. The second chapter discusses this process. Interestingly, the so-called victim's perspective does not rely solely on the actual presence of testimonies and photos of Jews in the Information Center, and the sole dedication of the memorial to them. It is mobilized also by the connectivity of digital technology and media. The Information Center has five archival presentations, four of them present information that is also partially or fully available online, among which are the Yad Vashem names database, and the Yale Fortunoff archive of survivors' testimonies. Visitors to the memorial browse them on their visit, as they can do at home, but doing so in the memorial then becomes part of the larger self-search and moral proclamation. The fourth chapter will discuss the role of media and mediation in the memorial.

The message transmitted by the presentation of archives is first one of openness to individual interest and the larger phenomenon of the

Figure 0.3 Memorial to the Murdered Jews of Europe: Room of Dimensions in the Information Center
Photo: Yara Lemke de Faria 2005 © Memorial Foundation.

interactive museum, to which the Memorial Foundation also has to adhere like other contemporary museums. But more specifically, the staging of the individual visitor in search of individual stories occurs in the context of a necessary examination of other German and non-German visitors. This is part of a larger phenomenon, described by other scholars as memory work happening in a transnational context, in which memories and their languages of representation get synchronized (Levy and Schneider 2002). These are the mechanisms through which European nationals construct a European Identity made of their separate national collective memories (Eder 2005).

Current available media that enables the storage and retrieval of more information about the past makes it necessary to ask whether this also leads to more intense memory work in and off the site, and how much of this memory work then enters the community's imaginative, or is reflected in it. As we know, the archives located in the personal computer stands in the Information Center are open for individual searches. I asked memorial workers what the common search interests are that visitors show. For instance, many young German visitors look for Anne Frank in the Yad Vashem names database. Is it an interest in individuals such as Frank? Given that those search engines offer the opportunity to also search the meaning of terms such as 'Ghetto,' 'camps' and 'Sobibor' – is it a way to learn about wider events?

I suggest that the interest in 'famous' victims is connected to the fact that, for most visitors, knowledge about the Holocaust derives from having read their stories or watched films about them. It is therefore a self-affirming interest both of the former knowledge of the events presented and in substantiating the relations between the memorial, the visitor and the past. Notwithstanding, the Memorial Foundation wishes to distinguish itself from other museums and memorial sites. In its introductory booklet, they write: 'However, the video archive in the Information Center is different. This archive is open to all: not only to researchers or those interested in a specific historical event or a particular town but also to those who come "just to have a look".'

Interestingly, the sense used to describe the action of browsing the testimonials archive is 'look.' Indeed, it does not attempt or threaten to make one delve into hours of testimony hearing, just to have a look at the room, perhaps at the computer. Then, as we will see in the creation of speakability through witnessing, the visitor is meant to find something familiar about the victims and the content of the testimonies. The words of a guide introducing the Fortunoff archive to visitors in the Information Center are indicative: 'However hard it is to listen to what he goes on to say, the listener does not feel detached from the account. This is because he speaks about Auschwitz in the same Berlin dialect.' Finding oneself familiar with a survivor's dialect makes one feel closer in time, place, language and culture to that survivor, perhaps, like in the Berlin Jewish museum, 'not what you expected.'

With the creation of this specific memorial, individuals and groups who would otherwise not choose to come to a memorial for murdered Jews visit, indeed sometimes stumble upon this one, while also performing different personal positions *vis-à-vis* the past, which to them may stand in conflict with the memory of the Holocaust. A pendulum is then created between the invented space located on and citing old, historical forms of public memory action, and a monument one stumbles into sometimes as an accidental visitor forced into the present.

The memorial was not a Jewish initiative. Jews in Germany were, however, consulted in the long process of its realization and, although many – like Ignatz Bubis, the president of the Central Council of Jews in Germany between 1992 and 1999, and 'the Jewish Group' in the 1980s – claimed that it is not 'for them,' they have been the most important group to look toward both in terms of the symbolism of the site and in terms of seeking legitimacy. Among other legitimatizing mechanisms, making the memorial 'a place with no things,' made it possible for the memorial workers to claim that it presents and represents a victim's perspective that is not only Jewish. It also includes the perspective of the visitors to the memorial in their memories of their experience. This perspective has been developing in recent years through the proliferation of other memorials stemming from this one, first, in archives presenting other victim groups, and second, in actual memorials adjacent to the Holocaust Memorial: the Homosexuals Memorial, the Memorial to victims of National Socialist T4 'Euthanasia' and the Memorial for Sinti and Roma opened in the fall of 2012. The fact that a memorial site bears no evidence is part of a dialectical memory work, in which the reference to the absence of objects is blended with the proliferation of reworked and represented materials (in all these instances made of concrete), and together they form a unity of experience, emotional engagement and moral transformation, to be performed and explored in the memorial.

Already broken

'Oh look, over there a stone is already broken' is a sentence I often overheard in German when standing in the *Stelenfeld*. The memorial as a site for the performance of memory work rests on the assumption that it should hold for many years, metaphorically as the ground to perform memory work. In this sense, memory gets embodied in the body of the moved visitors as well as in the 'body' of the memorial itself, and both are seen as carrying meaning beyond their time and place. We will see how this focus on visitors and the site as facilitating change, is both sought after and considered dangerous. A danger made clear through the repeated reference to immoral, dangerous action in the site, above all in the rules of conduct written on its ground (where it is stated that one should walk in the site quietly, not play music, sunbathe or bring in pets, and that the safety of visitors is their own responsibility).

The literal reference to the cracked stones in the German press, illustrates the safety of visitors, the memorial and memory at large. For instance, on 6 December 2011 the most popular Berlin tabloid, the *Berliner Zeitung*, carried the following headline: 'Now the emergency stairs in the Holocaust Memorial also disintegrate.' The article opened with the following statement: Again there are damages at the Holocaust Memorial. For years the stelae have been disintegrating, now the underground museum also has to be repaired'. In Chapter 2, I will analyze a few such articles, all warning about the crumbling memorial stones, alluding to Holocaust memory itself. I found no evidence of this worry in the international press or in tourist blogs. However, moral assessment of the memorial is not bound to its form only, but instead reflects what is expected from visitors. The most prevalent answer I received, in German, Hebrew and English, when I asked visitors what they thought about the memorial, was some version of: 'People jump on the stones. They do not respect the site or the memory of the Holocaust.' In 2005–6, I often heard: 'People do not know where they are.'

By suggesting that the site serves as metaphor for memory work I do not claim that people who use this metaphor all believe that this memorial or memorials in general are the site for this kind of work, or that it is actually being performed (whatever that could mean also remains open). I suggest instead that the site both offers a look into the symbolic index of memory work or at the various ways through which it is performed, and that it has thus gained iconic performative power (Alexander 2011). Its iconicity should be analyzed in the symbolic framework it is embedded in; metaphoric language about personal experience and transformation in the present. We will see in Chapter 1 how the site serves as a metaphor for the fragility of memory work in Germany, which is then extended to discussions about its own fragility in newspaper articles discussing cracks in the concrete stones.

I do not offer an evaluation of the project and use the vast literature about the history of the memorial and the discussions preceding it as a discourse which gets performed, reverberates and is a source of articulation in action at the site. This is done, I suggest, mainly through metaphorical talk which uses the aesthetics and history of the site as an entry point for talking about being in the site and about Holocaust memory in Germany. Books that were published both before and around its time of opening discuss debates about it and illuminate major political issues that were raised in it in light of memory politics in Germany after World War II and specifically after 1989 (Cullen 1999; Jeismann 1999; Stavginski 1999).

Other books and chapters discuss its architectural and aesthetic evaluation (Godfrey 2007; Young 2004), reflections on the project by its initiators (Quack 2002; Rosh 1999), and analysis of political and historical processes around its realization (Leggewie and Meyer 2005;

Till 2005; Young 2003). Carrier (2005) evaluates the memorial as a potential space for action, national identity production and incorporation of the past into public memory. Jordan (2006) offers an analysis of the relations between the place's landscape and sociological processes that caused its realization, including state and group actors. Kirsch (2003) develops an ethical evaluation of the debate as lacking collective 'mourning.' My work departs from the conversations preceding the site's realization and the myriad discussions about its functionality and legitimacy, focusing instead on political action, interpretation and the development of an arena for individual and social transformation at the site.

Bennett, in thinking about contemporary museums as exhibitionary complexes (2006) identifies changes that are consistent with their role in transforming people through their own self-activity, encouraging an individualized and innovative self rather than a self bound by custom (Kirshenblatt Gimblett 2006: 39–40). According to Kaschuba (2001), the new memorial sites and museums erected after the fall of the Berlin Wall created a landscape of memory, or a network of places of history; places of memory and places of 'working off' the past. For Kaschuba (2001), they have a central meaning for the rearrangement of German memory politics, but are not sufficient to develop a praxis of collective memory. My work is an attempt to think about the 'praxis' of memory politics in its larger context of memory work, in and around sites of memory as exhibitionary complexes, where individuals present themselves and perform transformation. My perspective has to do first and foremost with the memorial being a site of Holocaust memory, but no less with the urban, tourist, media and economic aspects of this engagement as a means of self-achievement.

As Carrier (2005) argues, the memorial is not a 'site of memory' in Nora's sense (1997) that it unifies the whole around a shared meaning. In its abstract form, it is open to interpretation, and as such is not a locus that reflects a unitary national identity or promotes one (Wagner-Pacifici and Schwartz 1991). However, the fact that it does not have a single figurative meaning does not mean that it does not allude to the lengthy deliberations that developed around the disagreements, embarrassment and fragmented views regarding Holocaust memory, which are fundamental to explaining the creation of the memorial and direct much of the action in it. Carrier (like Young 2003) sees the 18-year pre-history of the memorial as a site of memory in itself.

My research was thus directed at explaining contemporary engagement with memory as a field of social action and participation. The literature on memory and memorials tends to take both for granted as starting points for analysis, assuming that public action revolves around memory and how memory operates for collectives (Assmann 1995; Halbwachs 1992; Nora 1997; Young 2004). In this way, the literature substantiates its products as loci of agreement or conflict, or both. I depart from this presumption and suggest that what we should look for in examining a 'memory site' is action in it: what it 'does' (Eyal 2004) together with its form (Wagner-Pacifici and Schwartz 1991; Zolberg 1998).

Studies of memory politics in Germany look at memory spaces, memorials and the action, and interpretation in former sites of murder, as present politics in Germany is still very much entangled with the memory of its past (Savelsberg and King 2005). According to Judt (2005: 803), Holocaust recognition is an entry ticket to contemporary Europe. Within it, recognizing Jewish suffering is a necessary condition. Judt sees the Berlin memorial as the most explicit among those built to commemorate the Holocaust since the 1990s. The Holocaust Memorial has thus been a litmus paper for the examination of memory politics, German engagement with its past, and present German political maturity and responsibility in light of that past. It is a site around which Germans could ask themselves whether a memorial, with its symbolism, dedication and form, is necessary and legitimate, and how they would envisage engagement with it. Hence, looking at action in it may illuminate old and new patterns of engagement with the past, but also how this action opens up forms of political self-realization that are new to this sphere of action and thus to this field of inquiry.

The field of memory politics in Germany after World War II explores German engagement with the past through a plethora of topics pertaining to its viability as part of post-war German civil society and democracy. Through this lens, the discussion is mainly of:

1. Identity formation and representation of the past (Borneman 1992; Confino 1997; Jarausch 1995)
2. Single and generational views of the past and their ramifications for German political culture in the present (Assmann 2007; Geyer and Hansen 1994; Welzer et al. 2002)
3. Democratization from the European perspective (Eder 2005)
4. Attention to the victim's voice in testimony (La Capra 2003)
5. Inclusion of other minority groups, past and present, in the legitimate work of memory (Rothberg and Yildiz 2011).

All reflect on tensions around these issues in the German discourse on memory.

I examine the political and cultural sphere in which the memorial debates occurred as commented on in studies of German victimhood, history writing and museums since German re-unification. Some point to the blurring of boundaries between perpetrators and victims (Niven 2006; Olick 2007a,b; Schmitz 2007), and the treatment of minority groups in memory discourse, the most prevalent being the Jews (Bodemann 1996, 2002). The memorial developed as a prolonged discussion (as opposed to a finite product) into the political, cultural and geographical voids that Huyssen (2003) identifies in post-1989 Berlin. After its opening, the possibilities of engagement with the past proliferated, along with practices of engagement stemming from those discussions, but exceeding them into new forms of articulation that grew independent of the need to retell the past, shame, guilt of the actual perpetrators and victims as bearers of that past. What we will see in studying the memorial, alongside reflections of these traditional themes, is a discussion of individual experience of one's own 'memory way' and a constructed confusion in regards to interpretations of the past and their relations to contemporary local, national and international politics.

Spectatorship and mediation

Visitors publicly interpret their experience of, and at, the memorial, chafing with formal visions prevalent in the German press of what it ought 'to do' to them. The first challenge expressed in 2005–6 in visiting the memorial was its newness as a means of engagement with the past. Therefore, most observations of the site used to start with what it is not; that is, it is not an authentic place where the events of the Holocaust took place; it does not imply figuratively what it stands for, and the rules of conduct were the only text on the site above ground bearing its full name.[3] Visitors of all origins then asked, 'What is this?' regarding both the form of the memorial and the action in it. Interestingly, the short accumulated history of the site and discussions of it in the local and international press have minimized the centrality of the question 'What is it?' and, from an objective stance instead raised questions on visit practices at the memorial, along the lines of 'Is this right?' In other words, visitors reflect less on 'What we are doing here' and rather more about 'What happens here?' meaning, what others do. The playfulness of roles in visiting the site was introduced in my earlier analysis of games and etiquette (Dekel 2008, 2009a). I will discuss aspects of it here through Hegelian dialectics, the framework of theater and double spectatorship, which enables further understanding of the implied spectator's position of power. This spectator, or the moved and moving visitor, adheres to the rules of watching the distant suffering 'I' (as opposed to the bystander); in following these rules, we gain a structure of face-to-face encounter that involves recreation, but calls upon a practice of spectatorship similar to that of suffering, in which individuals talk about what happened to others, what other spectators do, and the moral connection between the two. This form of spectatorship mixes the media of distant spectatorship, the theater (with fellow spectators) and a game (which 'we' all play together).

According to Boltanski (1999), the spectator is affected by what he or she sees, and talks about it in emotional terms that involve three topics: the topic of denunciation; the topic of sentiment; and the topic of aesthetics. Alexander (2011) combines moral and aesthetic dimensions with material understanding. He suggests looking at the aesthetic dimension on the surface of the object through an understanding of the performative power of iconic objects; whereas its discursive and moral meaning come from a source external to the object, namely from society and socially held convictions which are then performed in the ways people engage with the object. In our case, the site has a performative

Figure 0.4 Man photographing in the memorial
Photo: David Dekel.

power as an iconic object whose moral meaning, or the moralizing meaning of being in it, comes from external sources such as memory discourses in Germany, the locations and forms of their performance.

Alexander (2011: 206) stresses the 'series of mediations' that intercede 'between projected meaning and audience response.' Iconic power, however, often resists institutional inscriptions and cannot be directly mediated by critics and experts, however keen they may be to serve as its illuminators or engineers. This fleeting nature of the production and distribution of meaning around the site is a challenge as well as a promise. It is a political challenge for those who, even dialectically and through a declared failure to comprehend, can offer various ways to engage with the Holocaust. It is promising precisely for this reason, that as a seemingly elusive site (icons become elusive once they are launched and gain independence from the powers that produced them), one can study institutionalized practices of engagement with memory and the various relations they share with socially held convictions about the past and dealing with it. Understanding the realm of performance around the Holocaust Memorial can thus teach us about the construction of meaning in a material site around which there is a 'scene' and hence various interactions and forms of performance. Those forms of performance reflect not only the state of engagement with Holocaust memory in Germany, but also transformations in the forms and structure of public action.

Here we see the vital importance of the possibility to change perspectives, as well as the roles of spectatorship objectivity, where impartiality is achieved without having outside objective observers, by means of the imagination of a moral order of observing memory shared among subjective observers, which is discussed in the second chapter. There, I hope to make clear how and why it is more likely that the spectator *cum* witness will identify with, or be sympathetic to, the victims, as opposed to imagining what it felt like to be a perpetrator and inflict pain on the victims. Thus, as Boltanski (1999) shows, the power of imagination is central to understanding the act of spectatorship, and it is one thing to imagine the pain of the victim in different stages, yet another and a much less practiced act of imagination to think about the orderly culture of dictatorship under Nazism, as the orderly *Stelenfeld* is also said to invite. And it is something else again to think of being the one following, giving or executing this order in a larger social context, or getting crushed by it. The imagination of past suffering and present lack of perspective then merge in the moral and aesthetic act of observation in the memorial.

With Boltanski (1999), we here confront the discursive apparatus of morally acceptable forms for the communication of suffering. Evaluative and emotive terms are used to communicate others' suffering (we will see ample examples of communication about Jewish suffering in visitors' book entries, workshops and guided tours). We have to remember, however, that at the memorial there is no suffering to be witnessed above ground, and the representation of suffering underground. This makes the emotive work address the act of leisure as if it were supposed to be an act of witnessing, or in other words, it is the witnessing of non-suffering that becomes an object of discussion and a topic for the performance of sentiment which, if one visits the Information Center, gets entwined with the witnessing of suffering in the dialectics of above versus underground that the visit affords the visitors, as of a community of spectators lacking the spectacle of the unfortunate. Boltanski (1999, 39) adds a crucial component to the act of spectatorship, which becomes triadic through 'the spectator of the spectator'. This third party, who gazes at the spectator's own judgment, brings others into the schema. Acting as spectator by motion and photography at the memorial then creates a dynamic sphere of impartial spectators.

The book's structure

The chapters are divided thematically according to four central themes. All utilize several sources and do not, for instance, offer one discussion of guides and another one of visitors; one of the installation and another of its reception. Instead, the various voices and performers in and around the site are studies through different analytical frameworks ranging from Goffman's sociology of interaction to narrative analysis, around four themes which comprise the book chapters.

Chapter 1.   Transformation or a transformative experience that is personal, corporeal and is done in motion. The experience of the memorial analyzed in all the book's chapters is introduced in the first through the structure of the moral, recreational and emotional expectations that flow from it; how its space and landscape are employed in the creation and performance of that experience; and how new practices of memory actions develop in it. The chapter uses Goffman's (1966) dramaturgical theory and Habermas's (1984) concept of deliberation in the public sphere to offer conceptual tools for understanding encounters and interpretation acts in the memorial. The chapter ends with a description of a shift from thinking about memory action through the lens of trauma and post trauma literature to understanding it through speakability, or new practices of performing Holocaust memory and mediation.

Chapter 2. Speakability and its four types are introduced and discussed in the second chapter. Speakability is a social condition developed and performed in the memorial, which rests on old forms of discussion and memory work, and departs from the conviction previously held in Germany, Eastern Europe and Israel regarding the inability to speak which is also informed by trauma theory. Here I will ask how institutions and individuals emerge out of certain forms of interaction, specifically institutionalizes memory cultures, and different, also critical, readings of it, and how the history of an interaction affects its current and future forms.

Chapter 3. I discuss here the ethics of engagement in the memorial through the prevalent performance of one's moral career in relation to Holocaust memory. I depart from the imperative to speak presented in the second chapter and analyze the engagement through articulation, specifically in direct and indirect moralizing practiced by visitors conversing, with guides and among themselves, about fellow visitors and their own engagement with Holocaust memory as a private making of sense within a tight grid of engagement rules summarized in the stages of 'getting in,' 'getting lost,' and 'getting it.' In this chapter we also look into the narrative and performance of disclosing emotions at the site as one strong and central mechanism of action in it.

Chapter 4. In the concluding chapter I look at mediation, at the ways the site is experienced through the various media used in it and in reflection on experiences at the site, such as from new archives, photography and film. I also examine how experience at the site is mediated by the experience of other media, in the expectation of visitors undergoing a personal transformation in a concise time and place. I thus suggest that the site's mediation rests not so much on actions but on reflection, through metaphors, on the transformation of emotions in facing the abstract memorial.

Throughout this work, by studying reflexive civic action, one can identify processes of agency production in changing democratic arenas and the ways publics correspond with them. This process is attached to state institutions as well as to civil society initiatives such as that which initiated erection of the memorial, 'Perspective Berlin,' and is studied through interaction between all those agents, their commentary, visiting the site and its various presentations as a case for the study of memory action in the public sphere.

1
Navigating Experience

§1 Studying the Holocaust Memorial

This chapter begins by defining what it means to experience the memorial, so as to lay bare the emotional and moral expectations the site has for its visitors and visitors have from the site. We will then look at the ways the memorial's space (§2) and landscape (§3) are employed in its experience, and how, as an invented, new memorial, new practices of revisiting memory develop in it. This will provide the basis for the theoretical shift I propose (in §4) from thinking about memory work through the lens of trauma transference, to thinking about it through acts of mediation and speakability.

1.1 Defining experience: entering the memorial

The memorial is a site of urban tourism, and particularly memory tourism around several eras in the history of Berlin, Germany and Europe, including: the history of Prussian architecture (Koshar 2000); World War II (Confino 2006; Jordan 2006); and the GDR (Boym 2001; Ladd 1997; Till 2005). The developing practice of memory tourism within the new Holocaust Memorial quarter is closely linked both to the history of Berlin and to exhibitionary complexes in and around Berlin. It is a space that enables wandering in the discourse about memory, leisure and pastime, accidental tourism, and play (Dekel 2009a). These acts of wandering do not disconnect visitors from the urban surrounding, which Stock (2007) argues undergoes a recreational turn; an environment used by mobile individuals, located in an area full of other new memory sites such as the new Memorial to Homosexuals Murdered in the Holocaust, the Jewish Museum and the Memorial to the Murdered Sinti and Roma.

The conditions of entry to the memorial and the action in it are non-explicit by design This sets a pendulum between the embarrassment of facing a conventional void and tolerance toward practices such as running, playing hide and seek, eating, sunbathing, and their interpretation by visitors and employees alike. Guides often encourage their groups to talk about their experience of the memorial: 'Here everything goes. There are no wrong answers.' By so doing, they ask for a public sense-making in the memorial, which then becomes an enactment of discourse. The utterance 'Everything goes' implies openness for interpretation, while also avoiding any fixed interpretation that may be an obstacle both to the role of the guides and to that of the memorial.

In writing about the memorial as a space of personal transformation through photography, play and observation (Dekel 2009a), I addressed the ways in which those activities formulate rules of engagement with the site and with the Holocaust, and showed that certain forms of questioning the legitimacy and necessity of the memorial are in fact deemed inappropriate and some, such as total obliviousness about the Holocaust or blunt anti-Semitic reactions, make the guides and hosts invite the visitors into the Information Center. Most of the emotional responses from memorial workers I have encountered were directed at Germans, exceptions made for Israelis and Jews. Hosts and guides in the site either say that the it is not for Israelis or Jews or that it is there to respect them, and thus that it is 'for them' in a form of *Wiedergutmachung*.[1] In any case, Jews and Israelis in particular are not seen as part of the memorial's fabric. As such, they can act according to their own rules, are not asked to respect the rules of the site, and are observed only insofar as they state that they like the place or are moved by it.

The particular architecture of agency that develops at the memorial is manifold and conveyed in dialogical exhibition (databases), oral history (testimonies) and what is required from visitors: first, the movement, in space, between past and present; then the need, and often failure, to feel or express one's feelings about the site, which visitors often then reflect on with guides in guided tours and workshops. My analysis here is grounded, on the one hand, on the audience-oriented performance that the dramaturgical theory illuminates (Goffman 1961, 1974) and, on the other, on the subject at the core of Habermas's (1984) communicative action theory, one that directs action toward shared understanding. At the center of dramaturgical action and communicative action stand the means and forms of communication, with their outcomes for agents, social structures and institutions. Through this lens, I will examine texts that communicate about the Holocaust Memorial, its exhibits and its architectural form. This analysis takes into account the acting subject, whose actions and utterances are self-conscious insofar as they respond to other forms of action at the site and not necessarily to social constraints (Warfield Rawls 1987). At the same time, it considers her speech acts within a certain communal and historical context. Communicative action occurs among actors capable of speech, and is both located in, and dynamically corresponds with, the site. The visitors' ability to create a new style for action in the memorial, perform this style, face the circumstances of this act and direct it toward visible or imagined others, are crucial in the analysis of engagement with the memorial.

Goffman (1961) divides face-to-face interaction into focused interaction, or encounter, where two or more people actively agree to sustain a single focus of cognitive and visual attention, as in a conversation or a board game. Unfocused interactions are interpersonal communication that occurs solely by virtue of people being in one another's presence, observing each other. At first glance, it seems that in the Holocaust Memorial visitors are engaged in unfocused interaction. They did not agree to meet there, and they usually do not talk to each other. However, its routinized manner, the shared visual and cognitive focus of attention (as evidenced in the act of constant self- and site documentation) and the rituals of entrance to the site, all blur the boundaries between the two and point to a multi-focused encounter.

There are actions related to memory that are expected in the site, and many visitors discuss their adequacy, proliferation or lack. The question 'What yields the action – visitors encounters or their consciousness?' is at the basis of the discussion of the site's work. For instance, an article in the Berlin daily *Tagesspiegel* celebrating one year since the opening of the memorial, the writer describes possible activities in the memorial as having to do with the visitor's choice, personifying the memorial and connecting its newness to new practices of action developed in it.[2]

> The memorial is a central point. Sometimes the tourists hop into the Field of Stelae, a little reminiscent of the skyline of Manhattan, to photograph or walk into the nothingness, in which one feels powerless, or can be afraid, or unafraid. [...] Memory is also set free between the stelae. 'The memorial casually gets a face through the people'. [...] The stelae-jumpers have become seldom. It seems that school classes, differently from a year ago, know where they are. It is not a cemetery but a memorial.

The search for the proper set of actions results from the widespread belief that memory is itself institutionalized, or tends to get institutionalized. The most accepted model for analyzing collective memory action in Germany is the Assmanns' Cultural Memory (Erll 2011: 27), which analyzes the interrelations between collective memory, political action and legitimation, and identity. New frames for understanding memory work are influenced and inspired by Aleida and Jan Assmann term 'Cultural Memory,' which stands for institutionalized forms of collective memory resting on media and rituals. 'Communicative memory distinguishes and studies institutionalized memory forms that are based on everyday interaction and communication' (Erll 2011: 28). The search for meaning, self-documentation and play seem to fall into the second category. In Chapter 4 we will discuss German memory politics in light of this assumed institutionalized culture of memory, and I illuminate a pendulum between the cultural and the communicative that endures and institutionalizes the latter. I will thus suggest turning our attention from institutionalized memory culture toward multidirectional memory (Rothberg 2009), while also attending to the processes of mediation which alter visitors' memories and relations to them. I will further suggest that this procedure can be cast as the cyclical performance of routinizing dis-closure, meaning both the (well-discussed) issue of the strategy of avoidance to close off discussion about Holocaust memory in Germany and disclosure of one's intimate relations to this memory.

Becoming engaged in activity at the memorial takes place in the performance of affect (or its lack thereof), and its documentation. My research, as well as that of a study of schoolchildren reacting to the memorial (Klein 2012), shows that the documentation of self-transformation complements the performance of affect. If they have not sufficiently reflected on their feelings, visitors to the memorial feel that they have not engaged with it properly. This was most starkly evident in guided tours and workshops for school groups: both the performance of feeling and reflection were routinized, but not shared with visitors that one does not know. In the process of becoming a routine, focused and unfocused interactions about memory and about other issues are publically discussed as related to memory. Such discussions about the moral career of the visitor in her ability to enter the site and undergo a proper mourning, contemplative experience will be analyzed in Chapter 3, and the discussions on minorities and how 'they' relate to the place will be delineated in Chapter 2.

An example from an interview with young visitors, who were part of a school trip from Bavaria to the memorial in July 2012, can demonstrate the presentation of feeling in relation to the site experience. I asked, 'What do you think about the site' and one pupil answered, 'it is an impressive field, with lots of power. Through the jumping one loses the perspective.' To my question, 'What do you take from the memorial' the same pupil answered, 'people go into the memorial and through the concrete stone they experience hopelessness. It somehow has depth. There people are moved (affected/hurt); there people were marked and labeled.' The pupil links visitors' feelings in the site (impressed, losing perspective) to feelings experienced by victims, such as hopelessness, all tied to the experience in the *Stelenfeld* and its aesthetics.

This 'propriety of feeling' in visiting the memorial can be understood through the way that Goffman (1961) discuses spontaneous involvement in an encounter in terms of the degree to which one demonstrates a visible emotional entrenchment in a situation, rather than as a fundamental level of experience (Ostrow 1996: 342). Getting involved in an action can carry the actor into a situation that he can be aware of without the necessity to reflect on his action. As a special example of Habermas's communicative action theory, the actor is aware of his action but is not willing to reflect on it rationally, even when communicating about it.

In the Holocaust Memorial visitors utter questions and assertions that seem silly even to them, and say that others say 'silly', unsatisfying things, as some told me, 'just to say something.' The utterances and attempts at assigning meaning are centered on the *affect* that the memorial arouses or fails to create in the visitor. Thus, many public activities in the memorial, whether rendered game-like or not, cannot be constrained to shared deliberation, in or outside of that activity. Moreover, we will see how 'performed perplexity' rules the interaction and delays deliberation, connecting the questions concerning what does one feel about and in the memorial, to what does one feel about the Holocaust. This question is the subject of much deliberation in other venues, such as the broadcast media, newspapers, books about the memory of the Holocaust and public surveys. In this, it is employed in its bare form of performed 'speakability': first about one's feelings and action; and second, if at all, through a special symbolic index, about the Holocaust.

Before we connect the deliberative and the non-deliberative parts of the communication in the site, I would like to dwell on Goffman's claims regarding the *rules of irrelevance* in focused encounters. In asking, 'what perspective does a definition of the situation exclude when it is being satisfactory sustained?' Goffman (1961: 19) looks at games and how their participants are willing to foreswear, for the duration of the play, their interest in aesthetic, sentimental or moral value of the equipment or rules employed. In applying Bateson's (1955) 'frame' of play to such encounters, Goffman helps us see that the contours of movement and action in the memorial have to do not only with the aesthetics of the site, but with the developing rules of what being in it entails. Playing tag and then reflecting on that act are two forms of entering and leaving the game, or more interestingly, entering, then playing the game. Those who do not play hide and seek, as well as those who do play, use the rules of irrelevance as a boundary that seals them off from many potential worlds of meaning and action. As Goffman claims, just like in games, serious activities are world-building activities. In our case, the proximity of the serious and seriously performed and the game creates a third space of encounter. In this space, certain individuals are invited to play, some are deemed as not needing to take part, and some exclude themselves from activity or are excluded from it for lack of understanding and adherence to its rules.

Differently from a shared and mutually agreed-upon game, the participants-visitors in the memorial are not all playing together in the same 'game'. Here we have to go beyond the limitation of the game metaphor and talk about 'communicative activity' (Goffman 1961: 35). In this light, Goffman (1961: 38) claims, we can see how a visitor to the memorial, through 'spontaneous involvement in the joint activity,' and in encountering the manner in which their fellow visitors experience the space 'becomes an integral part of the situation, lodged in it and exposed to it, infusing himself into the encounter in a manner quite different from the way an ideally rational player commits his side to a position in an ideally abstract game.'

Throughout the seven years of its operation, how visitors behave in the site is the most reflected-on practice by all visitors and therefore interesting for us as a central loci of self-transformation, specifically as the performed liberation from old memory practices and connecting to other recreational touristy activities. Goffman (1974: 249) recognizes a paradox in the relations between play and its surroundings: 'the assumptions that cut an activity off from the external surround also mark the ways in which this activity is inevitably bound to the surrounding world.' In our case, the beginning of a visit is marked by entering the site, the time it takes to walk in it, play hide and seek, or rest on a stele from a walk and the rules of conduct written on the ground, available light and the touristy pavilion's supply of refreshments: all shape the contours of action in it and how it is framed by those seemingly mundane spatial and temporal terms.

1.2 The transformation of experience: pedagogy in the Information Center

Upon entering the Information Center visitors encounter a quote from Primo Levi, the largest text in the site, written on the wall which opens the exhibition: 'It happened, and therefore it can happen again. This is the core of what we have to say.' If experience above ground at the *Stelenfeld* is facilitated by the distance between what one knows or encountered in places of atrocity, and what can be found in the Field of Stelae aesthetically, the Information Center also collapses the distance in time with this quote from Levi, adopting Levi's survivors' voice: this is the core of what *we* have to say. The visitors, together with the Memorial Foundation, enter the realm of observation of that which happened, with two additional statements in mind: (1) it can happen again; (2) the claim that this fact is the 'core' of what is to be said about what happened. This facilitates an immediate need for sustained reflection on that which happened but more so, on the danger that it will happen again, and what one can or should say about it. This practice of reflection in speech is situated in the experience of the site above ground, when most visitors, in guided tours as well as in interaction with hosts or in responding to the press, ask what this site is supposed to mean, what it symbolizes and how one ought to feel walking in it, searching, mournful or playful.

For German tourists, this site is part of a growing number of new sites they encounter in homeland tourism, in sites of memory in which atrocities did not take place. According to a public survey carried out in the Information Center in 2009,[3] about half of the visitors to the Information Center are German and the other half from other countries. Since 2005 the number of visitors to the Information Center annually is steady at between 445,000 in 2007 and 468,500 in 2006. After 2007 the number of visitors has been growing, and in 2010 it was 461,000.[4] There are no official numbers of visitors to the *Stelenfeld* as it is open at all times.

The pedagogical possibilities available to visitors at the memorial are:

1. Group guided tours
2. Audio tour through the Information Center
3. Workshops
4. Videoarchiv search and workshop
5. Materials for preparation and after-tour discussion

Workshops on offer include: 'The fates of families'; 'Self-testimony'; 'Art'; 'Why did it happen?'; 'Places of killing'; Sinti and Roma' 'Homosexuals memorial'; 'City walking tour of the memorial and other memorials'; 'project day in the video archive.' The most popular workshop is the one on families. The workshops take about three hours and are delivered in the Information Center's seminar rooms, where the groups meet, hear an introduction to the memorial as a project and its history, and then focus on the topic of their choice. The students are then sent in small groups to the Information Center with worksheets. Following this, they are expected to summarize their findings and present them to the larger group. Until 2007 there were guided tours with or without a following discussion and no workshops on offer. Worksheets were used before the workshops to try to engage the pupils personally with the Holocaust and the history of the memorial debate. Online materials for teachers and pupils before and after the visit are available on the following subjects: history of Jewish extermination, families' history, memorials in Germany, post-Holocaust memory in Germany, and an hour dedicated to discussion of the visit at its end.

Since I found booked tours and workshops to be the most informative and fruitful for my understanding of the site, I focus on tours in German, although examples of tours in English and Hebrew will also be discussed with respect to the differences between different groups' reactions to the site.

1.3   Making the feelings concrete: the rule of experience

I define *the rule of experience* as the rules that organize and frame action in the site, as well as the indefinite call to undergo transformation with respect to memory of the Holocaust. It is thus a condition for entry to the site, as one must engage with it and reflect on one's engagement and how moved one is. Through this form of engagement, I suggest, a new performative space is created, where one should present, document and discuss one's feelings and thoughts; specifically, those feelings and thoughts that the place itself provokes in relation to other sites of Holocaust memory. This experience is an *individual* capacity, facilitated by the presentation of individual stories both in the Information Center and in guided tours and workshops, where individual stories of victims and survivors are central components that coalesce with the personal experience, then story, of visiting the site. The rule of experience, both in visiting the site and in the materials presented in its underground Information Center, is directed by the wish for a transformative experience for the visitors. This characteristic, the transformative experience, is threefold: (1) a possible transformation from a certain community of memory to another; (2) a transformation from a certain emotional realm (of shame and guilt) to a different one of performing sadness, and through it, discussion of responsibility and engagement; and (3) a transformation from the performed realm of difficulty and sorrow to one of performed self-search. Touring the memorial makes visitors confront the tension between what the place stands for and offers in terms of experience, and what it does not: it was designed to be part of the everyday fabric of the city, yet it is a distinct field of slabs.[5] It relates to other places of Holocaust memory, but does not look like them. One can enjoy oneself in it, yet it is the memorial to the murdered Jews of Europe.

It is gazed upon (Urry 2002), observed and experienced differently, precisely because of these contrasts between the work of memory and the 'work of leisure.' It is a place that mixes *Bildung*, which McIsaac (2007: 3) defines as the 'contemplative aesthetic cultivation of the self,' with the legacies of the past like a museum, only with the harsh legacies of a murderous past presented by the perpetrators' children and grandchildren (Young 2003). It also offers an aesthetic experience that is generated not by exhibited art works, but by moving through the field of slabs above ground and by observing information that one has probably encountered in other memorials, media, films and books, together with fragments of letters and family narratives that one sees for the first time in the Information Center. Thus, questions regarding appropriate engagement and inappropriate behavior arise, normatively linking concerns as to how one appreciates art in a museum, how one mourns the murder of Jews, and how one appreciates the memory of the murdered Jews. In the 2010 and 2011 workshops, I also often heard connections made between understanding what happened to Jews in the Holocaust as a link to human rights violation and racism today. In the Memorial Foundation-commissioned survey, the results for September 2009 and April 2010 showed that the topic most visitors of the educational programs would be interested in attending is that of human rights (86 percent). They would be least interested in learning about anti-Semitism before 1933 (64 percent) and very interested in learning about other victim groups (79 percent). We will see how visitors react to the position of Jews and other victim groups during and after the Holocaust in Chapter 2.

As guides indicate in interviews and conversations, the most important element of their role is to make communication possible with and about the site. Since, they hold, the memorial is (1) abstract and (2) located in an 'inauthentic' place (in the sense that it is not the site where the events of extermination took place but where the political leaders orchestrated it), the controversy about its locale and dedication should reverberate in tours so as to enact and keep alive the discussion about the Holocaust. There are no rituals held in the site above or underground,[6] and the few calls for ritualized practices, such as sitting in silence or enabling a whole group to be emotionally aroused and cry together, are stopped by either guides or the groups themselves. This is consistent with Katriel (1997), who argues that museums as memory sites turned their orientation from enhancing knowledge to affording an experience, although interestingly, a large number of visitors name walking the ground to the visit in the Information Center and participation in educational programs as acquiring new knowledge. This does not necessarily stand in contrast to the recreational character of the visit, which is perhaps framed by those visitors as 'learning'.

Guides may direct the tourist's gaze and frame the tourist experience (Feldman 2008; MacCannell 1973). They can endow certain elements and artifacts with authority, omit others, and add yet further personal flavor to the visit, invoking feelings and provoking thought. Guides at the memorial are personally affected when visitors challenge the premises of the memorial. For example, a guide told me that an elderly woman asked him in a guided tour, 'So where are the Jews now?' His answer was, 'The ghettos and camps are closed now.' He told me in a later conversation that he felt that the woman, more than showing ignorance, was expressing anti-Semitism, which could not be tolerated at the site. When guides express their dismay due to a visitor's reactions they act as being part of the site which can also be shamed, and try to moralize the visitors in the same manner that visitors indirectly and directly moralize each other. We will see examples of this in Chapter 3.

When one assumes that a true memorial experience cannot be recreational, one encounters a conflict that is central to analyzing the mix of existential and recreational modes of touristic behavior at the site (Cohen 1979). Instead of looking for meaning in other places or cultural centers, here the quest is literally for meaning within oneself, yet in public; for German nationals, in one's own state capital. Visitors situate themselves within the visit and reflect on what they felt, as compared to what they wished to feel: 'I wish I was totally lost.' They wish to draw upon the absence of clear symbolic meaning in the abstract Field of Stelae above ground, to feel something clearly, and to be able to communicate just that. In this respect, there is also a wish to end the period in which identity is kept open for one's own interpretation (Bauman 1996), hence not only to feel a bit lost, but at the same time not necessarily to make one's identity solid, or to feel one knows all the answers, and thus one is not lost in the Field of Stelae.

The unique self-understanding of the memorial is as both transcending space and time and being non-immediate or inauthentic. The Information Center mediates and directs the experience of the memorial and knowledge about it and the Holocaust, both in its content, the focus on individual fates of Jewish victims, and the European dimension of annihilation and its form, the presentation in its four rooms, as well as in its archives (Quack 2002). The information taken from other sites – photos, texts, recorded testimonies and archival materials – is presented, and adheres to the wish of visitors[7] to be alone, in a meditative mode. It happens in what Hall (2006) calls an 'experiential complex' in themed exhibitions that engage the senses in a manner that connects the authentic and the simulated (or the display of artifacts, objects, which are not authentic).

The Information Center achieves this state through the effects of light and darkness, voice, texts located on the ground, on the wall high by the ceiling and in front of the visitors' eyes, as well as audiovisual engagement and the archives. In this way, the displayed information about the Holocaust gives rise to knowledge and emotions and alludes to other known images, iconic representations of the Holocaust and their meaning in the place and time of their display (Zelizer 1998). These means of representation also create a precarious proximity to the time of the Holocaust, to victims and survivors, while keeping distance from the authentic places of memory precisely through new modes of presentations and the experience they afford the visitor.

Exhibitionary complexes (Bennett 1995, 2006), such as museums, memorial sites, themed exhibitions and fairs, have been distinguished in their capacity to offer a transformative experience for individuals, while engaging them in reflecting on the exhibit, architecture of the site and its dynamic relations to other sites. They engage the senses in different ways, entailing movement and calling for various forms of interaction with their exhibits, space, guides and visitors. In studying the tourist experience at the Holocaust Memorial we can specifically ask how the economy of experience sets its goals around emotional experience and how emotional experience is believed (or not) to cause political and personal transformation through the 'search for meaning,' leaving the question about what that visitor's search for meaning means for later. In this section I focus on meaning construction and implosion activities performed by guides on guided tours and in workshops that took place in February 2010.

My analysis relies on the understanding of performance in and around the site by individuals, German citizens particularly, who are meaning-assigning subjects producing and consuming experiences of the site. From a study done by Klein (2012) on school groups visiting the site, visitors' surveys taken in the Information Center, and from my observations and conversations with visitors and people working in the site, the single form of reflection on the site that all German visitors share is the need to talk about it being a sad place, or a place for mourning. In what follows, I will focus on the visitor's performance of their need to feel sad.

In a conversation between a memorial guide and a class teacher following the workshop 'Why did it happen?' in February 2010, the guide talked about possibilities of tolerance and self-moderation that the memorial might open up 'when parents say to their children to be quiet and not to jump around.' The teacher said later on that 'the pupils have to come with their parents and figure out for themselves what this place means.' Here again, we can see the symbolic allusion to the question what it means to be in a place of Holocaust memory, even without going to the underground Information Center. The teacher, guide and pupils all think that the experience of the site can, and will, cause transformation for visitors.

In a few guided tours in 2006, guides indicated that there is nothing concrete to do with the Holocaust, or to take from it in terms of under-standing its experience, and that the memorial reflects this inability and tries to make the visitors struggle with it in trying to understand what it means for them. Similar to a phenomenon that Feldman (2008) analyzes in his ethnography of Israeli youth voyages to Poland is the following example of this kind of emptying experience that points to absence with respect to both: (1) what can be learned from the Holocaust and the visit to the Holocaust Memorial; and (2) the nullifying of the less attractive parts of Holocaust stories.

As a partial answer to what the search for 'meaning' means in the memorial, I would suggest that visitors and guides at the memorial per-form and reproduce an inability to assign meaning to the events of the Holocaust, at a site that itself makes it difficult to accept its own authen-ticity and the sincerity of its visitors intentions. This is a disintegrating process that questions a sense of shared identity so long as the narrative of commemorating the Holocausts' victims through the transmission of historical knowledge about it is popular. However, most visitors seem integrated around the belief in what is seen as the performance of a responsible and mature engagement in the public sphere. In saying this, I see meaning as both 'emerging from the contingencies of individual and collective action' (Alexander 2006: 29) and as a pattern emerging from narrative construction, and at times enabling relative autonomy within the confines of a narrative.

The 2009 visitors' survey at the Information Center provides an example of the conflicting demands and expectations that rest on a visit to the memorial. If visitors had expectations from the Information Center (50 percent) it was either to get more information about World War II, personal fates (about 10 percent) or the Holocaust. Here the differences among age groups are interesting, as none of the German visitors over 50 years old said that they wanted to find out more about personal fates. About half of the visitors said that they would prefer not to use the educational offers in the Information Center. Germans because they would like to experience it (as well as the Field of Stelae) alone and remain quiet, and tourists from other countries since they did not have time. The survey toys with the role of the Information Center as an 'attraction' as well as a service center. We can see that, on the one hand, its utility still needs to be justified and, on the other, it must complement and add to the formula of Holocaust memory experience by providing information, images and historical background.

§2   The memorial space

In thinking about the experience of memorial places, space becomes salient insofar as it is assigned to a certain group with a certain history (or histories), and as it projects onto others or is projected by them. Massey's (2005) description of space as a multiplicity, constituted through relations, calls for understanding the political implications of studying the built environment. Her work is particularly helpful in seeing the double articulation in the reading *of* space and *by* space through visiting and being in it. We will proceed to explore the relations between space, narration and practice, which consist in Certeau's (1984) analysis of the field of action and the verbal field through observation of the practices developed in and around the Holocaust Memorial. The memorial is dedicated to the Jewish victims of the Holocaust, while standing in a space adjacent to where decisions regarding their and others' persecution took place; that is, by the Reichstag building and close to Wilhelmstrasse and Hitler's bunker. Sited in the new 'memory quarter' (Till 2005), it is also a reference point for memorials to other victim groups: the memorials for Homosexuals and for the Sinti and Roma.

Through its locale, together with its exclusive dedication to 'murdered Jews' (and concomitant dispersion of other victims' groups) and the narratives in guided tours and in visitors' reactions about the site, the memorial produces a new model for Holocaust memory. Namely that of the newly created memorial space that is central, urban and 'open' (to physical access and to interpretation), standing in contrast to other memorial sites which, relying on 'authentic' objects, produce different effects. In devising and deploying this model – comprised of form, narration and developing practices – the Memorial Foundation and its official presentations focus attention on two characteristics above all: abstractness and openness. See, for instance, this description, taken from a booklet published in July 2006 by the Press and Information Office of the German Parliament, 'The Political Berlin: A City Tour':

> The feeling of being lost in a wide field is his [Eisenman's] basic idea. The visitor soon becomes disoriented and experiences powerlessness. The above-ground abstract level of the memorial is open to interpretation and is directed toward emotional experience, while architectonically entangled with the underground 'Information Center': here the emphasis is on the concrete histories [also stories], singular fates, of the murdered.[8]

The focus on feelings and interpretation, or recasting the form of the memorial by its visitors in their narration of its openness, is a starting point for the analysis of the relations between the space, its organization, narration and practices. Alongside this literal call for feeling, or 'emotional experience', visitors to the memorial first project on the tension between the non-authentic character of the site, with its abstract aesthetics, and their need to experience an authentic feeling there. They say to guides and hosts in the site, 'I wish I felt totally lost here,' or 'I am not touched yet,' or 'this is not sad enough.' We will return to this tension in our later discussion of the feelings and emotions performed in the site. For now, I would like to dwell on the ways the space is presented, experienced and consumed.

To that end, I suggest thinking of the memorial space in three dimensions: (1) the *invented*: relating to its physical openness and abstractness; (2) *emptied* or void of remnants of the past, visitors and instructions; and potentially, (3) *accidental*, or a space where a visit may occur accidentally, and behavior is directed by this fundamental touristy capacity. I base my analysis on the educational materials assisting workshops for German school classes in the memorial's Information Center, as well as on visitors' book entries, and on the majority of the postcards sold on its premises, depicting the site as empty.

2.1 Invented space

The site is considered and presented by memorial workers as invented and that relations to its ground's history are reframed by it, and by the discussion of its palimpsest-like nature. This characteristic is true when we think of any other memorial, or built place. The narration of the memorial's inception and invention presents the site as new and expressly connected to other new and invented sites in its vicinity for two reasons. First, it expresses itself as a memorial site located on a 'non-authentic' ground. Second, it is interwoven with the history of this specific ground. Moreover, as an invented space, the memorial legitimates references to topics other than the Holocaust, such as human rights violations, Jewish life and persecution in Germany and Europe before World War II, and to minorities in Germany. I heard these references more often in guided tours and workshops in 2010–11 than in previous years, suggesting that the respectability of such connections is related to some political and structural changes: (1) the opening of the Homosexuals Memorial and the memorial to Sinti and Roma, which entailed the extension of the Foundation's role to caring for all three victim groups; (2) the hiring of more guides with a background in education and communication rather than historians, who were more committed to protecting the Holocaust as a singular event, incompatible with comparisons to other genocides and human rights violations; and (3) the more widespread human rights discourse in relation to the Holocaust as the ground upon which to study German history of World War II, following a 'cosmopolitan' approach to memory in Germany.[9] We will discuss this at length in Chapter 2.

To be sure, the central location of the memorial by what is nowadays, and used to be between 1933 and 1945, the symbolic and practical center of German politics and administration, is a political statement and should be understood as such.[10] In other words, presenting the space as inauthentic insofar as 'the Holocaust did not happen here' reinforces this 'other' authenticity as a new memorial site: the memorial space is not inauthentic when considered as a space awaiting or enabling the narrative of the memorial. This 'invented' quality of the space allows the memorial, in its educational programs, to create a pendulum of distance and proximity to the Holocaust and Jews, by the symbolic, materialistic and ritualized means of using photographs and metaphors. I thus want to suggest that in the case of the Holocaust Memorial, we can see a move that Hirsch and Spitzer (2009) describe in their writing on post-memory and mediation: namely a move away from intergenerational transference, toward performing civility. There is an inherent tension between increasing and offering knowledge and enhancing an experience, the role of which the Memorial Foundation's staff is quite aware. This tension between creating and historically grounding knowledge is connected to another goal, that of creating a public civil space. This is *not* done through the appreciation of artworks, but here, and increasingly in other memorial museums, through creating some atmosphere, or experience, which is moving for the visitor.

In the 'Art' workshop pupils are asked to reflect on their feelings above and underground. The examples are taken from workshops held in October and November 2010. The first worksheet asks the pupils to reflect on their feelings in the memorial above ground:

Use all your senses!	
What do you see? (Eyes)	Common answers: stones, differently sized blocks, tourists
What do you feel? (Hands)	Common answers: stones, concrete, sleek surface
What do you hear? (Ears)	Common answers: autos, traffic, tourists
What do you sense? (Skin, feet)	Common answers: cold, no sunlight, uneven ground

The pupils are further asked to answer the question 'what is your favorite side or place to look at the memorial.' The pupils answer that from outside they like it better, because they see more of it, while they recognize that probably the center, where it is cold and dark, is the best location to experience the memorial. We saw also in the visitor's survey that visitors preferred to walk alone and be contemplative, a message that schoolchildren immediately get and employ in their reactions. Before we proceed it is important to dwell on how prevalent and agreed on the practice of engaging sensually with the site is, then to talk about one's quite visceral and mundane findings in metaphorical terms. We will return to this point in the discussions of emotional transformation and moral career performed in the site.

In the art workshop, the same manner of reflection on form is expected from pupils. Indeed, in the ways the worksheets are filled in, we see how the pupils react to the call to use metaphorical thinking in conceptualizing Holocaust memory and their relation to it. They are then asked to create a memorial either from words (haiku or writing a poem are the two options) or from artistic materials given to them in the workshop: photos of the memorial, empty and full of people, with a flower-made Star of David on one stele, as well as with leisurely looking visitors. They are also given large paper sheets, scissors, glue and colors. Many of the art works contain Jewish symbolism such as the Star of David, filled with or made of a part of memorial photos. The art works often contain text, clarifying it in the form of the poem the pupils are asked to write. Figure 1.1 shows an example of their art work.

The group wrote 'and what makes you happy?' around the central circle (see Figure 1.1). In smaller writing, 'be a part,' 'think about it,' 'work along'. Inside the main circle are the words 'families,' 'friendship,' 'memory'; the names of the pupils in class (including 'non-German' names); and the words 'hope' and 'love' (in English). The symbols are a rainbow, flowers, Stars of David, a cloud, question marks, female and male signs, the anti-nuclear symbol and smiling faces. In their presentation of this work, the pupils told the group that when the rays tucked under the main circle layer, there is less light and hope, and when they open, like sunshine, there is more hope.

Figure 1.1   Artwork by pupils in the Information Center
Photo: Irit Dekel.

The invented character of the memorial not only allows for a variety of strategies for filling the space with meaning, but also of various legitimate intersecting memory and identity narratives. This particular example mixed old memory symbols such as the Star of David, which was also very popular in the suggested designs for the memorial, with cosmopolitan advertising symbols of happiness, freedom, peace and the rainbow, and calls to individuals to participate and cooperate. However, and as we will see in Chapter 2, there is a distance between this apparent openness and the focus on symbols of mourning the dead Jews, which the pupils write about when asked to reflect on the memorial in words.

2.2   Empty space

The memorial space is officially presented in photos as empty of people, or as hosting three or four, due in part to the fact that photographers try to catch a large segment of it (where people might at times be invisible between the stelae). However, I suggest that this is also because the preferred way to represent the site is as barren and timeless. The few people that are seen in it are icons and types for its success and of the various activities in it. In order to take a photo in which the memorial appears empty, one has either to be far from the site or stand above it on the second floor of the food pavilion or fly above. Otherwise, a close up photo can also depict the site as empty, catching a few stelae, cutting off or blurring the rest. Devoid of people or other objects, those popular photos look like old black and white photography, a classical monument and a clean artwork. Postcards depicting its premises produced by the Memorial Foundation present it as empty of people, and at times containing trees or with Tiergarten in its background (see Figure 1.2). Here its newness is related to the nature it bears in the midst of its surroundings, as of the city and country.

Both postcards (Figure 1.2) were produced by the Memorial Foundation and sold in the memorial's bookstore. The first shows the Field of Stelae and on the right side one can see photos of all four rooms of the Information Center, filled with people listening, reading and in other inquiring positions. The emptiness above ground and lack of color is met with the colorful liveliness underground. The second photo leaves the Field of Stelae out of focus while a mature looking tree trunk is in focus, again on the right-hand side of the postcard. Here the memorial is filled with a fragment of nature so that one may ask oneself if it has been there for a long time (in fact, it was planned and planted with the memorial); about the relations between the natural, the surrounding

Figure 1.2   Postcards produced by the Memorial Foundation:
Above: View over the *Stelenfeld* and pictures from the underground exhibition
Photos: *Stelenfeld* by Yara Lemke 2005; Exhibition by Marko Priske 2009 © Memorial Foundation.
Below: Close-up of a tree in the *Stelenfeld*
Photo: Klaus Raabe 2009 © Memorial Foundation.

city and the memorial; and also about how aesthetically pleasing they both are, together, and what that might mean.

2.3   Accidental space

The memorial is also a site of *accidental tourism*: its central location and physical openness mean that tourists often stumble upon it, en route to or from the Brandenburg Gate, the Reichstag building or Potsdamer Platz. The standardized survey at the Information Center about the reasons for visiting the memorial carried out in September 2009 showed that 17–20 percent came spontaneously or walked by, while 33 percent came in a group tour, 11 percent came to commemorate the victims and 38 percent came for 'other reason,' such as personal interest, a visit to Berlin or to show the place to others. From this we can glean that a proportion larger than 20 percent was 'accidental' or 'wandering,' since the segment of visitors that actually enter the Information Center are already well informed, interested and highly educated visitors. When visitors realize that they are 'there' they usually enter a realm of performed contemplation. In looking at memorabilia produced in and of the site, one can see how accidental tourism is one of the ways the site is mediated both as Jewish and as non-Jewish. For instance, in an exhibition presented on the site, celebrating five years from its opening and 20 years from the civil initiative to build it, the central focus was on what a citizen's initiative can achieve when persistent. Alongside those official narratives, on the promenade adjacent to the memorial as well as in the bookstore in the Information Center, Jewish memorabilia, such as dreidels and books about Jewish Berlin, are sold. Both the professionals working in the memorial and visitors that expressly intend to go there reflect on this 'accidental tourism.' Guides and hosts at the site often reflect on the question for whom the site is meant and works the best, or for whom the abstraction is meant. It is either for people who know very little about its history and the history of the Holocaust and would be drawn into it for its aesthetics, or for those who would be willing to discuss it as a site and a project. This is clearly not the only site of accidental tourism in Berlin. The Jewish Museum advertises itself as 'not what you expected,' offering a mostly feel-good experience.[11] Its architecture invites wandering, a displacement that echoes the rupture in Jewish life and German–Jewish relations but also Jewish life after the Holocaust, and thus a visceral experience (Heckner 2007).

Based on the assumption that people have to know what the site stands for, and the history of its realization, the Holocaust Memorial develops a form of *interactive staging*. The site stages its history in its current form of culmination through absence of information above ground, with the underground Information Center supposedly there to clarify this absence. This duality depicts the tension between history which is symbolized underground, and memory enacted in the *Stelenfeld* above ground. This then becomes an interactive staging ground because people become spectators and are subjects to the gaze of others once they get in the vicinity of the memorial. Being both observing spectators and subject to others' observation adds to the feeling expressed by many of being lost in the memorial and its interpretation. An Israeli guide at the memorial told me in an interview (December 2005):

> Eisenman was against the writing that identifies the site as a Memorial to the Murdered Jews of Europe. But the Foundation wanted it and in the end they compromised on the rules of conduct. So, people read them to look for meaning. They even ask whether the stones that do not absorb the rain– whether this has a meaning. There's so much, they don't know what to do.

The guide talks about the essential feeling of losing ground or being lost and ascribes it to German visitors, reflecting on the abstractness of the site. The accidental character of encounter in the memorial is therefore also of conduct, and action, since new rules of conduct apply to the site in comparison to other memorial sites. Accidental tourism is also made possible by the fact that the site calls for the mixing of activities of play, leisure, learning and piety. The performance of accidental tourism happens through the invocation of emotions, and it is an example of performance as a dramaturgical act that may involve speech acts as in the declarations: 'I wish I was totally lost'; 'Does the grid symbolize Nazi order or moral escalation?'; 'Do the 2711 stones have a Jewish meaning?'; 'Is it right that this is exactly the number of pages in the Talmud?' Here we can see how being lost within the maze of the actual memorial is also reflected upon with reference to being lost in relation to Jewish culture and heritage. This feeling of losing ground is tied to feeling helpless in regard to victims.

Visitors often ask themselves if 'perhaps this is how the Jews felt,' reflecting on the feeling of disorientation in the Field of Stelae. We can see how they make reference to history and to victims and victimhood (old narratives about Holocaust memory), while also asking about Jews' 'feelings' in a comparative manner, alluding to theirs. They might be toying with what Habermas (1984) calls 'extra-conventional norms' that do not yet exist but are imaginable, and which might be formed through discursive acts of communicative rationality around the site. This question, however, does not mark a commitment to explore the life of Jews then or now; or for that matter, a mature 'perpetrators' narrative.' Instead, it marks the distance between different forms of memory engagement, or the different focuses one puts on references to the Holocaust, be they of Jews, of hopelessness in a state of war or hopelessness in addressing what happened to the Jews then and Jewish life before and after the war. This self-questioning is widely reflected on in the German press and goes back to Schröder's wish that 'this is a place to which people would like to go.' The tension between what the press calls 'serious' and 'fun'[12] is a potent one, which developed in the narration of its invention and emptiness.

The accidental characteristic also flashes new topics and facilitates the creation of new memorials citing this one. The memorials to homosexuals and Sinti and Roma persecuted under the National Socialist regime cite it in form (though they are much smaller in size) and are located as centrally as this one, enabling walking tours between all three at the center of contemporary political power. Accidentally, when walking from the memorial toward Potsdamer Platz, visitors are likely to see the Homosexuals Memorial, where they can watch a short video of two men kissing. Since early 2012 a new film in the memorial shows various gay couples kissing and other, 'normative' people look at the act and move on, all recognizing the tension in the moment of gazing, which is immediately released by both the kissing couple and the spectators accepting the situation. The memorial to the Murdered Sinti and Roma is also managed by the Memorial Foundation. Thus, the institutional link between the three will add to the narrative network on victims groups and it is yet to be seen how the space of the Holocaust Memorial will be reflected in both, and how it will in turn reflect them. A further outcome of accidental tourism is that of accumulative experience. Visiting the site and comparing one's feelings in it to other sites of remembrance becomes the backdrop to visiting Berlin's Holocaust memory landscape (Blumer 2011).

§3 Landscape and history[13]

We will now move from thinking about the memorial experience and the ways to study it, to the narratives grounding this experience in history, that of a charged landscape, which leans on the assistance provided by old memory narratives in authentic memorial sites, in order to build a narrative structure that can depart from both those sites and those narratives.

The Holocaust Memorial is built on historically charged ground: it had been the Ministers' Gardens in imperial times, the center of Nazi power, and during the GDR the death path (or 'no man's land') by the Berlin Wall. This physical ground serves as a basis for discussing the German past, layered under the memorial's abstract architecture. Guides, hosts and visitors in the memorial often talk about the topography of the area, and every publication about the memorial dwells on the history of its ground.

Scholars evaluating the project refer to this topography and landscape as part of the chronotopia leading to its realization in its current form, dedicated exclusively to Jewish victims, at this particular place between the Brandenburg Gate, the Reichstag building and by Potsdamer Platz (Carrier 2005; Cullen 1999; Leggewie and Meyer 2005; Quack 2002). Carrier (2005: 102) states: 'the significance of the site of the Berlin monument was consistently perceived in general and imprecise terms.' Its dedication to Jews was a constant source of dispute. The popular name 'Holocaust Memorial' suggests commemoration of the Holocaust in general, and even the references to the land of its erection described the multiplicity of past uses of the site. The site has developed historical specificity from the moment of opening it to the public as a 'Holocaust Memorial.'

The Holocaust Memorial is thus on territory that is now, for the first time since imperial rule, accessible to citizens. Questions regarding the actual 'filling' of this site with the particular memorial, joined questions regarding renaming streets; the fate of Nazi architecture and objects, and those of grand historical importance such as the Church of Our Lady in Dresden and the Royal Palace in Berlin (Koshar 2000). Evoking the political monuments of the GDR and reusing old war monuments, such as the *Neue Wach* in Berlin, set the ground for multilayered thinking regarding how to commemorate the past and to what extent to mold it with the present and future of Berlin (Ladd 1997; Varvantakis 2009). The process by which new and old memories are represented and reorganized in the urban landscape follows from the construction of the 'new Berlin' (Till 2005). Guided tours, as well as leaflets given to visitors at the site, exploit this embroidered past and present, informing the visitor about the *'Führer Bunker'* and 'Göbbels Villa' that existed there during the Nazi era, and about the history of the site during the Kaiser's rule and the GDR. All contemporary maps of the site demonstrate that its history precedes it: the space had been empty for years, and the memorial filled it, making it an integral and universally accessible part of the city for the first time. In this sense, the presentation of the site's topography is crucially *not* as a 'topography of terror,' but corresponds with places of horror by reflecting on the foundations of past places, and its proximity to sites of killing and torture that are now gone.

3.1 From abundance to absence of meaning

The relation between individual stories and stories of landscape, between people and topography, is established in the memorial through the discussion of individual personal experience. However central the former buildings on the memorial ground to the discussions at the memorial may be, no map of the memorial site conveys those historical locales from different eras. Nonetheless and as stated above, it remains clear that the site had indeed been empty for many years, and that the memorial filled it. Presenting and discussing the site's historical landscape together with its abstract form sets the ground for a deliberation-oriented engagement with memory and its uses.

If architecture is considered the most 'social' of art forms, presenting 'ethics in stone' (Erll 2008: 231), we will see how the construction of a memorial that does not resemble others in its thematic and geographic vicinity produces various sites of memory. It morally calls for a new ethic of individual engagement with memory, and as we saw earlier in this chapter, this ethic can best be found in acts of interpretation which focus on plurality and openness instead of one 'proper' way to remember the Holocaust. Guides describe the site's 2711 stones as a random 'meaningless' number, encouraging visitors to think about its history and the history of commemorating the Holocaust and the murdered Jews in a way that avoids closure and produces more interpretations. This meaninglessness then mobilizes visitors to consider the memory of the Holocaust morally, as these thoughts, and their action in this site, 'charge' the memorial with meaning.

Guided tours relate to Wilhelm Street (*Wilhelmstrasse*) as the center of Nazi power, moving from that street and Hitler's bunker to the memorial today, the Reichstag building and the tourist center of Berlin after 1989. The memorial's area has also yielded new sites and streets. Three counterpart streets were named after Jewish women on two sides of the memorial. On the eastern part of the memorial runs the new Cora Berliner Street. It is crossed by the new Hannah Arendt Street. On its south end there is the new Gertrude Kolmer Street. Sybille Quack, the first executive director of the Memorial Foundation to the Murdered Jews of Europe, writes: 'We are in Germany. The *Stelenfeld* symbolizes part of our history [...]. The murder belongs to us. The three new streets are short, as well as the history of deciding to give them these names.' According to Quack (2005), remembrance through street names of Jewish women scientists who suffered expulsion and persecution under the Nazi regime goes beyond mere geographic orientation. It is the first framework of concrete historical orientation around the abstract memorial, even before one descends to the Information Center and encounters more information about the Holocaust:

> It neither admonishes, nor warns. It does not monumentalize humi-
> liation, fear or festering wounds. It even belies description as an

undulating Field of Stelae, for all that is to be seen is a heap of big, grey stones, scattered far and wide, quietly unassuming. If you didn't know it was there, you might drive past thinking it was a huge construction site. And that may be exactly what it is: a place that presents nothing, where nothing is finished, and with which the Germans may not so easily find closure.

We are not confronted with the presence of history but with the present itself. What has been created here is not a landscape of remembrance but a landscape of experience.[14]

These two excerpts are taken from a book published with the opening of the Memorial in 2005. Hanno Rauterberg is an art historian and writes for the center-left weekly *Die Zeit* about art and architecture. He first presents what the memorial is not. It does not educate and warn (as other memorials might attempt). It hinders description and as such is a construction site for nothing – and can therefore never be finished. It thus stands for presence, present and experience.

Peter Eisenman writes in the same book:

The experience of being present in presence, of being without the conventional markers of experience, of being potentially lost in space, of an un-material materiality: that is the memorial's uncertainty. When such a project can overcome its seeming diagrammatic abstraction, in its excess, in the excess of reason gone mad, then such a work becomes a warning, a Mahnmal,[15] not to be judged on its meaning or its aesthetic, but on the impossibility of its own success.

These excerpts constitute the attempt, in which guides and hosts also participate, to collapse the meaning that one might infer from the memorial. Whereas the guides and hosts are often frustrated in trying to communicate these messages and facilitate this experience; the writers manifest the ground on which the place should be (un)understood.

In January 2001 there were extensive discussions about the right to demonstrate in the future memorial. These debates connected issues of security and the wish to facilitate democratic participation in the site. Eisenman gave an interview to the *Zeit* in which he was asked whether he, as a Jew and the memorial's architect, would allow demonstrations. He replied that if there is right-wing radicalism, then it won't help to repress it. Why should not the 'Holocaust Mahnmal' be the place where this energy is visible and released?[16] He said that the place should not look like a concentration camp with wire-fence and a watchtower. The interviewers asked him if he sees the memorial, then, as a catalyst for social conflicts. His answer was that he did not want to represent or illustrate the Holocaust but to originate an experience that generates insecurity. The visitors should ask themselves: What is it here? What does this mean? Where am I actually? Eisenman: 'I want to originate exactly this feeling of being lost and lack of orientation; this search, in vain, for a clear sense. The cognitive experience abdicates the affective one'.[17]

Ball connects Eisenman's architecture with the political discussion of proper memorialization and the sentiments expected in a Holocaust memorial:

> Eisenman's 'deconstructed minimalism' marks the power of the rhet-oric of sublime unrepresentability associated with Adorno's negative aesthetics. The emergence of this arguably 'Jewish' style as a nega-tive memorial genre indicates that moral protocols have bled into aesthetic conventions that regulate the kind of sentiments viewers should experience while reflecting on the contemporary significance of German responsibility for the Third Reich's crimes.
>
> (2008: 12)

The discussions regarding the aesthetic propriety of this work of art as the German national Holocaust Memorial dealt with the gigantic, mon-umental figures around the site, alongside speculations about securing the site. After the opening, when it became clear that there were to be very few and random cases of graffiti, and no right-wing demonstra-tions, the focus shifted to the security of the visitors themselves, who tend to jump on and between the stelae. That led to the view that 'anything goes' in the memorial visit. Whatever comes to one's senses is welcome.[18] As noted earlier, newspaper articles celebrating it being a year from the memorial's opening related to Schröder's famous wish that the memorial should be a place people wanted to go to. Journalists reflected on the large number of visitors through the lens of that saying, and seized upon the notion that this is the case: the memorial is indeed a place where people like to go.[19]

Two discursive means are constructed around the process of going to the site and touring it. The initiators, builders and guides try to create an event located in a negative space (visceral, devoid of an inherent message), which reflects the absence of meaning and the inability to represent the historical event it alludes to. The memorial site, in this particular landscape, thus serves to recall and transform experiences of this and other historically charged grounds and make them habitable for discussion for Germans as well as for other visitors from all walks of society. In that sense it is crucial for the guides and visitors alike to keep it in its multiplicity not only for the positive chronological and moral ascendance from Hitler's bunker to the Holocaust Memorial, but as a framework for keeping competing and sometimes conflicting memories open for revisits. For this reason, the landscape of the memorial is open to interpretation that delves into the possible qualities of the memorial built on this ground, and of new memorials in its surroundings, which bear many of its physical traits (such as those dedicated to other victims of National Socialism, the homosexuals memorial, and the memorial for Sinti and Roma).

In presenting the topography of the site, guides at the memorial discuss 'real' sites of violence now destroyed or buried, such as the center of Nazi power and Hitler's bunker – sites which should not become sacred (indeed, should be kept in their profanity) because they epitomize violence, albeit violence that occurred elsewhere. They discuss those places together with authentic, classical memorial sites in concentration camps where violence did occur. It is crucial to these discussions to not attempt to unearth the past in some kind of archeological excavation, as it is close to the surface of knowledge, not too remote in time, and dwells in other 'authentic' sites. The moral task here is to expose one's dealings with the past to others touring the site.

Erik Meyer[20] attends to the question of the non-authentic nature of the memorial, its form and its possible influence on memory action:

> The conception that the Holocaust Memorial is virtually a lapidary inscription of a final line of which some were afraid and some perhaps even hoped for, is not true. This Field of Stelae is quite open in meaning and has no clear message. One cannot read off the stelae what they should mediate to us. The visitor wandering through the stones is in the end directed by his own perception.

Meyer claims that it does not mark a finish line over the Germans' dealing with their past, as its 'readers' are left to their own devices there. They wander in it as if on a project test. Opposition to the building of the memorial focused on fears of it serving as a closure device (Young 2004); that once a memorial was built in the center of Berlin in an area in which 'nothing actually happened,' people would not go to sites where crimes had been perpetrated, that it would be like drawing a

Schlussstreich, or a bottom line, under Germany's past and discussions of it (Till 2005). It would trivialize memory and encourage its misuses in adding yet another site to the already saturated endeavor called Holocaust memory. The fear of reaching an end of German engagement with memory of the Holocaust was at the center of historians' debate in the late 1980s. Maier argued in his discussion of the debate that this fear led to insistence on the left that the Holocaust was a unique genocide, incomparable to other genocides, and should be kept vivid in German memory (1997 [1988]: 55). This insistence led to the focus of the memorial on the Jews as a single victim group, in order to avoid relativizing their case.

3.2   Creating the palimpsest of meaning

Participants in guided tours are familiar with some of the discussions that preceded the building of the site and the discussions following its opening that refer to the historical topography of the site. Guides offer a sacralizing experience of this site through what it is *not*; making this sacralization both possible and bound to fail (as we saw in a guide's assertion: 'This place is not authentic. There is nothing concrete you can do with the Holocaust.'

   This failure to comprehend the task of commemoration is akin to the inability to represent 'the Holocaust.' This is necessary because there is still the danger that the former 'real' sites will attract 'authentic' pilgrimage, and more importantly, because it could bring closure to the discussion about memory that this site strives to facilitate (Young 2004). This inherently open-ended discussion, based on the inability to grasp the memorial and its site as a whole, calls for constant motion and metaphorization, and thus cannot abide the closure that sacralization would entail. Discussions about the topography of the place between visitors, workers and scholars create an alternative landscape of memory work, based on the tension on the axes of presence (the remnants of the Nazi period such as Hitler's bunker) and absence, sacred and profane, real and unreal.

   Nevertheless, the abstract and visceral qualities of the memorial should not necessarily lead us to assume plurality in the legitimate approaches to it, but rather the multiplicity of encounters that the site facilitates for different visitors, which then become grounds for moral collusion, which we will discuss in the next chapter. The palimpsest of the memorial's meanings – it resembles a graveyard and a labyrinth, visitors as well as Eisenman himself say – and the palimpsest in its topography – former site of Nazi power, on top of which rested the wall, on top of which came the memorial – collide, as guides insist that an entry point to discussing the memorial is knowledge about its topography and about the chronology of its realization.

3.3 Attempts toward comprehension

The following excerpt is taken from a guided tour in the memorial in March 2006. Standing in the *Stelenfeld*, the guide asks the pupils to reflect about the memorial after walking in it:

GUIDE.   What do you think about the memorial? How did you feel in it?
PUPIL.   How does it look like from above?
GUIDE.   Like a wheat field. This is one of the only things that Eisenman agreed to say about the memorial. I'll show you a picture taken from the air inside the Information Center.
PUPIL.   It is narrow, one feels lost.
PUPIL.   Yes, it is like a labyrinth
GUIDE.   Anyone can feel what they wish here.

In this short interaction we can identify the conflict the visitors face between the lack of guiding text in the site, built around the authority of Eisenman, and their will to comprehend what it means, or how one can grasp its experience. As the guide avoids providing interpretation to the memorial form, he offers an official one, and hurries to blur it when stating 'anyone can feel what they wish here.' The question, 'How does this look like from above?' also reflects the double wish to be walking in this maze together with experiencing it 'not from within.'

The same guided tour proceeded:

GUIDE.   So many ask me: where was the *Führer bunker*? *[imitates an old voice, the pupils laugh]* the bunker was there, near the trees, and Göbbels Villa on the other side. Decisions were taken here, but the Holocaust did not happen here. This is not an authentic place in this regard. You can run, hide, jump, anything goes here.
GUIDE.   No one asks me how much it cost? – 3.3 km. *Autobahn [imitates an old voice]* 'It is taken from my Renta [retirement payment]' some people say. Then I tell them it is 3.3 km autobahn.
TEACHER.   It is really ok. We need them both equally.

The idea that, since it is not an authentic place and since it is also abstract and urban, all is possible in the memorial is very intriguing.

At the same time, the moral standing of the visitors and their families is constantly tested through references to popular interest in Nazi history and its heroes and the questioning of the memorial's necessity. Tracing the history of the German ground is an activity embedded in West German memory politics since the 1970s (Koshar 2000). Paradoxically, both the guide's references to the *Autobahn* (highway) and to the memorial bring in history unwittingly, as the Autobahn was one of the major successes of Nazi architecture. Maintaining it will enable mobility in the present and the future, but also allows the maintenance of a trace – far removed from its origin, and resembling the Holocaust Memorial's relations – to exist along with extinct traces of the past on its land.

We saw how the abundance of historical evidence of Nazi terrorism instills the memorial ground with legitimacy and meaning and makes possible the search for significance outside of it, in the memorial's abstract structure, with its absent figurative and instructive meaning. This tension between the wealth of the palimpsest on which the memorial is constructed and its form, which calls for different engagement than is expected in other Holocaust memorials, was crucial to the understanding of visitor action in and around it. We saw how the act of exposing oneself and others to questions regarding what one thinks and feels in the memorial stems from the knowledge of the site's historical landscape, and that in turn, it is vital to present it as emptied, and then to recharge it with meaning.

§4　Transferring trauma?

As has become clear from discussion of the memorial space, we cannot think about it merely as a space where transmission of historical knowledge concerning atrocities takes place, as in other sites of Holocaust remembrance. We now move from the developing practices of memory action in the site, which rest on old narratives about the ethics of visiting other 'authentic' sites, toward the question of transference itself, or what kinds of affects are created in the memorial and how. I claim that transference of Holocaust history in the mode of trauma memory, both in the memorial above ground and in the Information Center, is neither attempted nor achieved. Much like the description of trauma memories, the site provides an emotional visceral experience, and at times facilitates critical reflection on ways to remember (and forget) the Holocaust. It cannot, however, serve as an example for intergenerational transference or 'post-memory.' Post-memory is a dynamic form of transference calling for different forms of engagement with the past. I thus suggest that the memorial communicates a post-memorial aesthetics and experience that draws attention to the body as a site of interpretation, without the trauma discourse present elsewhere.

Erll and Rigney (2009a,b), in their dynamic approach to the relations between collective memory, media and mediation, advance the study of experience embedded in the present. With this approach we see that sense-making is also anchored in past forms of talking about the Holocaust and its various mediations in print, spoken and broadcast media, photos and films. Understanding these memory mechanisms, and with our discussion in this chapter departing from questions of memory transmission, we go beyond the theoretical lens of trauma theory in explaining the work of memory (Giesen 2004; Hirsch 2008). This approach relies on an experimental ground for transformation in public, rather than representation or the secondary witnessing of a traumatic event. The Holocaust Memorial as a site, with its specific aesthetics, in this specific point in time of the first and second decade of the millennium, allows us to see not only changes in the modes by which mnemonic action embedded in sites produces various experiences of the past and through them of oneself, but also the political manifestations of changes in the ways to fulfill the moral commitment to keep memory 'alive.' Looking at what people do at the memorial reveals the exploration of oneself as part of a nationally, transnationally and locally definable group. Rather than the widespread normative viewing of facing trauma, we observe the performative dimension of translating aesthetics into ethics. The exploration of oneself is evoked not so much by the memory of one's facing of trauma or suffering, or more specifically by the expectation to be saddened by an authentic feeling, which could be aroused by facing a traumatizing space, photo, or testimony. Instead, one's performed self-exploration is primarily facilitated by the condition of getting cut off from the world that the trauma discourse surely enables, together with the widespread practice of playing and exploring one's feeling in the site.

4.1   From architecture of trauma to architecture of feelings

However 'trauma free'[21] the structure of relations with the past at the memorial may be, Hirsch's question of how to create ethical, critical, relations to the Holocaust in the post-memorial age is at the center of our discussion, since some of the ethical implications of post-memory, such as tentative identification with the victims, are indeed performed in the memorial (Heckner 2008). It is important to try to find a different explanatory mechanism for the ways visitors experience the memorial, and not only because the reality of their experience is not of transmitted trauma. In post-memory, the experience itself does not have to be traumatic, though it can be, and we see that it is sometimes liberating. Finding new tools to explain memory work around new memorials will also advance our understanding of the directions the interest in memory studies are taking. As Radstone (2005: 138) argues: 'The rise of interest in memory is associated [...] both with the emphasis in trauma studies on that which exceeds representation and with oral history's quest to retrieve the memories of groups whose histories had previously been neglected.' Within certain social, historical and political conditions, museums and memorials are institutions that partake in constructing and sustaining certain ways to remember the past, and as we see in the case of the memorial, no longer through trauma, though still using testimony and victims' personalization as means of telling and generating feelings about the Holocaust.

Hirsch and Spitzer (2009) rightly argue that there has been a widespread reliance on witness testimony as a mode of transmitting trauma. This tendency is also carried into the presumed experience of the memorial. Heckner (2008) shows how Hirsch presents an individualized visceral experience in her understanding of Holocaust photography. Eisenman's memorial offers a visceral experience and is experienced as such. However, the lens of mediation offered here captures, first, the ways both memorial workers and visitors talk about a failed experience of feeling sad or moved and about the memorial's role as a mediator in facilitating this experience. Both the aesthetics of the site and the Information Center's content create distance and present second- and third-order information about the Holocaust.

What Eisenman (2007) terms the 'architecture of affect' builds not only on the lack of figurative meaning which endorse certain *effects*, but on a transformative experience that promotes feeling through mediation.[22] The original effect in memorials and sites of atrocities is known to the visitors, and they employ it in this new site, where they are also aware of the fact that they are supposed to feel sadness, alongside other feelings. In the memorial above ground the visitor is supposed to stumble; then grasp some unmediated truth about herself; then about her community; perhaps then about the Holocaust. Eisenman's resistance to any form of literal, imitative experience is evidently followed here, and reflects Habermas's model of the memorial as a 'deliberative space' that the Bundestag adopted in its resolution to build the memorial in 1999.

We have to separately distinguish the potential Heckner (2008) sees in the post-memory experience of Holocaust photos or of Libeskind's Jewish Museum in Berlin as a material difference which discusses its own failure to connect generations to the past. Furthermore, in the memorial, there is not necessarily a victim's bodily enactment of a testimony, but the visitor's bodily enactment of experience. With visitors to the memorial, it is not a generation once removed from the ability to practice recollection, instead relying on imagination of traumatic experiences. Rather, we find individuals building on the experiential model of post-memory to depart from old modes of transmission altogether. In post-memory, the imagination and creation is of a lost world. In the Holocaust Memorial, it is of an invented space made for the performance of emotional transformation. Lastly, post-memory presumes a rupture, of people whose places of memory were destroyed and their parents' memory expelled. Here we do not have the rupture, or a narrative of rupture, but a movement between narratives of memory action, and not of the unmediated past. To be sure, this is not a phenomenon that is special to the memorial I studied. We can see it in pupils reacting to parts of the Jewish Museum in Berlin. For instance, the Holocaust tower is sometimes confused by young visitors with 'the gas chambers' (Bishop-Kendzia 2013). In the same manner, I often heard visitors to the memorial compare the security check in the memorial to a ghetto with Kappos or to a line guard by Stasi agents. Applying actual historical meaning to memory architecture is accompanied by visitors' apprehension regarding their relations and feelings; first, with the referred to histories and, second, in visiting the site invoking it.

Hirsch leaves the question of witnessing authenticity that Liss (1998, in Heckner 2008) raises as grounds for her skepticism of the potential of post-memory in Holocaust photography. However, as much as I agree with the techniques of affording a memorial experience through representation, projection and reinscription of a visceral experience, I would like to reiterate that it is not the experience of trauma, and that it is not achieved in modes of transmission, however productive they may be, but instead of transformation.

Upon its opening, the Holocaust Memorial did not invite, nor did it produce, a response to survivors' memories, even though those memories exist in some of its archives and rooms, together with representations of newly found victims' testimonies. Since 2010 there have been more possibilities to engage with survivors' narratives in the Fortunoff archive and through publication of books by the Memorial

Foundation which focus on the experience of one survivor. Most visitors, however, do not go to the Information Center and thus do not respond to Holocaust memories or experience, but to their own experience of the site and if they talk about the Holocaust at all, it is through this experience. For example, a teacher from Bavaria visiting the memorial with a group of pupils answered my question 'What do you think about the memorial?' thus: 'The exhibition is very good. It is an extension of the memorial. I learned about fates [...]. This gets under the skin [...]. But the pupils are overwhelmed.' To my question 'What do you take from your visit,' she answered: 'I learned about one or two families that survived, and that many went to Israel or to America and left Germany.'

The teacher assesses the Information Center through her interest in German Jewish victims ('fates', 'many went to Israel or America') and the ways the Information Center complements the *Stelenfeld* together with what she thinks about other visitors' experience ('the pupils are overwhelmed'). She concluded the description of her own impression of the memorial with an emotional statement: 'it gets under the skin.' It is a bodily, visceral experience that stands in contrast to the condition of the pupils who are clearly also moved, but too much, or too little; in any case, the place, according to the teacher, does not work for them, or does 'work' to overwhelm them.

In the third and fourth chapters I will show that the building blocks of conversation in the memorial are discussing feelings and the abstract. Narrative analysis often discusses events as the building blocks of more abstract categories in stories that people tell about themselves. The Holocaust Memorial is a case in which the opposite is true: talking about the abstract and through it about feelings constitute the building blocks of the conversation, with very little reference to events outside of the visit, which is less alluded to as an event but rather as a reference point to expressing personal transformation.

In a discussion in November 2005 with history students from the Technical University in Berlin, Uwe Neumärker, the director of the Holocaust Memorial, said, 'People can find horror stories and pictures elsewhere,' differentiating the Holocaust Memorial both from historical sites of mass murder and from the possibility that the Information Center could offer the same 'traumatizing' experience. We see the declared negation of the traumatic experience interwoven with a statement that the memorial will offer something different, which comes out of the necessity to not be like the other 'authentic' sites and not offer the experience of events in the same manner they do.

An additional 'newness' that Neumärker offers in the description of what the memorial does differently is the return to the victim's perspective, again separating it from the popular instances of Topography of Terror or the House of the Wannsee Conference, which present the perpetrators' deeds.[23] An outcome of the Memorial Foundation's insistence to present the victim's perspective, or speak in their voice, is the mixed categories of perpetrators and victims, which found its way both into the discussions regarding the memorial before its inception and to current views regarding its functioning as 'returning their names to the victims,' Lea Rosh, the initiator of the memorial together with Eberhard Jäckel and the chair of its association, often ascribes this as one of the main goals of the memorial together with speaking in the name of the victim, or from the victim's perspective. This is also seen in the quote from Primo Levi that is the motto of the Information Center exhibition, as discussed above. Frei (2004)[24] points to the mix of victim and perpetrator categories in his commentary on the sixtieth anniversary of World War II in Germany. In his piece 'felt victim' (*Gefuehlte Opfer*) published in the weekly *Zeit*, Frei discusses the rush to hear the victims as an empathic attempt to meet the war generation, which also disregards the differences between perpetrators, victims and bystanders.

This is not merely a sign of the categorical confusion between perpetrators and victims that Olick (2007a,b) and Niven (2006) discuss, but a fundamental shift from learning history, to witnessing moving personal stories and undergoing a comparable emotional transformation. In his description of 'vicarious memories,' Bartov (2003) claims that in the past three decades, people do not only 'feel' themselves into the past but also 'remember' a past that they never experienced. Besides illuminating a historical phenomenon of fabricated memories, and the sociological one of the primacy of experience in memory work, Bartov refers to the expansion of the category of victimhood both among Germans and among second and third generations to survivors (Olick 2006a,b).

The expansion of the category of victimhood was historically connected to the unification of Germany (Habermas 1997; Möller 2006), and to a widespread tendency to personalize the experience of victimhood (Gillis 1994a; Lowenthal 1994), seen in Holocaust memorial museums and their performative narration (Carrier 2005; Stier 2005). La Capra (2001) criticizes the indiscriminate generalization of the category of the survivor and the overall conflation of history with trauma, which obscures historical distinctions while enabling the first move in that shift – of learning to experience the after-effects of trauma from history. According to La Capra (2001), in the wake of writing about trauma, the universalization of the victim occurs and blurs the boundaries not only between victims and perpetrators, but also within the testimony itself, which then ceases to be historically grounded. Trans-historical trauma (as opposed to historical trauma) should be correlated with the absence of individual origins, in contrast to loss. La Capra calls not for identification, but for empathy when someone does not feel compelled or authorized to speak in the other's voice. Thus, the conflation of perpetrators and victims, of trans-historical traumatic categories with historical ones, creates interest in well-known victims, like Anne Frank, and the righteous speech 'from the victim's perspective' that is practiced in the memorial alongside their 'individualization' and 'personalization,' an affect-producing mechanism for provoking feelings in the visitor.

But since there are pictures and descriptions of Holocaust horror in the Information Center, why not understand action in the site in terms of trauma? Insisting on the abstract, unique and non-representable character of the traumatic limits events, according to La Capra (2001: 93), may lead to their construction through the hyperbolic aesthetics of the sublime. This process may prompt an inadequate account not only of representation but also of ethically responsible agency, which is what we see in both the collapse of a distinction between perpetrators and victims (and the subsequent shrinking interest in the perpetrators), and in the rush to feel for the victims, as well as to feel oneself into and out of the site at its center.

The tension between the narration of meaningful memory as historical transmission and that of engagement in a mature political entity can be heard in public reactions in and around the site and in a personal interview in February 2010 with Ms Lea Rosh, the initiator of the memorial. I asked what pleases her about the ways people visit the memorial (and what does not). Her reply was, 'when they go underground they no longer ask how much it cost.' Rosh reflects on the 17-year-long controversy and discussion that preceded the memorial's realization, which she herself was very much part of fueling, but also about the way the Information Center literally grounds the memorial experience, so that people don't question its necessity, dedication and form, when they see 'what happened.' This reference to the site's cost was prevalent in guided tours in 2006, and in every discussion of the deteriorating state of the stones. We can also read in Rosh's answer her reflection on accidental visitors. Their experience, for Rosh and many others in the Memorial Foundation, becomes intelligible in the Information Center.

Neumärker takes a slightly different position *vis-à-vis* visitor's legitimate activities in the site. When asked about visitor's actions in the site (for instance, in an interview held for the celebration of the first five years of the memorial in May 2010), he said: 'with the *Stelenfeld* there are creative ways of dealing, and different reactions. Many play hide and seek, many break into tears. The *Stelenfeld* is a mirror of the community, a mirror of the city, and it is ok.'[25] Neumärker employs Eisenman's approach to the memorial's success as a living and breathing entity with two distinctions: he connects it to the Berlin and German community, and he adds the act of crying to the acts of play. So long as this expected outcome of the visit, namely feeling sad and letting it show is taking place, playing is seen by many commentators as a harmless balancing act. Not something they wished for, but also not anything to be ashamed of. On the contrary: it shows a vibrant and engaged community.

The physical condition of the memorial has been the focus of many articles in German newspapers, especially in connection with cracks in the stones. These cracks are contrasted with the 'success story' of memory work in Berlin and become a metaphor for the memory work carried out in the memorial. For instance, articles in May 2010 celebrating its first five years discussed the memorial's success as a 'visitor magnet' alongside a grim description of the cracks. 'Around 1900 of the 2711 *Stelen* are affected (*Betroffen*[26]), but we also could 'not expect, that all parts of the memorial would look as they did on the first day,' said the director, Neumärker, in an interview to the local, freely disseminated *Berliner Woche*.[27] The tabloid *Bild* asked in March of 2010, 'can the Holocaust Memorial be saved'[28] in its description of the breaks in the concrete. The center-left *Sueddeutsche Zeitung* reported on 7 August 2007[29]: 'Memorial with fractures: the memorial must be renovated,' the article complains about the very expensive memorial already having cracks emerging, using language to describe the cracked concrete stones that can also be used to describe emotions (*Betroffenheit*). The memorial's director was interviewed and said that the problem is aesthetic and not a danger to the visitors. Elsewhere (Dekel 2009a), I analyzed the transformation from the question of what would shame the memorial, which came about in thinking about right-wing graffiti and protecting the site from it around the time of the Degussa affair in 2003, toward whether visitors would be acting shamefully when they play hide and seek, toward the larger question of what shames memory, which we can see in the given examples. Referring to the cracked stones in emotional, personal terms as 'affected and to be saved' alludes to the expectation of timelessness, both of the site and memory work, and by the same token on the vulnerability of both as they merge in the memorial – a position we can see with the mixing of categories of danger to the memorial and danger to the visitor.

We have thus far read descriptions of how visitors engage with the site along with the transitions of the site itself. However, the second most discussed topic in and about the site is whether it arouses the right emotions in visitors. In a February 2010 interview with the memorial's pedagogue, Dr Barbara Köster, she reflected on what many guides said, namely that 'the young visitors do not show much affection' and it is 'hard for the guides [...] if they have any interest, it is in the human rights discourse, which is, in the eyes of many guides, problematic.' What is the tension between showing no affection and that of being interested in human rights implications, alongside what guides often describe as a danger of relativization? It is the breaking off from old forms of memory engagement that formerly were performed around the inability to talk about the past (Jarausch and Geyer 2003), and newly developed abilities to act around just that silence in a site of memory that simultaneously invokes old, 'authentic' sites and memories. More importantly, it serves to provide a new narrative construction about the position of individuals in relation to the past, from present local, national and cosmopolitan perspectives (Eder 2005).

The construction of meaning is referential both as regards the site's abstract aesthetics and as regards what distinguishes it from other memorial sites and museums. Kelner (2010: 97), following Urry (2002), identifies three forms of semiotic difference in the construction of the tourist's relationship to place: absolute difference, difference within similarity, and similarity within difference. The first, absolute difference, is alluded to in the aesthetics of the site as well as its location on a non-distinct Holocaust ground. Another form of absolute difference is achieved in the difference in time – then and now. However, Levi's quote, and the numerous references to images and historical facts on the Holocaust, blur this absolute difference and bring similarity within difference and difference within similarity to the forefront of the memorial experience.

In addition to these, we find two forms of engaging in self-search. First, spatially: *displacement*, or the wish that many visitors express above ground to 'feel lost' in it, to be able to render its experience within the grid of Holocaust Memorial visits. This will be discussed further in Chapter 3 in relation to the performed moral career of visitors to the site. The second form is that of *constructing and collapsing distance* from the World War II era through a variety of methods: by way of the quote from Levi seen on entering the Information Center and increasingly, by describing the marginalization of the Jews in terms of the contemporary marginalization of migrant minorities, as in the 'families' workshop,' through *universalizing strategies*, or the attempt to make Holocaust stories accessible to German visitors in their contemporary everyday lives.

The workshop on families in February 2010 began with a request that pupils choose from over 20 adjectives describing familial relations and what family means for them, and post it on the common board. Among the possibilities were 'love,' 'fun,' 'security,' 'generations,' 'tradition,' 'ritual,' 'siblings,' 'parents' and 'responsibility.' On the tables, for each of the five groups, there was the story of a Jewish family destroyed in the Holocaust. The guide introduced the workshop and the topic, saying, 'everyone knows families. We will see here how they were hurt.' After they had toured the exhibition (guided by their worksheets) and each group had presented the story they were given of the five used in the workshop (selected from a total of 15 families represented in the Information Center), the guide asked the pupils to say what is lost from the options they were given at the start of the workshop, and they indicated that almost all was lost, apart from 'love,' 'parents' and 'generations,' and discussed with the guides what was actually left, if anything, for the five families studied closely in the workshop. Among the adjectives and nouns describing families there were descriptive ones referring to the structure of a family, like 'parents' and 'generations'; actions performed by families, such as rituals; and 'keywords' that refer to feelings such as love, fun, security. In the pupils' choices of what is left, there was random omission of qualities not necessarily connected to historical facts they had just learned, such as the use of the term 'generations,' which is central to German discussions of Holocaust memory. Universalizing strategies help connect the pupils' everyday lives now to the history of the Holocaust, independent of the question of knowledge and only indirectly related to their emotions in the site.

This chapter focused on experience in a site of memory that departs from post-memory. As section §4 shows, in a post-post-memorial age that brings into being the memory of an experience that is only loosely related to its historical references, the visitors focus on the present rather than the past in their response to the site. This helps us depart from trauma as a main theoretical lens in studying memory action. Section §3 dealt with historically anchoring the site's experience in the tension between its authentic and non-authentic qualities as seen through the prevalent discussion of its landscape. Section §2 introduced the memorial's space in its various new forms of presentation and consumption, while in section §1, I introduced the topic of experience with which the chapter ends: a central category of the work of the memorial as a performative space.

2
Spheres of Speakability: Old and New Discursive Modes

The first chapter discussed the pendulum between abstractness and the seemingly new arena of interaction that is informed by the set of rules known from similar non-abstract sites of Holocaust memory, which determine a form of search and improvisation in the Holocaust Memorial and in most cases then deemed as having failed. In other words, the forms of action which work in and around other sites of Holocaust memory are found time and again to not match this one. This is why a visit to the memorial seems to call for improvisation. However, since the rules are not shared by all, improvisation also does not provide the solution to the question of how to act with Holocaust memory in this site, or how it can act as a mirror to a similar ethical question around Holocaust memory in general.

In this chapter I introduce the concept of speakability, so as to explore the discursive modes in which talking about the Holocaust is shaped, performed and transmitted in the Holocaust Memorial. To do so, I begin with a theoretical reading of memory work, going beyond seeing it as the aggregation of what people know about the past in relation to the time, context and milieu in which remembering occurs (the 'collected memory' described by Olick 1999). I, instead, propose to examine collective representation of the past and what Olick (2008: 376) describes as its performance, as a phenomenon *sui generis*. Such performance is *not* inherently connected to knowledge of that past, but rather to an emotional commitment regarding the act of memory performed and discussed in a group. The claim, in other words, is that in a place of performative, as opposed to collected, memory, what people know about the past matters less as a shared basis for memory action than what they perform as the right way to 'remember.' Now, how do they know what to 'perform,' and according to which and whose rules?

The institutionalization and acceptance of play in the *Stelenfeld* makes clear that the answer is not only 'improvisation,' which clearly rests on the specific rules of a game in the open space as opposed to non-game expectations in a closed, authentic space. The answer which this chapter offers is that based on the accumulated knowledge of performing feelings, especially those pertaining to transformation around Holocaust memory, visitors as well as Foundation workers perform transformations of feeling about the metaphoric and the abstract, through which a collective as well as a personal moral career can be assessed.

Before presenting the concept and forms of speakability, I would like to discuss the acts of my interpretations, or: how I differentiate my own understanding of action in the memorial from the shared context of the visit. In a few instances it was clear to me that I do not fully understand what moves the visitors to a heated discussion or why guides react in apprehension to certain topics, such as discussions of historical anti-Semitism which were interpreted by many guides as actual anti-Semitism. It was usually when visitors from the former East presented a viewpoint that seemed to be illegitimate to the guides and seemed to me to be an important description of their own relation to the past.

The first question to ask in that regard is how I gained access to the definitions of the situation expressed and presupposed by the participants and guides (Habermas 1984, vol. 1: 131). According to Habermas, 'the lifeworld forms the horizon of processes of reaching understanding in which participants agree upon or discuss something in the one objective world, in their common social world, or in a given subjective world.' At times I realized that there was a disagreement about something unspoken. After the discussion had ended, I would ask the visitors and the guides what made them uncomfortable or angry. It was the definition of the situation which the two sides did not share, such as whether Germans could be described as victims of World War II or criticism of the way that memory work at the memorial was being led through discussion of Jewish victims. Two examples are discussed at length in Chapter 3, of a group of elderly visitors who wanted to talk about their experience of anti-Semitism in Berlin before the war, which was interpreted as being symptomatic of old GDR attitudes against democracy and in that regard also anti-Semitic.

Moving on from questions of transmission, or whether the memorial consciousness is historical or departs from history and is set within the realm of emotions, I will discuss the conditions of speakability, or the realms of deliberate and non-deliberate assertions about memory in Germany that are opened up in and around the memorial. In looking at the spheres of speakability developed in the memorial, I also seek to illuminate a 'performative' lacuna within the theory of cultural and communicative memory (Assmann 1995) involving the institutionalization of memory action, and thus offer a more dynamic approach to memory work through analysis of actual manners of engagement with the memorial.

By developing the concept of speakability, we will see that to the visitors to the site, 'being there' in a certain way takes a more important role both in telling the site's story and in memory stories. Moreover, as evident in the specific case of speakability, the rituals of declaring guilt, shame or being proud of German public memory work (Olick 2007) paved two ways for seeing the memorial's desired functions, first as a site that acknowledges crimes, and second, as a site to be proud of that culminates Germany's commitment to commemorating the Holocaust and the Jewish victims. But the memorial's Foundation and visitors wish to gain more from the site, to make it a site of moral transformation, as we will see in the next chapter, as well as to make it a site of perpetual discussion.

Speakability is the condition and outcome of engaging with the memorial: the ability to speak, which stores in it dense social knowledge put to work in talking about memory of the past. This statement and what follows is about the relations constructed around talking about the past, and is based on Tilly's (2000) observation that 'social relations store histories', or that instead of asking how histories inform social locations, we can ask *how institutions and individuals emerge out of certain forms of interaction and how the history of an interaction affect its future forms*. More specifically, I will delineate a middle-way between what Tilly calls *creative interaction* and *cultural ecology*. The former occurs in sites where there is a rough agreement about procedures and outcomes, such as in play, which enables improvisatory interaction. The latter concerns transactions among social sites which, for Tilly, 'create interdependence among extensively connected sites, deposit related cultural material in those sites, transform shared understanding in the process and thus makes large stores of culture available to any particular site through its connections with other sites' (2000: 723).

The second form of interaction is called *cultural ecology*, and focuses on transactional interaction. However, Tilly describes relations between social sites, none of which contains all knowledge about their relations, but are interdependent through shared cultural material that connects one to another and transforms shared understandings in the process, so that 'Relations store histories in this dispersed way' (2000: 723).

One can thus see in the Holocaust Memorial the relations between creative memory work within as yet unclear relational rules are celebratory as such within a self-validating 'play-like' sphere. In this sphere, the special transactions that take place between social sites that are different Holocaust-memory, tourist sites and the open public arena are quoted or referred to in an inherently incoherent style. I thus suggest that the very nature of this new mnemonic site is to validate the existence of memory work – based on and at the same time questioning practices of public memory that invent new types, and citing strategies from other kinds of site, such as the museum, the beach, the playground, the park and the mall. To the extent that visitors use play and creativity that some deem inappropriate, then cite a repertoire from other social sites as available examples for action in this one, it is located between creative interaction and cultural ecology.

I described the practices of institutional memory production, or how the sphere of memory work stores histories, among which is knowledge of other mnemonic practices. We will next look more closely at the specific site of German memory work performed in the memorial. I do not assume a coherently 'German' mnemonic practice or culture. However, since public memory work relies on normative modes of justification which are usually made of grand narratives (Boltanski and Thévenot 1999, in Eder 2009), I suggest that the spheres of speakability, which construct the mnemonic practices, will reflect well-known remembrance frames such as silence, guilt, shame and responsibility, through which memory work becomes convincing and indeed 'real.' Both state memorials and initiatives and civil initiatives, such as the one that brought the Holocaust Memorial into realization, use these categories. Thus, understanding how the spheres of speakability work can frame our understanding of what Eder calls Civil Society IV, in which it 'turned from an instance of defense against state power to a partner of political power' (2009: 25). We will see how what actors say and do in the memorial and the institutionalization of memory work on the state and the civil society level are indivisible.

Eder's (2009) discussion of civil society as imagined, practiced and staged, describes relations between civil society and state actors as a competition between at least two scripts pertaining to the role of the performers. According to him, civil society is a script which is context-sensitive and which is embedded in permanent movement in time and space. In our case, the performance of relations between civil society and state narratives is practiced and staged in the memorial as an ever-shifting boundary between groups and individuals performing and observing memory work. As Olick (2008) notes, memory 'has a history', and historical debates and their performance, too, can be studied as the events they commemorate are studied. With this statement in mind, we can understand the ways old memory practices influence the ones discussed here and also how new modes of experiencing the past can develop.

The action of initiating speech is instigated in opposition to the well-worn claim concerning the inability to speak, or need for silence, about the Holocaust experienced by the first two generations post-World War II. This endeavor, however, becomes a site of performance that is no longer connected to the historical events to which it relates, but rather to the visitor's moral standing in relation to memory work and the presumed positions of fellow visitors in relation to the past. In connecting civil society's performance and the public sphere, or the site and time of action, we can refer to the context in which those actions are embedded as that of assuming a coherent 'culture of memory.' We will also, following Eder's question of how the public 'civilizes civil society', look at the perspective the public takes on civil society performance, focus on the relations between the emotional realm of interpretation in this specific memory performance, and the differentiating mechanism between good and less favorable memory work. Eder claims that 'Civil society provides a stage for performing diversity without violating the principle of equality. Civil society is a form of staging differences' (2009: 31).

The Holocaust Memorial hosts different performing publics, who do not always care how their actions are evaluated (or care to show that they don't care), but most play according to a bounded script about Holocaust memory, thus staging differences between different scripts in a stark manner. On the other hand, Memorial Foundation employees are civil society agents who partake in the perpetual process of evaluating action in the site and are closer to state agents. All these actors participate in the self-referentiality of civic action through the mechanism of learning, mediated by the force of continuing a narration once started (Eder, 2009: 32), while re-evaluating, adding to, omitting and playing with it. We will analyze the interplay of the organizing narrative of memory work and the specific time and space mechanisms which provide its context.

§1   From cultural to communicative memory and back

Assmann's (1995) distinction between communicative and cultural memory as a means of institutionalizing memory action is helpful in explaining the transformative terrain of the memorial for visitors and, at the same time for the discourse on German memory work. Using Assmann's distinction, I show how the memorial operates as a transformative device from communicative to cultural memory, and back again to the communicative, simple-to-mold level. I first introduce the theory, then criticism on the question of whether there is, or could be, one 'memory culture' in today's Germany, and then, through the discussions of Jews and minorities in the memorial, I suggest that we should look more at the open-endedness of multi-vocal memory work.

According to Assmann (1995), communicative memory is the everyday, flowing, unstable and not yet institutionalized perception of the past; while cultural memory dwells in the realm of institutionalized culture with the potential to be elevated from the everyday. For Assmann, cultural memory has the capacity to reconstruct the past through available frames of reference. Cultural memory is inherently of things past, while communicative memory is of the still (at least potentially) enfolding past, and as such brings together individuals and collectives who give meaning to reality in their memory work. Assmann distinguishes between two modes in which cultural memory exists: potentiality, where accumulated texts act as the horizon; and actuality, 'whereby each contemporary context puts the objectivized meaning into its own perspective, giving it its own relevance' (1995: 130).

I suggest that in the memorial, communicative memory is transformed into cultural memory that *is* located in the everyday. Symbolic representations of the institutionalized ways to deal with the past, mediated by established culture, can be seen in the memorial and in the ways people react to it. That this performance of institutionalized memory again turns communicative is due in part to the ambiguous conditions of entry to the memorial that are non-explicit by design, calling for a perpetual search for meaning above ground, which can then also lead to a discussion of the meaning of remembering the Holocaust, or the Holocaust itself. Guides encourage public sense-making in the memorial, a public, staged interpretation of discourse, as the desired praxis at the site.

In observing the movement from cultural to communicative memory, one can see in the memorial the establishment of virtual communicative memory, which utilizes new media to create interactivity around photos and fragments of testimony, and enables a combination of the indexical and the archival forms together with the familial form seen in family albums. Former frames of memory personalization that create effects of authentication (Huyssen 2003, in Hirsch 2008: 120) of the past are presented in the Information Center. These frames, however, collide with two new affect-oriented mechanisms: the authentic experience above ground and the inauthentic nature of the exhibits, which are taken from other archives and museums and are directed at illuminating two aspects of knowledge about the Holocaust: the European and the personal dimensions of annihilation. Mediation enables the pendulum between communicative and cultural memory.

Levy and Sznaider (2002) introduced the term *cosmopolitan memory* regarding Holocaust memory beyond the nation-state in the age of globalization, which indicates the common ground of memory symbolism with respect to human rights and genocide in recent decades. Although I encountered very few attempts at comparing the Holocaust to other genocides in the memorial (guides and Memorial Foundation workers would vehemently oppose it as a form of Holocaust relativization), the growing interest of visitors in human rights and other victim groups and the reference made by visitors to other historical and current atrocities makes the concept relevant to the discussion of the memorial. As a special case, it is located in an area that derives its authenticity from the urban history of National Socialist power. It is literally the site of (other) sites of memory and as such adheres to the relative openness of cosmopolitan memory.[1] The term I offer of *virtual communicative memory* refers to the possibility of articulation that is facilitated both in and outside of the memorial through various media (archives, testimony, conversation about the site), which escapes the phase of cultural, more established memory, and enables different forms of engagement with the past.

While communicative, everyday memory does not need specialists because it is biographical (Hirsch 2008) and is transmitted within the family and among living individuals who have experienced that which they remember, cultural memory always depends on a specialized 'cultivation' practice. Assmann (1995: 131) distinguishes three levels of cultivation that are relevant to the present discussion: (1) the *cultivation of text* as can be seen in the Foundation's insistence on the accuracy of records in the place of information[2]; (2) the *cultivation of meaning* as manifested in hermeneutic and moral judgment within the memorial, or in acts of assessing engagement with the site and its forms – for example, asking 'what is it' or 'is it OK to enjoy oneself in the memorial' are forms of judgment within the memorial, expressed by visitors, and are part of the cultivation of meaning that signals cultural memory; and (3) *mediation*, or the translation of text into life, which is what the guides try to do in guided tours both in the site above ground and in Information Center underground. Lastly, Assmann argues that the binding character of knowledge preserved in cultural memory has two aspects: the formative one with its educative, civilizing and humanizing functions, and a normative one, providing rules of conduct mediated by symbolic systems.

In line with the more recently developed distinction of Aleida Assmann (2006), according to which cultural memory is archival and national, in the memorial the formative and the normative functions of this institutional memory collide, since both dwell in the sphere of present action that relies on experience. The guides and workers, as well as the media and the visitors have an idea of the *implied visitor*[3] who searches for meanings in the space created between herself and the memorial. This space is composed of her knowledge of the site and of the history of its and other memorial sites' realization. In the act of touring and searching, her judgment will reveal something about her norms as well as about the larger context of her visit. This revelation then becomes a source for further search, which aims at bringing about transformation in the visitor's experience of the past and communication of it.

This description has departed from an underlying assumption of both cultural and communicative memory – that of a certain relationship to a certain past. I would suggest that aside both from the passage of time and generation crucial for Assmann's account, and from trauma, or rupture of the possibility of remembrance, discussed in Chapter 1 with reference to Hirsch's instructive discussion of *post-memory*, we can find an established connection to memory, with very periodic and indexical connections to the past, because they function as a symbolic grid of the ways people ascribe meaning, and inter-generational transmission of knowledge cannot be presumed. Hirsch (2008) argues that the concept of post-memory is a generational structure of emphatic transmission. I would now like to present the modes of transmission that do not rely on first- or second-hand experiencing of the past, but on publically performed discussions in the memorial that use fragmented knowledge about the past as well as about the victims to enable personal transformation.

When talking with visitors about their experience at the memorial and what they thought about it, I have tried to probe the presumptions of the processes by which speakability is achieved deliberately and non-deliberately. I did not presume any former knowledge or relationship with the site. I asked not, 'What do you feel?' or 'What most impresses you?' that guides asked their groups, but instead 'What do you take from the memorial?', 'How do you find/What do you think about the memorial?' The shift from talking about feelings to talking about the experience in the site enabled a reflection on the processes by which spheres of speakability are created and maintained. Short interviews with visitors were carried out in both research periods and reflected similar views to those of visitors on guided tours with a few exceptions. The interviews were carried out in the *Stelenfeld* in German, English and Hebrew, and I did not ask or assume that the visitors had been or intended going to the Information Center or to any other memorial site. The reactions about it as mediating tools for the experience of the memorial were therefore scarce, but distinctly, those who were in the underground Information Center talked directly about facts related to the Holocaust in comparison to those who were not. The location of the interview in the *Stelenfeld* itself did not affect the answers as far as I could tell. I initially assumed that the further away physically the interview was from the Information Center, the less likely it would be that people would talk about the Holocaust, which was not the case.

However, age group and nationality differences were apparent: young German visitors expressed their views in metaphorical terms, older visitors made direct references to the history of the Holocaust and to Holocaust memory in Germany. Visitors in 2006 from other countries spoke more about 'the German memorial' or 'the German memory project' in comparison to 2010–12. Six years after the opening of the memorial, visitors reflected on 'tragic history' with less assessment of Germany's memory project. In all cases, I asked two open-ended questions and received answers that lasted between two and five minutes.

For example, in July 2012 from among a group of ten people in their twenties coming from the Balkans on a German Foundation study tour, one student answered the questions as follows:

1. **'What do you think about the memorial?'**: 'Great, tragic history. I mean great, it stands for history.'
2. **'What do you or others take from the visit/from the site?'**: 'It makes me uncomfortable. I don't know what people take from it. People take advantage of this they are laughing and jumping on "stones."'

This student referred indirectly to the Holocaust ('history,' 'tragic history') and directly to other visitor's activities, which to him hindered the task of the memorial and made him feel uncomfortable, even angry in the way he related to the other visitors perception of 'stones.'

A couple from Romania in their fifties, sitting on a stele on the south-west part of the memorial answered the first question 'What do you think about the memorial?': 'We knew it, we knew about it from the tourist guide' and 'But we were surprised by the architecture. The idea of the architect was of a cemetery, of something dark, definitive'.

Their answer to the second question was 'People take thoughts about what happened, and that somebody was capable of doing it.' This couple related to the metaphor of the cemetery in the memorial. The second answer connected more directly to the Holocaust: 'people take thoughts about what happened,' with direct reference to agency, 'someone was capable of doing it'.

The search for meaning becomes a search for the validity of one's own interpretation along with an attempt to interpret, pointing to the question whether consciousness can be historical, or how relations around memory relate and build on their own history, with which I opened the chapter. Somewhat similarly to what Till (2005) expected – that within the *new memory district* of Topography of Terror, the memorial and the Jewish Museum – the memorial will offer visitors a space for transforming horror into hope. On the grounds this is indeed a space for performing transformation, and visitors engage in a search for meaning in the abstract by asking what the conditions are through which it could make sense to them and to others, and in what context the claim for meaning can be accepted. This is a case of action in the public sphere that is highly dependent on context, but at the same time perpetuates the age-old narratives of perpetrators and victims held in common by Germans, Israelis and visitors from other countries, suspending the immediate redemptive outcome but keeping it an open possibility through the (failed) chance to understand and the call to serve as a witness to Levi's dictum, making sure that 'this will never happen again.'

1.1   What is speakability?

Speakability is a social condition enabled by discussions in and around the memorial, and a larger discursive change which relies on the rules of democratic articulation and at the same time serves as a negative to the inability to speak about the Holocaust (Jarausch and Geyer 2002). Given the understanding that all memory is social, dependant on physical objects, surroundings and other humans (Halbwachs [1925] 1992) and communicative in as much as it does not exist within but between people (Welzer 2010), we will explore the changing experience of the memorial as presented and discussed by visitors in guided tours and workshops, in conversation with me and in the visitors' book. We will take into account the various media shaping the experience: print, broadcast, spoken, photos and film. The speakability which has so far been developed in the memorial with its non-discursive mode, abundant with symbols, references and voids, is connected to the understanding of oneself as a potential victim of the war, either as a Jew or as identifying with the Jew. It is signified by speech acts based on former symbolic universals signifying the Holocaust, such as comparing the Field of Stelae to a graveyard that then shifts into signifying proper or improper memory work in that space. The prevalence of the graveyard metaphor points to Crownshaw's observation that 'The universalization of the victim compounds the otherness of the perpetrator and obfuscates the process of perpetration' (2011, 77). Without getting into the question of closure that is also signified in the graveyard metaphor, the nameless graves for the nameless victims (whose names are then searched and, when known, presented underground); the perpetrators are not alluded to, but the acts of perpetration have to be told and shown in order to be represented.

I recognize four types of speakability:

1. **Witnessing.** The most prevalent form, which allows one to talk about the past and thus of the right ways to engage with it.
2. **Guilt/shame.** The mirror case to the post-war thesis that guilt and shame have not actually been the most productive mechanism in making people engage with the past.
3. **Performing silence.** In which sorrow and grief are united in the announcement of the need to be silent, alone and together.
4. **Provoking knowledge.** Where personal engagement with Holocaust memory today, following knowledge accumulated in the visit, is expected from visitors walking in the Information Center and the *Stelenfeld*.

Visitors to the memorial speak very little about actual remembering and more about 'dealing with the past.' This form of action puts pressure on present memory work, for it is not only that narratives about the past change slowly, or that the public knows less about the Holocaust. Rather, what is mostly reflected on in a memorial visit is the framework for experiencing a proper memory of the past, legitimatizing the state-recognized division of labor between institutions commemorating that past and the memorial's genres: invented and authentic. In other words, visitors of different age groups react to the Information Center and the memorial above ground through their relations to the past, the ways it is transmitted to them in the family, school and media, and what they know about and expect from the memorial in relation to what they experienced in other Holocaust memorial and historical sites. This argument is historically specific in its attempt to demonstrate that it is no longer a debate about how much memory is good for the public, as I claimed earlier (Dekel 2008), following Benz's, the head of the center for anti-Semitism Research and the spokesperson of the Memorial's Advisory Board, assertion in a public discussion about the memorial in 2006 that 'the public needs more than they want', and his reading of the historians' debate, which Olick summarized thus: 'it often seemed as if the right wanted identity without history and the left wanted history without identity' (2008: 377).

This question is less relevant in 2011, since the public flock to memorials, as well as initiate new ones in Berlin and in other urban centers (Huyssen 2003), and visitors to these memorials deal neither with history nor with 'identity' (here meaning national and collective) that the historians debate. They use both terms as self-referential symbols in speech acts pertaining to their own experience of the site. As Wagner-Pacifici (2005) shows in her sociological analysis of surrender, the performative is one semiotic phase in the deep structure of surrender, which then gets represented. In between the performance and its representation there is the semiotic phase of demonstration, which is dependent on the witnessing of the very performance of surrender. This demonstrative phase is crucial to understanding the possible terrain of performing emotional transformation in the memorial through the four forms of speakability and its demonstrated failure.

How are we to see memory studies in an era with fewer, shorter lasting controversies, in which memory is a product not of the chafing of history, but of consuming and performing feelings in invented, public sites or around newly written texts?[4] These sites now partake in a staged activity whose rules and outcomes are shared and concern the de-legitimatization of former state memorial initiatives (such as the Neue Wache), together with favoring discussion of new ones which define their work on dealing with the difficult and shameful German past as a national duty. Thus, the first phase of performing speakability after departing from the 'inability to speak' pertains to a collective, national but also cosmopolitan, duty.

§2   Witnessing

Could we call visiting the memorial a witnessing act? The 'classical' witness is an external party observing the actions of others, who, as

Wagner-Pacifici puts it, 'survive, render and remember [...] give lie to the distinction between action and observation in the sphere if history' (2005: 303). Further, according to Wagner-Pacifici, all witnessing involves some ratio of performative, demonstrative and representational acts. The term witness means participating or being inside the event and testimony, or being a third party. It seems to me that in the memorial there is a movement between the two kinds of witnessing, since on the one hand, mostly in the *Stelenfeld*, the witness is a participant, while underground, attenuated by Primo Levi's citation, they are third-party observers of history, making sure that 'it does not happen again.' Of course, the passage of time from the events of the Holocaust, to which visitors are called to bear witness, makes the case even more complicated, since they easily get implicated in the events, in a position that I and others observed as an amalgamated perspective, comprising both that of perpetrators and that of victims (Crownshaw 2011; Dekel 2011; Radstone 2001). Wagner-Pacifici (2005: 397) further shows that all witnesses are both inside and outside of an event: they are implicated in it and freed from its mandates. Witnessing is thus prevalent in the memorial, connecting its above ground and underground experience and creating the first form of speakability, or the first shared form of mediating this actual as well as metaphorical space. Wagner-Pacifici illuminates the form of exchange she calls 'cross witnessing': 'witnesses witness actors engaging in the actions on the stage. Witnesses also witness other witnesses witnessing the action' (2005: 309). Wagner-Pacifici adds that the relation of witnesses to the scene is a function of proximity, point of view and perception. The first two are spatio-temporal and the last has to do with the social context, past perception and other actors and witnesses in this memory act and past ones.

In the Holocaust Memorial, becoming a witness of public as well as private stories of one person, or a family, impels one to talk about the past and then of the right ways to engage with it. I discussed elsewhere (Dekel 2009a) the witnessing of other individuals at the memorial itself and their actions as both a trigger and predicament of speech. As a trigger, talking about the legitimacy of certain actions in the site connects its location on a mental map of Holocaust memorials to that of 'authentic' sites where one is expected to act solemnly. This is precisely the predicament: discussing the possibility of playing tag or eating in the Field of Stelae marks the Holocaust as a lamentable event disconnected from politics and history.

Observing visitors, guides and media reflections on the site reveals that witnessing is the most prevalent form of speakability in the memorial. It is also the most common activity in the Information Center, where one encounters personal and family stories, photos and film. Through these one witnesses the normalcy and 'everyday' aspect of Jewish life before the war, and then the scope of annihilation from that personal perspective. As stated earlier, the largest text opening the installation, written on the wall leading to the first corridor, is the quote we've already encountered from Primo Levi: 'It happened, and therefore it can happen again. This is the core of what we have to say.' This quote calls for all forms of speakability. It creates a witness to Primo Levi's personal story and symbolic meaning of a survivor warning against a second Holocaust from his particular moral standpoint. It also creates witnessing to the quoting body, the Memorial Foundation, stressing its mission statement upon entering the Information Center. A statement that amounts to: beware; what we are talking about here is history and its possible outcomes. We will see how this works within the other three spheres of speakability.

The following excerpt is taken from a guided tour in March 2006. The two guides ask the pupils to say what they thought about the installations in the Information Center:

PUPIL 1.   In my view the best room was the room with the statements [testimonies].

GUIDE 1.   Room 1.

PUPIL 1.   Yes.

GUIDE 1.   So people find themselves in such conditions and write.

PUPIL 1.   People write.

GUIDE 1.   Yes, people write. It was not always easy, especially in situations where people were deported, or running away. It is crazily fascinating how people had the pen and the paper to write in such conditions, and anyhow the whereabouts this, writing must stay secret. Maybe hidden, or in one's clothes that were found later, or in the pockets, or one can give it to someone one trusts, who can bring it further. And one must also know that these documents were not thought through. They are singular, and so a very authentic look into the person and how they felt in the moment of writing and seeing death with one's own eyes.

GUIDE 2.   People wanted to leave something behind, and then, why, for what purpose?

PUPIL 2.   People were transported all over Europe, they wanted to reach out to others maybe.

GUIDE 2.   Yes, somehow to inform. When one saw death in front of one's eyes, knowing that there would be no help any more, one wanted maybe to leave a testimony, something that would stay behind. There is no history without testimony. (*Pause*)

Discussing the quality of the installation and what moves people in it is a tool for discussing people's knowledge of the past and relationship to it. We will see how the fourth form of speakability, provoking knowledge, operates on this basic level of creating a threshold for discussion, as well as enabling the highest form of engagement – informed, endless search and discussion. The 'self-testimonies' in the Room of Dimensions (room 1) enlarge the possibility of witnessing on the visitor's part, which is why these testimonies are so successful and moving in their view. The letters are so moving because they reveal something about the victims' knowledge of their own imminent death. Moreover, they enlarge the visitor's credibility as a witness without endangering either role: that of the victims who registered their experience against all odds, and that of the witnesses, today, who recognize what happened and thereby also give a testimony about their relationship to the past.

The literature of witnessing a traumatic event or an account of such an event relies on psychoanalytic theory (Caruth 1993; Felman and Laub, 1992; La Capra 1998). In Chapter 1, I suggested going beyond the terminology of post-trauma in getting to grips with understanding memory action in the site. I would here, nonetheless, use its literature on testimony to account for the appeal of witnessing, precisely because of the prevalence of psychoanalytic theory in the discourse on memory. Felman argues that testimony became a crucial mode of our relating to events of our time: 'As a relation to events, testimony seems to be composed of bits and pieces of a memory that has been overwhelmed by occurrences that have not settled into understanding or remembrance, nor assimilated into full cognition, events in excess of our frames of reference' (1991: 5). Testimony, Felman suggests, is a discursive practice, not a full account. As such, the practice of witnessing testimony, in either text or image, consequent to bearing witness to the murdered Jews' fates, is used in the memorial to create speech acts about the past. This practice, I suggest in this chapter, is one form of speakability, and as for the three others, it is performative and may stir more accounts by visitors describing their experience, or more rarely, a discussion. Even if not fully discussed, testimony can achieve a form of engagement with history. It makes the visitor a witness to a personal fate that then follows her in the exhibition until she verbalizes it.

A worksheet given to pupils in guided tours upon entering the Information in 2007 reads:

> The goal is to *give back*[5] their names and histories to the murdered. In the four exhibition rooms you will meet different paths to the fates of the murdered Jews of Europe.
>
> Please stay in the foyer. Take some time for yourself and review the six single portraits in front of you. These portraits represent the six million Jewish victims. In these photos you meet women, men and children from different Jewish life-worlds.
>
> Which of these persons talks to you? Choose one of the six persons and note for yourself the information written underneath.[6]
>
> Together with this person you will now experience the installation. During the tour you'll meet again some points in the life of the person you chose.

As the visitor makes herself familiar with each person and his or her fate, she is supposed to choose one who speaks to her the most, someone whose face, or place of birth, age, or place of death, they find compelling. They 'meet' them and through the installation they will 'meet' again at some points on that person's life trajectory. Similar to touring the Holocaust Memorial Museum in Washington, D.C., an individual follows another individual's fate.[7] However, in the Berlin memorial the visitor chooses 'her/his person' who, first, represents victims for her and, second, represents different 'life-worlds.' Thus, the described tasks create a clear distinction and distance between the visitor, who is presumably not Jewish, and the victim. These worksheets have not been in use since 2009, as pupils were asked to retrieve information about a victim or a family and present it on a timeline, but not to say how and whether they relate to these persons. We will see later in this chapter the modes of class and leisure, birth date and town of origin, through which visitors relate to specific personal stories and fates.

2.1   Witnessing ourselves: Jews as ordinary people

A prevalent topic in the guided tours is that of showing Jews as ordinary people. This is done through telling the personal and family stories of Jews who perished in the Holocaust, as well as telling about an experience of meeting with survivors in the memorial itself. I will present here only the aspect connecting witnessing and testimony to the presentation of Jews.

In a guided tour with Year 11 secondary school pupils in May 2005, the guide tries to blur the boundaries between the Jew as an 'other' and the German audience. She confronts the pupils with personal similarities between a potential Jew and themselves:

GUIDE.　This is a memorial built by Germans. Actually, Jews were against it. Could you think why the Jews were against the building of the memorial in Berlin?

PUPIL.　They were afraid.

GUIDE.　Of what? If your grandparents were murdered in another country, would not you like them to be remembered?

PUPIL.　Sure I would.

GUIDE.　So what are they afraid of? Maybe they are against the memorial being built in the land of the perpetrators because they don't need it there? Maybe they say: 'How dare you build a memorial for us here? We don't need it. It happened to us. We think about it everyday.'

The guide, who is German-Jewish, attempts to decode the boundaries between Germans and Jews and then rebuilds them. She brings the Jew back in as an ordinary person seeking remembrance of his loved ones. She is talking about Jews today, not necessarily victims or survivors of the war, but then confronts the German audience by speaking in those Jews' names when quoting their critique of the memorial project done by Germans to honor the Jews. By challenging this particular facet of German identity, still defined by distance from the 'other' (the representation of a Jew as a victim), the guide includes them as potential group members. She also offers a tool to relate differently to other European groups, as well as minority groups in Germany.

This guide, in her guided tours, is one of few to reflect on the absence of perpetrators from the installation. She said in another guided tour with adults from the Left Party (*die Linke*) that she thinks that 'as much as Jews, as individual persons, are shown in the memorial Information Center so should the perpetrators be discussed personally.' One visitor said in response: 'Yes, why, in fact, do we not have a memorial to the perpetrators, featuring their names and addresses?' This call to balance the stress put on victims with as much dexterity in exposing the perpetrators is often discussed by and among memorial workers. Most of them agree that there is not enough emphasis on perpetrators, because of the division of labor with other institutions commemorating the Holocaust and dictatorship in Berlin-Brandenburg.

When asked by non-German visitors and myself about the reception of the memorial by 'visitors who were on the side of the perpetrators,' guides and hosts often reply that it is hard to react to this: 'Once an old man came who said that he dealt with the topic for many years and he is now ashamed. It was hard to deal with it.'[8] All memorial workers admit that the memorial does not sufficiently deal with perpetrators, but whereas for this guide and a few others this is a topic to be raised through the presentation of Holocaust atrocities and their memories, other guides avoid confrontation on these issues and actually think it is inappropriate, mostly because they respect the division of labor in memorial institutions, in which the Memorial Foundation took upon itself the role of representing the murdered Jews. If this is the case, why is there so much symbolic work in making the Jew an ordinary person with which one can easily identify? One answer would direct us to the second part of the memorial's name: of Europe. In order to represent the dead Jews as European (and not all migrants in Germany, even after two and three generations, get this privileged status), one has to be able to see them as such. But perhaps the other grounds for the importance of witnessing is the fact that only through that level of relations with the victims, will visitors be able to personally relate to the Jews' and other minorities' fates.

2.2 Guilt/shame

This form of speakability corresponds with the post-war thesis that guilt and shame have not been the most productive mechanism for making people engage with the past, or more broadly, that remembering a difficult past is important and achievable, but through productive means of engagement and not through guilt and shame, which were in any case rendered irrelevant from the second generation onward (Olick 2007a,b; Welzer 2002). Most guides identify as Germans in the memorial, and only a few invoke shame among the visitors, or talk about their own guilt feelings with the visitors. Till (2005:179) notes that representing German guilt was one of the goals listed in the first competition, and artists mostly undertook to fulfill this goal through the commonly expected forms of Jewish symbols, references to graves, concentration camp icons and biblical scripts. After the first chosen design was rejected, the goals of the memorial, together with the need to literally represent guilt were better contextualized. However, although we can see the shift from the language of guilt to that of responsibility in the memorial itself, guides often commented to me about feeling guilty, mainly through the need to deal with the Holocaust, study and teach it and by talking about their family history as the ground for their engagement with the Holocaust. I never asked directly about their grandparents and parents and never offered my account before I was asked about it.

This form of speakability thus recalls the inability to speak or talk about the Holocaust because of shame and guilt, which at the same time situates this historical mechanism for silence about the Holocaust within the family (Welzer et al. 2002). It is worth considering an example from the memorial's visitors' book and two from guided tours. The visitors' book entry relates to someone's family history while the first guided tour example invokes shame in the visitors and the second sheds light on the shame and guilt that the guide feels.

The entry, in German, in the visitors' book reads: 'Both of my grandfathers were Nazis, and I am deeply ashamed. But I cannot change it.' The writer wrote only this sentence in the visitors' book. It implies that the visit was an opportunity for him to reveal this – but not a redemptive one, not because stating one's guilt is not redemptive, but because one cannot change the fact. The possibility of closure without redemption is a very potent one. It rests on the liberating conflict with Christian values embedded in European memory culture, especially in German memory culture that used universal Christian values to look at all victims evenly, and to assess anti-Semitism not as racism, but as a problem between Christians and Jews (Olick and Levy 1997). A. Dirk Moses (2007) thus suggests that the terms 'guilt' and 'shame' cannot 'account for the intergenerational transmission of moral pollution signified by Holocaust memory.' He offers instead the concepts of stigma and sacrifice. Pointing to what Germans feel about their past (as described in their accounts), Moses turns to the use of concepts that presume the signifying of Germans as guilty, hence carrying a stigma. The whole notion of guilt, Moses points out, is biblical, using the idea of inherited sin. The language of moral pollution used by politicians describing German guilt makes Moses choose the concept of stigma, recognizing that it is not a sentiment like guilt. According to Moses, in order to cope with the stigma, Germans had to view the murdered Jews as sacrificed, which made it easier first to see them as victims and second to identify with them.

Thinking of oneself as a victim is one kind of redemption, but thinking of closure without redeeming the deed can be a powerful mechanism of coping with the Holocaust as Germans. James (2006) describes how East Germans redeem their German identity after unification through the reconstruction of sites that were destroyed in the war. In the visitors' book entry there is no such attempt at undoing the wrongdoing. However, by stating that the writer cannot change the fact that his grandfathers were Nazis, even with his shame, his standpoint is that of the self-assessing of one's relationship to the past, whether through guilt, shame or other forms of engagement. In this example, the very statement connects personal German history that could also be shared in other sites of Holocaust memory, to this one, when a third-generation German reveals that he knows his family's history, then that he is ashamed of it, but since it is a matter of the past, there is nothing he or she could do to change it. In this sense, what the memorials' supporters wanted it to be: a place for Germans to recognize the murder of the Jews, is realized. The question remains, of course, whether this sense of the sacrificed Jews will take the German collective memory of the genocide beyond identification with the victims, toward a more diverse and tolerant community, which can be performed at the memorial (Habermas 1997, in Moses 2007).

A German guide at the memorial in March 2011 conveyed the same message of stating one's clear relations to the perpetrators' side, this time on a more general level connecting German identity with the difficulty of constructing the Holocaust Memorial. The guided tour was given in English to American university students visiting Berlin. The guide began by making three statements refuting some common perceptions about how the guided tour itself would go: (1) he is not a historian; (2) the tour at the Holocaust Memorial will not be about the Holocaust; and (3) it took 'us Germans' 60 years to build this memorial because we were not ready to talk about what we did. These three statements counter what a representative visitor would assume about a German guide to the Holocaust Memorial: instead there will be no discussion of history, or the Holocaust; the guide speaks openly about his German identity and about the Germans' problem with the past. The visitors seemed unmoved by these counter-intuitive statements, and the guide proceeded to describe the history of the site, then the destruction of Germany and its 'liberation' in 1945, its reconstruction and division into two states. He then talked about German unification. He repeated the third statement with a slight change, namely 'it took us Germans quite a long time to view this as liberation.' The third time the guide talks about 'us Germans' is when he talks about the erection of the memorial itself. He asks, 'how did it come to our society' to finally build a central memorial for the murdered Jews? A student answers with the assumption that the generation of Nazis had to die out first. The guide later confirms: 'Maybe these things take their time, until the perpetrators die.' He offers a different perspective, however, on why and how the memorial was realized, stating that it had a lot to do with emotional relations to the Holocaust and how it was mediated in the TV mini-series *Holocaust*: '1978 was the first time that the Germans confronted mass murder emotionally, through a story of a German-Jewish family in the American TV mini-series Holocaust.' In the Information Center the guide repeated the importance of emotional relations to the Holocaust, now potentially practiced and shared by all nationalities: 'we don't only give facts but also the personal dimension. We present the Holocaust not only through facts and statistics but also through emotions.'

The guide refutes the presumption that a German will talk favorably about his own culture, by presenting the shortcomings of German society in remembering its own deeds. He then presents the idea that through emotions, Germans relate most strongly and efficiently to the Holocaust, in line with what Levy and Sznaider (2006) term the 'cosmopolitanism' of Holocaust memory as a universal story of victims. In Chapter 3 we will discuss the use of sentiments of sorrow in visitors' performance at the site, and ask how the position of German guilt is countered by the construction of Germans as victims of totalitarianism. Here, I would like to concentrate on the presentation of German guilt that facilitates speakability, first about the memorial and, through it, about memory of the Holocaust (and sometimes atrocities of other nations at other times).

We saw how guilt and shame are coupled in stating one's position in relation to the Holocaust, then the guide's statement about how German guilt and emotional angst blocks acknowledgement as the country of the perpetrators. We will now move to see how the terms 'guilt' and 'shame' have been substituted by those of 'responsibility'. The visitors are motivated by the very act of the visit to the memorial to engage in '*Auseinandersetzung*'[9] with the Holocaust. This term is the one most used by memorial staff in describing expected action in the site. This form of engaging with the past is a very personal one, and presumes, primarily, not the willingness to remember – the discourse shifts from memory to experience – but the willingness to deal with issues of remembrance and representation of the past. Responsibility is a concept in which one can become guilty if failing to care about the outcomes of one's deeds. Responsibility can make guilt possible. The concurrence is thus between obligation and relations oriented morals. The writer of the example taken from the visitors' book is not responsible for the grandfathers' deeds, though the expression of shame shows an obligation for a different set of morals. Richard von Weiszäcker expressed this structure of speech over responsibility and future oriented morals in a heavily cited speech on World War II remembrance: 'the generation that was born after the war is not responsible for what happened but of the historical consequences' (quoted in Hartman 1986).

The following example is of a guided tour of German pupils in April 2011, which was followed by a discussion in the seminar room at the Information Center. Here we will see that the guide, a German woman in her forties, spoke about 'the Germans' not in terms of 'we', and opposed the terms of 'shame' with that of 'responsibility' in her description of the long time it had taken to realize the memorial. Guide: 'How long do you think the memorial has existed? The pupils' answers are of between 20 and 50 years. The guide then says that it has existed for six years and asks why it took so long to realize. A pupil answers that it had taken a long time 'to talk about it.' The guide says that the nature of the talking also changed. In the 1960s young adults asked their parents, 'What was your role?' 'What did you do? Why did you not do anything?' However, the memorial took even longer, another generation, to be discussed, and for a citizen's initiative to be created. After the civic initiative was formed, it still took many years. Why was this? A pupil answers, 'Maybe the older people did not want to face history?' The guide asks; But why do we need this?:

PUPIL.   So that people do not forget.
GUIDE.   People in Germany asked: 'Will it be a memorial that will shame us?' People said: 'We have to be able to forget.' It was all very emotional. And after a long time and much discussion it was realized that the memorial is about respect and responsibility, not shame. It had taken years to realize that it is about the future.

The guide follows the conviction expressed by Richard von Weiszäcker that German memory work of the Holocaust is the civic concern of a healthy, future-oriented community. Notwithstanding, the guide raises the issue of shame, which is presented as parallel to forgetfulness: those who wish to be no longer ashamed by the past could also be those who wish to forget. She thus presents the discussion as 'emotional,' culminating in a realization that a built memorial will reflect respect (to whom?) and responsibility (toward what and of whom?), echoing the discussions regarding the memorial's role in building a healthy society by and for Germans that were reviewed in the first chapter. Those questions remained open in this guided tour, and the guide moved on to discuss the fact that the memorial was dedicated solely to Jews.

This guided tour ended with a conversation in the seminar room, in which the guide asked the pupils to reflect on their feelings and thoughts at the memorial, especially the Information Center. At first, no pupil spoke, but the guide then gave them a pen and asked them to pass it between them, so that each person that talks holds it, then passes it on to the next. In this way, all the pupils talked about their experience of the Information Center.

GUIDE. Perhaps there is a room that spoke to you?

PUPIL 1. I found it very good, eh, the room with the statements and the room where you could see the families [...]

GUIDE. Is there anything that stayed in your memory? Or that you read?

PUPIL 1. Yes, with the statements there was a person, I don't remember what his name was, he wrote in his diary that he would like that someone will remember his name.

GUIDE. It was personal.

PUPIL 1. Yes, it was, it was also a little strange, and there was, children, they sat somehow there, I don't know, and they cried the whole time, because they wanted to eat, and then came a soldier and shot around and then the children turned quiet. That was also, I don't know, impressive.

PUPIL 2. Yes, I found it very interesting, and the room with the families where one could get the history itself, how does one know what happened then and in relation to the families? I found it all very impressive. And in the room with the statements on the floor, it stayed in my memory, that, a woman sent a postcard to her daughter and in the end, ah, there is a sentence where she said, 'Children, I will probably not see you again.' That stayed with me.

PUPIL 3. Yes, I also found the room with the statements impressive, because there one could see all the bad things that happened and also, the statement that she said also stayed in my head because it is, yes, simply one could see what terrible things happened when one reads 'I will probably never see you again.'

PUPIL 4. I also found the room with the statements the best, because there one could see how the Jews themselves saw it.

PUPIL 5. I also found the room with the statements impressive, because one could see first what terrible things were happening, and one statement stayed with me that a rabbi wrote that, yes, 'I will not see you again'.

PUPIL 6.	I understood how young the children were when they understood that they were about to die.
GUIDE.	Irit can perhaps help us with the number. There were about 2 million children who were murdered in the Holocaust?
IRIT.	The estimates are around 1.5 million.
PUPIL 7.	I found everything very interesting, but found it really terrible to see the room with the photos of people who had to walk to their death.
GUIDE.	Also naked.
PUPIL 7.	Or where the women were forced to be naked, also terrible.
TEACHER (WOMAN).	The room of families was very good. You could see a family sitting in a beer garden with their children. It could be a photo of my parents. So it is very close and very familiar.
PUPILS.	Or where the women in the picture are naked, I find this totally bad.
GUIDE.	There is a map you might have seen, of the family Toteltaub, the name is also very beautiful, family Toteltaub. It is in the last row in the room of families, and there is a picture that I always find very impressive, because the family sits in a beer garden. I don't know if others saw it [the male teacher hums positively], and there is a photo from the photo album, with the children's toys. It could be the photo album of my parents. So very near and very familiar.
TEACHER.	Yes, they are sitting on pillows at the auto.
GUIDE.	Yes, father, mother, son, who sit in this beer garden, and it's often asked why did this family not flee? And with this family you see that it was not that easy. They tried actually, and you can see on the map the zigzag of the journey they made. And then you see, when people escape... What can they actually take with them?
TEACHER (MAN).	And then the auto.
GUIDE.	And you ask yourself, why didn't they run away? Well, it was not easy, they tried. You see on the map the zigzag they took in trying to flee, but it is not easy! They had a house! Or

	an apartment, and things. What does it mean when a person does not have a home (or there is no place in which he can be at home) any longer? That they are not secure any longer?
GUIDE.	I guess that you did not have time to look at the computer databases. Did you?
TEACHER (WOMAN).	Yes, well, it was overburdening.
TEACHER (MAN).	Yes we did. My grandmother worked for a Jewish family in Dusseldorf. She took care of the children and cooked and so on. And they were taken. I don't know how, but perhaps through friends they got to New York, and they wrote after the war, family Loran. And they are there.
GUIDE.	But this is a databank for people who were murdered.
TEACHER.	Yes, partly.
GUIDE.	Did anyone look what happened in Duisburg? Perhaps you can, on the way out now.

We can see a plethora of topics having to do thematically with Jews as Holocaust victims, which are then thought of by the teachers in familiar terms in three different dimensions: (1) Jews look like their own older-generation family; (2) family members of theirs knew Jews personally; (3) 'normal' families were destroyed. The pupils related to this third dimension when they talked about the age of the children and youth who realized that they were going to die, or the mothers who were separated from their children. The guide moves back and forth between making the history familiar and accessible to the pupils, and making sure that the depth of cruelty and loss is not lost on them. She then encourages them to look for information about murdered Jews from their hometown. I, as the ethnographer, was brought into the discussion – this was quite atypical – when I was asked to contribute information about victims, after I was introduced as a social scientist coming from Israel.

The guide claims that the photo album and its vacation scene made her realize that the memory of the Toteltaub family could be the memory of her own family. It is not only that objects like a photo provoke memories (Urry 1998), not even the content of those photos itself which were surely 'Heimlich' to the guide and the visitors, but the combination of both, and the fact that they could be produced and presented by any family, in any family. We can thus recognize three levels of identification with the story of the photo:

1. The scenery and the people in the photo are familiar and provoke memories of familiar and comparable scenes in one's own family. It is crucial that the photo presents people seemingly at leisure, and this was the point of identification for the guide and the teacher.
2. Remembering oneself looking at one's own family photos, located in the home or within a family album, with family members recollecting together a specific experience they cherish.
3. Thinking what such people as those appearing in the photo and looking at such photos would do in real life once the viewer identifies with them, which lead to the question: why did they not flee?

The connection the guide makes between leisure and tourism and the possibility of fleeing can help us see not only the importance of tourism (and middle-class leisure activities) for the potentially cosmopolitan imagination of 'others,' as well as for everyday life-changing choices, but also the connection between traveling for leisure and traveling because one is actually forced out. If they could appear to be having such a good time in a beer garden, how come they could not use the same social capital to leave Germany. The guide then sticks to economy and politics in her explanation: one could not leave easily, and one could not take much.

The pupils spoke in distant terms about what they found to be 'good' in the installation through the criterion of what 'impressed' them and ostensibly, what they can already say that they remember from the visit. The attempt to historicize the visit's experience not only speaks volumes to the importance of this experience, but it is also used to describe the experience of Jews in the Holocaust. It is done here and in most discussions I heard, with minimal mention of the perpetrators (one pupil mentioned a 'soldier,' without saying whether he was a German or a Nazi, giving the impression that the Holocaust itself could be a war scene). Besides the vague description of what was impressive for the pupils, and the fact that they use a very positive language to describe what they remember from the installation, the description of the letters before death is itself cinematic, and uses a plot to portray the importance of 'seeing what happened.' The pupils thus present an impression both of the installation and of history as they understand it, with only random reference to agents or to specific times of the happenings.

Like Moses (2007) and Frei (2004), German political scientist, historians and sociologists point to the relation between the normative framework of memory work as emotional work or the 'felt victim' (Jureit 2010) and the wish to identify with the victims. Jureit takes the Holocaust Memorial to be the central example of this process, as the memorial is not only the central memory site for the history of the Holocaust, but also represents an image of the past that is politically and aesthetically shaped on identification with the victims. Similar to Till's (2005) view that the memorial will become a site of transformation into hope, in thinking about current practices of memory work, Jureit (2010: 11) also describes a promise for salvation as a major practice in memory work, where exploration of Jewish tradition of memory is occasionally confused with Christian salvation. I would like to make a connection between this moral layer of performed engagement and the physicality of the memorial, which is described in popular tour books as getting even deeper and darker than one feels alone, and that of standing under the warmth of the sun's rays with the city around, where they catch up with each other and offer hope. The guides, on the other hand, rarely offer this salvation and focus on telling actual Holocaust stories or insist on constant engagement with the site and the search for its meaning. See, in the following example, how the guide insists on engaging the pupils with historical facts.

In a discussion following a guided tour for tenth-grade pupils from a technical school in May 2006, the guide, a German Jew, refers to the horror of knowing of one's own imminent murder. She does so in relation to the fact that Germans knew about the persecution and murder of the Jews and did nothing:

GUIDE. In the Room of Dimensions [room 1] there is a text written by a small girl. She writes to her father: 'Dear father. I write this to say goodbye forever. They are going to kill us all. I very much want to live, but they would not let us. I kiss you warmly.' [pause] She knew exactly what was going on. Do you have an idea how human beings could do such a thing?

(The group is silent for a minute)

GUIDE. I too don't know. Even today, I still cannot understand how this could happen. What is even more striking is that for this scale of murder many Germans had to know and participate or help...

And the Jews in Germany, many of them were not religious. They wanted nothing to do with Judaism. They were totally

normal German citizens. So the Jew was a friend or a neighbor
and suddenly, they are enemies, and we are getting rid of
them, and perhaps hungry for their possessions.

GUIDE. What about shame? Who is responsible for what happened?
Only people who pulled the trigger? Those who looked and
did nothing? The operators of factories using slave labor?

PUPIL. People who took part.

GUIDE. But how can we determine who participated? You know,
there were also Germans who said they were not participating. There is an example that is also documented in the film
Rosenstrasse. A simple act of protest of wives who did not let
the Nazis take their Jewish husbands worked and saved lives.

GUIDE. Anything else about the installation? (The pupils are quiet)

There is something missing here for me in the installation. That is,
that there is very little about the perpetrators. It is really important to
show that there are not only crimes but also criminals. And this aspect
is not to be found here.

The guide leads the discussion through presentation of new information to questions of German shame and guilt, and finally to the
lack of information about perpetrators. She draws a parallel between
bearing witness as a victim and bearing witness as a perpetrator. She
cannot understand, and in that sense she also bears witness, how such
acts could be performed. She invites others to report on their failure to
understand. She first repeats (verbatim, and without the text at hand)
the testimony of the young girl. She uses the written text to create a
circle of people who bear witness to the girl's knowledge and sorrow at
her own imminent death. She then attempts to facilitate a discussion
about how this was possible and is faced with silence.

The written self-testimonies are a special form of testimony: they were
written by people who most likely thought that strangers, if anyone,
would find their statement, even if it was addressed to a loved one.
Many of these statements were indeed accidentally found by strangers and either were placed in archives after the war or were delivered
by those strangers to their destination. Their presentation is both a
medium for self-testimony, which creates witnessing, and a last account
that is placed, in the most original form available,[10] into an installation
at the Holocaust Memorial in Berlin. Thus, because of its originality as
a testimony, and in its triple presentation, the reader bears witness not
only to the cases themselves, but to herself reading a testimony and
then asking herself to account for it as an experience. But when guides

attempt to make the pupils repeat the act of testimony or deliver an account to it, the discussion is halted and the performative speech act of the pupils' testimony of experience stops, and can be resumed only in discussing the next room – the Room of Families, and not through questions of guilt.

2.3   Performing silence

The third form of speakability is the performance of sorrow and grief – related both to shame and guilt and to the historical inability to speak, broken here by the proclamation of the need to be silent, alone and together. It is the most elusive form of speakability as it uses the practice of calling for silence in order to prompt reflection and speech, not so much about the past but about experience. Aleida Assmann (2006: 176) reminds us that there are two sides to performed silence: that of the victim who is left without the ability to speak and sometimes without a voice, and that of the perpetrator, which can also be used as a form of power. There is also the silence of those who don't know what to say or do not care enough to express it. I think that both kinds can be mixed in their circumstances and outcomes, but that this division is helpful in understanding the performed silence in the memorial as confusing perpetrators and victims.

Here is a second example from the continued guided tour led by two guides in March 2006 that we discussed earlier:

PUPIL.   I liked the room with the family stories.
GUIDE.   Yes, what I find impressive here is the combination of ways in which one can get information. One can read letters, and hear [information about places of killing] in the Room of Places.
PUPIL 4.   For me it is very concrete. Clear.
GUIDE 2.   There are pictures that you may already know from Auschwitz of the smoke and the mountain of graves.[11] They are still important.
PUPIL 5.   It is important to raise attention, and these pictures are part of my past, I have realized that, but it is a part. I have it now. But there are other stories and one can get distanced from it.
GUIDE 2.   And the visit today…
PUPIL 4.   It was good. I took a lot from it.
GUIDE 2.   Right. Many people did not know that so much took place in Poland.
PUPIL 6.   For example, that people were deported from Greece to Auschwitz; that I did not know.

GUIDE 2.   Yes, this is very concrete here.

TEACHER.   I had already been here and find it very good. I did not know that there were so many concentration camps. I thought there were camps in Poland and Russia, but not all over.

GUIDE 1.   It is good to make concrete that these places were all over. Tragic history.

GUIDE 2.   And many people think that all were gassed and do not know about the shootings and the death during transport. And the solution to kill them all with gas was decided only at the Wannsee Conference, to make it easier on the 'poor soldiers.' So from the perspective of the perpetrators, they wanted to make killing more effective.

PUPIL 4.   For me it is very hard, Dachau and all, to talk about. That people were shot, and gassed, for me it is very hard. Maybe we can also be silent. As a visitor I am touched. I would like to be left alone now, quietly, maybe in the *Stelenfeld* [Field of Stelae]. I am so touched, and sad. It is OK that you have a discussion in the seminar, but for me it is something else.

GUIDE 1.   Maybe you can go there after the discussion.

TEACHER.   It also has to do with our other program today. It is very hard to take it all.

GUIDE 1.   The point of this conversation is to talk about what is hard to take and organize in one's mind.

TEACHER.   As a pedagogue I would say that after the visit in the Information Center, there will be quiet time in the *Stelenfeld*, maybe alone, and maybe that will satisfy the need to talk about it.

The pupil who talks about the difficult experience of being in the memorial actively frames his experience in memory,[12] through references to historical sites where atrocities took place and that he has probably visited or learned about, such as Dachau. Thus, the memory of visits to other memorials frames the scene and experience of this particular visit for him and for his classmates and teacher. We also saw references to this in the guides' earlier comments about Auschwitz. The pupil not only remembers that it is hard to face these facts in a place of memory (be it the original or a new one) but also is uncertain as to what one does in such a situation – and suggests that everybody be silent. He repeats the description of his own difficultly in dealing with what he saw and what that reminded him three times, adding that discussion is perhaps not the appropriate form of engagement with what he and his friends *saw* in the memorial. The preferred place of silence is outside the Information Center, in the *Stelenfeld*. The memorial thus serves as a transmitter of meaning (especially the Information Center, in line with the pupil's description of what was specifically difficult for him). The *Stelenfeld* can then serve as a place of contemplation and comfort. Another pupil talked about the fact that this is *his* past, but it is over, and he 'has' it now. He mentions that this is part of his past, among other parts, and that once he assimilates this into his identity, there is no way to change it – that is, the past. In this regard he said that he has taken a lot from the visit.

The other pupils' attempt to stop the discussion or to orient it toward sitting together in silence failed. The group agreed to the formula of silence and solitude connected to the moving, individual body – which should be practiced above ground, preferably as a second attempt to be in the memorial after its discussion underground in the Information Center. What would be the role of the pupil's classmates, the teacher, and other visitors in walking outside in silence, or in sitting in silence instead of discussing the visit to the memorial? This question remains open because the commemorative suggestion (Casey 1987) to act together in avoiding speech did not materialize (the pupils had to rush to their next tour in Berlin). Perhaps the mere suggestion is a commemorative act: the avoidance of others as a reaction to the suggestion, their maintaining silence, was part of the pupils' idea. They were familiar with this way of performing in memorials from other discussions and other visits to places where the Nazi past is commemorated.[13]

The guides proceed to verbalize the pupils' experience of the Information Center, and suggest that after the conversation, people can go out and be silent by themselves. The teacher thinks it will be hard to fit silence into the daily program that is already too full, and the first guide insists on talking about 'what is hard.' He then suggests that they incorporate the moment of silence in a second, now informed, visit to the *Stelenfeld*, which is what the group intends to do after the discussion.

In a visitor's survey carried out in April 2011 by a research group commissioned by the memorial foundation to find out how visitors see the Information Center, visitors expressed their contentment with the exhibition, as they generally did in the earlier runs of this same survey in 2009 and 2010, which I mentioned earlier. I interviewed the survey workers, who led only the survey interviews, between the times they were leading interviews and asked them how visitors like to conduct themselves in the Information Center. They answered that visitors would like to walk in it quietly, to respect the victims. Some visitors expressed their need to have an additional room in which they could just sit silently, perhaps even pray in respecting the victims. This 'respect to the victims' goes hand-in-hand with the division of labor between other sites commemorating World War II. Visitors stated that in the Holocaust Memorial, one should not display horrifying photos, as this is the place to respect the victims.[14] If one wants to see the acts of perpetration, one should go to the Topography of Terror. On the other hand, if one wants to find out more about Jewish history or anti-Semitism before 1933, they should go to the Jewish museum.

A third example of performing silence is taken from a series of reflections written by a group of English pupils from a Berlin bilingual school, some of them Jewish, who were asked to write a short essay after the visit, answering 'how one segment (room or area) of the exhibition uses design elements to have an effect on you, the visitor. Choose one that has the greatest effect on you.' Before we turn to the pupils' reactions, it is important to point to the way the educators presume that the pupils know that the site is designed to raise certain feelings. In other words, the pupils are, in fact, asked about the way the design, not history, creates feelings rather than knowledge. The pupils describe the emotions aroused in the site (sadness, hope, forgiving), alongside matters of design, such as lighting (dim), sound (silence or quiet color and texture): 'more of a texture that symbolizes hope.'

The description of emotions was accompanied by a description of physical feelings or the physical surroundings designed to move the visitors, which were also present in other reactions to the site above ground. For example, a pupil writes in reaction to the Room of Names: 'The room had to have been air conditioned because I felt myself getting colder and colder as I sat there and listened to stories of normal people's lives being torn apart in such relentless force.' Later on the same pupil writes: 'I found myself entranced by the stories of the victims and by the otherwise utter silence around me.' Later on she writes: 'As I listened to the stories I began to feel totally helpless [...] I became glad there were no images, I felt, otherwise, it would be too much.' She closes her reflection: 'In my opinion it is an excellently designed and thought-out room – one which invokes a series of emotions in me that no other room had been able to invoke.'

Positive reflection on the Room of Dimensions by a pupil, who identified himself as Jewish, focused on what he termed the 'peacefulness' of the room's design. 'The lighting gave the room a quiet, peaceful atmosphere, which I think can be interpreted as a symbol for the victims of the Holocaust, who wrote similar letters, to rest in peace.' The story of the room's design is interwoven with the pupils' search for metaphorical meaning connected to the historical stories, but also to their emotional resolution or its lack. As we will see in the following example, silence connects not only between atmosphere, metaphors and emotions, but also to a fourth component, moral standing, which we will analyze in Chapter 3. A pupil wrote about her impressions of the Room of Dimensions: 'It is to be observed that this room was the only one where not a voice was to be heard, and nobody dared to whisper, even though there was no aural component as in most of the other exhibits in the museum.' Another pupil chose to concentrate on a negative feeling in his reaction to the Room of Dimensions: 'The dark room and the ghostly light shone from the rectangular shapes in the ground gave an image of a graveyard. [...] It was like peeking inside the victim of the Holocausts' [*sic.*] grave and reading their last notice. The quietness and the solemn mood inside even brought tension in the room, creating a nervous atmosphere.'

Silence is used as a tactic of sensory austerity to invoke atmosphere that, together with design elements like darkness, enables a series of emotions to arise. Some culminate in conflict, as in the latter example, having to do with what the pupil thinks he is supposed to experience, his knowledge of forms of death (which exclude the option of actually not having a grave and a last note) and bits of knowledge about the Holocaust, which created an inner conflict. Other, more often described emotions are of sadness, peacefulness and awe. We can, thus far, see that visitor's talk about the need to be silent is connected to the content of commemoration and the desired feelings of sadness and catharsis (peacefulness) to identify with victims as persons, as well as what visitors often describe as feelings of hope and forgiveness, aroused during the visit. The same wish to 'respect/understand the victims' is reflected upon in visitors' book entries.

The form of speakability of performing silence, above all reflects how visitors construct stories about emotions. The normative position in regard to emotions should be separated from the act of telling about them and performing them in public. The normative position that German critics recognize is that of the need to show emotional engagement mixed with a wish for salvation, which we could also see in the examples combining the description of silence and peacefulness, hope and forgiveness. However, telling stories emotionally, or describing one's emotional engagement in a memorial museum, is a phenomenon that is not specific to this particular site.

2.4   Provoking knowledge

The fourth type of speakability involves personal engagement with Holocaust memory in the present, through knowledge accumulated in the visit. It is expected of visitors walking in the Information Center and the *Stelenfeld*. The work on this last kind of speakability occurs in all other forms of engagement, whether the guides assume that the visitors know about the Holocaust or not, both as a method of invoking questions, mostly about the memorial, but, in case the person asking seems interested and engaged, also about the Holocaust.[15]

In 2008, a survivors' testimony portal was opened in the Information Center and added an additional layer toward fostering knowledge in the memorial for interested individuals. I will write about it at length in Chapter 4. These testimonies are researched, labeled and offer additional information to interested visitors through links to additional and very specific information about the Holocaust, expanding opportunities to acquire knowledge via an advanced search according to the visitor's particular interest. The following example is taken from a worksheet for pupils in the 'families' workshop, directed at focusing attention while in the Room of Families by asking the pupils to collect information about the family who is related to the person they chose to follow earlier:

> Based on 15 Jewish families' fates, different social, national, cultural and religious life worlds are presented in this room. Photos and personal documents testify to dissolution, expulsion and annihilation of these families. Look in this room for a family that, for example, comes from the same region, land or country as *your* person from the foyer. Try to situate yourself in this specific life world.

As we saw earlier, the visitors are requested to relate to the families' stories through a person they have chosen at the beginning of the visit. Since 2009 a modification of the worksheet asks visitors to locate the fate of their chosen individual on a historical timeline. Through that person, they are asked to enter the life world of a time, a family and a region. It is hoped that the more personal the quest becomes, the closer one gets to putting oneself in that person's position. Knowledge is enhanced by the understanding and undergoing of a personal experience. The worksheet, however, ends with a future-oriented task (in looking at the memorials portal):

> In the large exit foyer of the Information Center you face, through the interactive 'memorials portal,' a virtual view of the historical

places of memory, research institutions and museums dedicated to changing themes in Germany and Europe. In the Room of Places you have already received some information about the place where *your* person was murdered. What happened after the war in this place? What is the use of this place today?

Here the visitor is supposed to come to terms with places of killing as present-day places of commemoration, or if they are (or have been) used otherwise, to acquaint herself with a deficit in commemoration that is related to *her* person, then hopefully to herself. The compilation and then personal search for this information in an archive-like portal creates a form of engagement similar to the one offered by online search elsewhere. Getting to know more about the past is a personal responsibility, much as it is a personal task to experience the memorial and learn about the Holocaust. Here speakability about what happened in the past is documentable, and asks what is being done to commemorate it in the present. It creates a sphere in which the visitor, who bears witness to atrocity, comes to terms with the ways society chose to commemorate it. We can thus see how *revisiting memory* is the main protagonist in knowledge acquisition about Holocaust commemoration in the memorial.

However, revisiting memory is not a monolithic, agreed-on action. Trouble and disagreement occur within the foundation, and between guides and the foundation regarding what the memorial should focus on, mainly on the question whether the foundation should engage with present politics in their educational activities.

The memorial pedagogue Dr Köster told me in an interview (March 2011): 'our visitors want to be part of a Berlin site and are less interested in the Holocaust. If they are, they go to Sachsenhausen, to Ravensbrück, to the villa in Wannsee. The initial igniting force for coming to the memorial is to come to an icon of Berlin. They want to have a photo there. Now, the teachers want to teach history, or use the site for this purpose, but the visitors as individuals are less interested in it'.

Köster describes visitors' conflicting interests around different sites of memory, where the authentic sites attract visitors interested in history while the invented site attracts visitors interested in iconic urban-tourist sites. She then connects this with the conflicting interests of school group educators who are closer in their aims to those of the Foundation: they want to teach history. The individual adult visitor is then compared to the individual pupil visitor and both are set apart from the interests of the Foundation and educators, standing for the community. This is then connected to larger economic and political agents:

> We are very cautious, as we hang on political factors for our finan-cial support. And so even in workshops that have to do with present problems such as Sinti and Roma or with homosexuals, we don't deal with homophobia. We have no answers for today. There were visitors here from Rwanda, educators working in memorials to the massacre. They asked 'where are we,' 'where is the fifth room' of the memorial that should deal with the present? This should be the pedagogical offering, but instead we hide behind history. Other colleagues are not interested in talking about the present. I ask myself what the themes for the future are, but we don't get more money to pay people to develop that, and there is not a curator for it, just us.

Köster portrays the current interest of visitors in connecting their visit to the memorial to other genocides as well as to minorities' issues in Europe and in Germany, which she and other foundation work-ers recognize as important but, due to their dependence on funders who presumably would not see this development positively, it is not institutionally pursued. Competing symbolic markers of the site such as urban tourism and iconic consumption meet with those political concerns. One can consider two implications of these concerns: (1) as in other museums, the dependence on funding-related factors, on the one hand, and on visitors' interests on the other, dictate the content and educational considerations of the institute.[16] (2) Those concerns are connected to the assumed popular interests of visitors and to con-temporary political affairs but are then detached from the others to the extent that a central site of Holocaust commemoration in Germany can-not afford to openly use the Holocaust as a case for the study of other genocides, xenophobia and racism. However, within the Foundation and among guides, this has been a recurring theme and guides often make references to current affairs in their guided tours.

As is the case with art as well as with historical museums, the Memorial Foundation invests value in objects differently from that of commodities (Myers 2006). The memorial establishes a special relationship between missing people, objects and meaning, and this relationship is at work in the production and use of knowledge as a form of speakability. I will now ask more precisely: what are the forms of information that are being provoked and how are they dealt with differently by guides, visitors, foundation workers and the press, who oscillate between making sense and provoking sentiment?

Welzer (2010) points to a fundamental difference between communication forms about the past. Emotional knowledge, for instance war stories or a grandfather, are different from knowledge mediated through history lessons, films and TV shows. This differentiation is indeed reflected in visitors when they differentiate their experience in the Information Center through the following hierarchy of emotional response: (1) most moving are stories of individuals; followed by (2) the stories of families; and then (3) places of killing. According to Welzer (2010: 6), 'communication in memory communities mainly transfers the emotional frames for the interpretation of narratives and images of the past.' Thus, the hierarchy of emotional experience is set within one's community and brought to the fore in memorials. Visitors evaluating the strength of experience in the Information Center told interviewers, commissioned in April 2011 by the Memorial Foundation, that they think that 'Schindler's List' is a bad film and they would like 'real documentaries,' as a reaction to the interviewer question 'What was impressive in the Room of Places' (where places of mass shooting and extermination are shown). Thus, the downward hierarchy relies first on personal experience of victimhood, where the personal written story is deemed the strongest; after which comes the family story, in text, accompanied by photos and short films; and only third in importance is the room with the proof of cruelty and killing, with supporting evidence provided by maps, large photos and drawings, and audio stations.

Reflection on the form and content of media focuses on whether it is valid historically and not only authentic or emotionally moving. Another form of reflection by way of media, which we encountered in the first chapter, is on whether the photos and information are shocking. The interviewees told the interviewer that they find it positive that the memorial does not show photos that are too hard to watch, because 'this is how one can respect the victims and not focus on the perpetrators.' This has been a repeated theme since the opening of the memorial, of whether it intends to, or should, 'shock'; now interpreted within the framework of which institutions should present shocking evidence that stands in the way of sympathizing with the victims since their aesthetic is estranging and since they make the average visitor think of the perpetrators. We learn that the division of labor between different memorial sites relies first and foremost on the question of who and what acts are being commemorated, which gives content to the form of memory action to be employed, and the reaction to new knowledge acquired in that site. Visitors from all backgrounds know that the Jews are commemorated in the memorial, and relate mostly to knowledge acquired in the site about them.

I will now analyze an April 2011 guided tour for a vocational school, with a follow up discussion. The guide opened with a presentation and discussion of the question, 'Why did it take Germans so long to build the memorial?' (assuming that it is indeed crucial to have one), and after the pupils stated that they think that it has probably existed for 50 or 20 years and not six, she states that it took the German public a while to figure out that the memorial is about 'the future.' 'It is about respect and responsibility, not shame.'

The form of speakability of guilt and shame is used as a mechanism to talk about other frames of relationship to Holocaust memory available these days, which were figured out throughout the long Holocaust Memorial public discussions in Germany and are raised after the initial discussion of the memorial's history and goals.

The guide, a historian and pedagogue, then moves on to talk about the question 'Why only for the Jews,' and asks, 'Who else was murdered by the Nazis?'

PUPILS. *(after a long pause)* Poles, soldiers.
GUIDE. Who else? Who was bought to Dachau? What was the political system?
> *(The pupils are quiet.)*
GUIDE. Communists, socialists, SPD too. Who else? Who is getting into this picture?
> *(The pupils are quiet.)*
GUIDE. Homosexuals, Roma and Sinti, so called a-social people, like prostitutes, alcoholics, Jehovah's witnesses. Why them, actually?
> *(The pupils are quiet.)*
GUIDE. They did not want to go to war.
GUIDE. But the civil initiative decided it will be only for the Jews. However, they gave the memorial a very long name, 'The Memorial for the Murdered Jews of Europe.' Why Europe?
> *(Guide waits and then provides the answer)*
GUIDE. Because the Nazis wanted to kill Jews from all over Europe. Do you know how many of the Jews that were killed came from Germany?
PUPILS. Two million, three million.
GUIDE. No, only 165,000. How could that be?

*(Talks about the exclusion of Jews in Germany since 1933
and their ability to leave.)*

GUIDE.   Why is it located here?

PUPIL.   Brandenburg Gate?

GUIDE.   Yes, and Potsdamer Platz and what is the building over there
with the dome?

(Pupils are quiet.)

GUIDE.   This is the Reichstag building, the site of the parliament. This
is the political center of Berlin.

We will further see how the discussion of other victim groups like the
ones mentioned in this fragment of the guided tour affects both the
experience of the memorial and the relating to history in it.

2.5   Projecting other groups and ourselves

This last type of speakability, provoking knowledge, is most strikingly
provocative through attention to other victim groups or their lack
thereof. The following examples illustrate the moralizing capacity of the
evocation of multidirectional memory (Rothberg 2009) in which the
Holocaust is an example to human rights violations elsewhere.

In guided tours and workshops, guides concentrate on the fate of
the Jews while in discussion they connect their persecution to the stig-
matization and exclusion of other 'others' between 1933 and 1945 as
well as, sometimes, to nowadays in Germany. Discussing the memorial
experience during and after the visit enables a search and construction
of narratives about Jews and their persecution that thus reflects dealing
with 'others' in Germany today.

Following are three visitors' book entries connecting the space of the
memorial to human rights violations at present, and offering a critique
of the memorial's mission and function in this way:

Six million people is a statistic but each death is a tragedy. For those
of you who are still suffering today, I hope that you find peace; but
I'll understand if you never can.

First name, last name, January 2008

What about the Palestinian victims?

No signature, January 2008

Very touching and moving and terribly scary, for I am sure this is
continuing to happen at present around the world – even if it is on

a smaller scale. Thank you for realizing the importance of learning from our past.

First name, last name, New Zealand

According to Macdonald (2005), visitors' book entries are sources of study that were produced by visitors without knowledge of the specific research. This is an advantage but also, according to Katriel (1997), a disadvantage as many of them turn into either a form of complaint or more often a praise which reflects the actual museum experience to a lesser extent. On the other hand, and for the same structural reasons, Macdonald suggests that they can be a source of visitor study against the grain as they reflect many forms of engagement with a tourist site. In what follows, each writer reflects on what they see as the task of the site, in relation to the memory of the Jews who perished in the Holocaust. Two compare the Holocaust in some way to human rights violations happening today (without, however, mention of the actual victim groups and the cause of violence), compatible with the sites own dictum borrowed from Levi,[17] that it is directed at preventing such events from happening again. In all three instances, the writers connect the Holocaust Memorial to atrocities which took place after the Holocaust.

The location of the visitors' book at the memorial is in the entrance and exit hall, where people are freer in their movement. The book is not bound to specific exhibits, media or text. Visitors leaf through it and usually write in it at some point before leaving the Information Center. There are two forms of visitors' book in the memorial: the first is for VIPs, and is kept with the hosts behind the reception desk and offered to important dignitaries and celebrities. The second, on display in the hall, is a folder containing blank white print paper. About ten pages (size A4) are filled every day and entries can vary between a drawing or a few words to a two–three paragraphs of text. Most entries are of a sentence or two. Noy (2008) thus claims that the visitors' book is a specifically situated medium of communication. I see it as a playful means of indirect communication between visitors, and between visitors and the institution or the museum. Noy further suggests that the visitors' book creates 'dynamic spaces of articulation and display that serve as channels of communication between – and the constitution of – various social actors and entities, both concrete and abstract' (2008: 176).

When I asked Foundation Memorial workers whether they ever systematically read the visitors' book they answered negatively, but were, nevertheless, curious about translations of what Israelis write and to hear my analysis of the various themes addressed in the book. The following examples, in English, with some translated from their original German, reflect on the museums and memorials that this one is being compared to in Germany, Israel and elsewhere, as well as on the historical referents and emotional depth imagined in the site. Through these examples one can also apprehend the intertextuality with other prevalent media in the memorial, such as the graffiti, the blog, an email, talk back and diary:

> The exhibition was very impressive. I really felt the architecture and design of the Mahnmal allowed me to reflect more, similar to how I felt in Yad Bashem [*sic*.] in Israel.
>
> Thank you. Name, USA

> There are two different feelings above ground and in the memorial. Architecture and light effect bring us to rethink the history.
>
> Name, name (Hong Kong, China), January 2008

> Dear Museum, There are Fotos from the concentration camp of Belzec on the internet.
>
> January 2008

> I am a bit disappointed with the database. Where is the Stih and Schnock one that's located in Neuköln? Or the monument against fascism in Hamburg, or even a stolperstein which is pictured but I can't find it in the database. Yes. This memorial is good + you can learn a lot here, but it's my belief that if you're going to have a database like this it should be exhaustive. Thanks.
>
> Name [German], January 2008

> What about the extinction of homosexuals and lesbians? More about those persons too. Thank you.
>
> Drawing of a pink triangle [German], January 2008

Following Raid, Macdonald suggests that a 'key analytical task is to try to identify the kinds of socially situated performances that are entailed in making a certain kind of entry in a visitor book' (2005: 122). The German visitors make more direct comments assessing the exhibition's content and do not take its choices or displayed knowledge as the sole truth. The Israeli visitors write in this visitors' book in a similar style to the one described by Katriel (1997), with the exception that we see base language directed at the Nazis and reference or quotes from poetry, which I assume communicate the distance in cultures and the marking of difference between Israelis as Jews living in Israel who are the offspring of the victims, and Germans as the offspring of perpetrators. The Germans assume that the memorial is a German undertaking and thus point to the existence of evidence from the extermination camp of Belzec and ask for more materials and representation of other European memorials and minorities. Both in the case of mentioning family members and asking for more information about camps and victim groups the visitors' book is used as both a commemorative device and a political one.

Rothberg (2009) discusses the widened spectrum of atrocities and their possible representation and learning goals, which he terms 'multidirectional memory,' to show that collective memory of the Holocaust is informed by other genocides, has many directions and directors. Multidirectional memory is shaped and carried by many actors and media not comparing the Holocaust to other genocides, but, rather, it 'recognizes the dynamic transfers that take place between diverse places and times during remembrance' (2009: 11). One surely finds the residues of postcolonial discourse in the texts written in the visitors' book and discussed here both about the Palestinian victims, in the language used ('victims'), as well as in comparison between the victimhood of Jews and the victimhood of Palestinians inflicted by those Jews' offspring. 'Name, M,' who directly addresses people suffering today, helps us see the shortcomings of multidirectional memory discourse which, taken to this extreme, turns a-historical and only uses the Christian symbolism of redeeming victimhood (find peace in acceptance).

Following the theme of Christian symbolism in the representation of the site, we will briefly divert from the visitors' book discussion. This symbolism is also conveyed in postcards and Memorial Foundation representations of the memorial. The first image (Figure 2.1) is of a postcard I bought in a book/stationary store in Berlin, while the second (Figure 2.2) is a scanned page from a book published by the Memorial Foundation in 2010, presenting the Information Center. The adjacent text on the postcard explains the attractive and accessible experience that the Information Center affords the visitor, transforming them and their experience of nameless victims above ground.

In the postcard (Figure 2.1) we see the form of the Star of David between the stelae and in its midst, the sewage system contains nine crosses. The upper part of the Star of David leads to a tunnel of light outside the memorial's confines.

Figure 2.1   Memorial postcard, view of floor forming a Star of David in the Field of Stelae

I see in this booklet's picture (Figure 2.2) an allusion to the crucifix. The child looks searching, he is a little dirty and his arms are raised in the air forming a cross. Again, behind him we see the light of day entering the memorial from without.

The third example of the prevalent Christian symbolism (Figure 2.3) is also in the form of the cross, this time with the sky above in a post-card I bought at the bookstore of the Jewish Museum in Berlin (run by the same museum gift shop organization in the Holocaust Memorial and in other Jewish museums in Germany, Cedon). In this postcard the cross is formed by looking on the skies through the high stelae. On its sides the allusion to the Star of David from the first example can be made. This photo is also sold in the memorial's book shop in a larger form and as a poster.

Another form of prevalent conventional symbolism in the memorial is that of national identity, and it is expressed vividly in visitors' book entries. Following are a few examples from entries in 2005, 2008 and 2010.

Figure 2.2 Boy in the Field of Stelae
Photo: Dirk Nazarenus, 2008 © Memorial Foundation.

Hebrew

It is good the state of Israel exists. We must guard it. People should know what happen, so that it will not happen again.

May 2005

This is a must for Jews and especially for Israelis, to visit such places, so we know that our place is in our country!!!

May 2005

This is our revenge! Never again!

July 2005

we won!

[The mayor of the city of Haifa] July 2005

Figure 2.3 Memorial postcard with a view of the sky forming a cross

This is a great commemoration. I wish that their sons (offspring) will come and see what their parents and grandparents did to the Jews and other nations.

26.5.05

It is good that they did this place after they did the Holocaust. It is good that I survived. Thanks to the state of Israel.

July 2005

I. and A. from Raanana, Israel, visited, were impressed, shed a tear and above all were scared.

July 2005

Grandma and grandpa, now I feel the pain and coldness that you felt. I am happy that you were saved and that the sons of bitches did not kill everybody.

Name, January 2008

The pain and coldness got into our bones and veins. The Israeli people/nation is alive forever and ever!

Full name, Israel, January 2008

We will never forget [a drawing of Star of David]. Beware of Lieberman and his friends.

Name, July 2010

In German, the reference to national identity is looser, though the victims are identified clearly. There is one reference to the perpetrators, with a general question about how one would act in such circumstances. See the following examples.

German

Every person should not forget what happened, so it will not happen again.

20.05.05

No forgiving! No forgetting!

20.05.05

What would you do then? Honestly!

May 2005

I would very much like to get lost, if I am allowed. Why so late?

May 2005

It was very interesting. The poor Jews.

May 2005

English

Forever and ever I will remember what they did to us.

17.07.05

It was not only the Nazis who killed the Jews.

17.07.05

We are still alive! We live on.

17.07.05

To the memory of my mother.

July 2005

In English there are also more general statements about war, other victim groups and peace:

> I come from China and want to tell all the Japanese to tell your people what you have seen here.
>
> > July 2005

> Peace & love.
>
> > name [July 2010]

> (drawing of a heart shape)
>
> > Name, Denmark, July 2010

> Respect, love & peace ya'll.
>
> > Name, name, Amsterdam, July 2010

We can also turn briefly to reading a small sample of general reflections and expressions of feeling:

> A moving and heartening experience, thank you!!!
>
> > Full name, Israel [Hebrew]

> my god, my god may it never end. The sand and the sea, the bright skies, the prayer of men. Hanna Szenes.
>
> > [A citation from the poem 'A walk to Caesarea' by Hanna Szenes[18]]

> This place is always moving, it is hard for me to capture my feelings in words. Greetings.
>
> > name [German, January 2008]

> Full Name. 'Shalom! After I came out of each presentation I had to write what I feel because of the thoughts that many Jews like me were killed. So what I felt is that everyone that was killed, they had a lot of dreams that simply shattered and I felt bad about it and I want to say to all the people who survived the war that they will stay alive and only happiness and prosperity I wish them.
>
> > [Hebrew, January 2008]

Recurring themes in Hebrew claim causal relations between the Holocaust and the state of Israel and its Jewish citizens, whose existence should be fortified for that reason, while sometimes mixing

Israel militaristic and commemorative language and history after 1948 with the Holocaust. The language style is often elevated as in the example of the cited Szenes poem, but can also be base, for the precise purpose of creating distance from the murderers' culture, either by framing the memorial experience through Israeli symbols relating to the Holocaust (coldness, sorrow, grief) and ritual text, or by referring to it through the base language of sport or war games, as in the examples of cursing and the 'we won.' Katriel (1997) suggests that through the visitors' book, visitors inscribe themselves into the museum text as an audience's gesture of closure. Noy observes further that at a commemorative site in Jerusalem, the visitors' book functions as a 'medium of inscriptive communication which is manipulated to serve as a cultural site of nationalist participation, commitment, and performance' (2008, 175).

As Macdonald (2005) observed, entries in the same language in the visitors' book correspond in style and themes. For this reason, I chose to analyze consecutive days in 2005, 2008 and 2010, and wrote the dates when the visitors wrote them in their entries. As Katriel (1997) showed and we have seen in other examples in this medium, visitors' book entries correspond on many issues and are used as a place to complain, make institutional suggestions for improving the exhibition and compare one museum to another. One characteristic of the memorial's visitors' book entries seems particular to this site; the reference visitors make to their own family history in all the three languages I analyzed, but especially in Hebrew, in which no entry I read dealt with other victim groups in the Holocaust, before or after. The reference of Jews and Germans to their family history is, I suggest, a form of closure to the experience of the memorial, which is not a narrative closure such as the one Macdonald (2005) observed through the entries (and interview requests) regarding the end of Hitler himself in the Nuremberg rally ground's visitors' book. This closure mechanism in the Holocaust Memorial has various forms. For the Israelis and the Jews writing in English, the focus is on their families and Jewish fates past and present. For the German-writing visitors, it could signify personal engagement with the past and the commitment to discussion, as well as closure as exemplified in the entry that stated, 'Both of my grandfathers were Nazis, and I am deeply ashamed. But I cannot change it.' In this instance, no further space of articulation is opened, but rather an implicit suggestion for the inclusion of the perpetrators in the memorial, an act corresponding to the wish that many German visitors expressed, especially to guides, of learning more about the perpetrators while in the site.

In the entries in German there are direct mentions of the Nazi past, assessment of the memorial and reiteration of dictum like 'never again.' German visitors echo all of the waves present in Holocaust memory debates in Germany since the end of World War II, often making it unclear from which standpoint they are speaking. Statements in English are often referred to a wider audience; sometimes written by Jews and very general, so that it is not clear who the perpetrators and victims were. Israelis often write as a family (whether they come in a group, as family or as individuals). From the signatures and handwriting, one could assume that women write in the name of their husbands. German writers almost never sign their full name, only the last name or initials.

The visitors' books provide a view of people's ideas regarding the memorial and Holocaust memory which usually remains unaltered by the visit, or at least not in the first text they write about it to the institution and to fellow visitors. Many entries look like short blogs, and in a way, are the only creative engagement with the Information Center's installation. Sometimes they write in the visitors' book what they do not dare say (or simply do not find the appropriate audience for their utterance) in the memorial. They are, however, encouraged to talk with each other and with hosts, guides and Foundation workers, who all see themselves as mediators. The topics of mediation and the experience encouraged in the site will be discussed in the following chapters through the themes of participation and agency presented here. To conclude this chapter, I would like to connect the views written in the visitors' book with its role in the installation, and its liminal role in the memorial.

The following examples are taken from instructions written for guides in the Information Center by senior guides who were engaged in developing the workshops. In the workshop *Denkmal und Gedächtnis* (Memorial and Memory), the pupils look at four memorials at four different memorial times in the history of Berlin: the Holocaust Memorial above ground, its information center, the Homosexuals Memorial, and a memorial for Goethe.

> The central goal of the workshop is not the presentation of each group's historical findings but rather formulating an answer to the question how does our community construct its memory? The groups are asked to answer (among many other questions) the following ones: 'What can the four memorials tell us about our present?'

In relation to the Holocaust Memorial, the expected answer is that

> The visitors have to show maturity, perceptual experience or sense, they have to be burdened.

As for the Homosexuals Memorial:

> minorities will be noticed and allowed, so long as they behave respectfully (Kiss in public, yes – more, please don't) to express and live with their orientation.

Here we see an interesting projection of the problems homophobes have with the visibility of homosexuality into a somewhat similar problem people express with the praxis of minorities' cultures in Germany.

The groups have to conclude that a pluralistic society both needs and has to cope with differentiated memory. Here, again, the movement is from the Holocaust Memorial, to thinking about minorities (albeit through still evidently unacceptable homosexual orientation), to the much sought after pluralistic discourse that going to and discussing memorials is believed to facilitate. The groups also have to ask themselves who should identify with the memorials and their messages and how. In the case of the Holocaust Memorial: it was initiated by non-Jewish Germans and is directed at them: they should identify with it so as to interpret it by themselves. Interpretation is thus believed to be a form of appreciation and appropriation.

The following example illustrates the centrality of different victim groups and central events for justifying the investment in memorials in the center of Berlin.

A newspaper article in the Berlin daily *Tagesspiegel* presented the future memorial for German unification ('Memorial for Freedom and Unification'), named 'Citizens in Motion' and designed by Johannes Milla and Sasha Waltz. It is planned to build it in Schlossplatz in the center of Berlin and to look like a see-saw that will move with at least 50 visitors walking on it. The journalist commented: 'Lately, with the Eisenman's stones-forest that is supposed to serve the memory of the Holocaust, the wishes of countless interest groups have proliferated that also their victims, suffering, or acts of heroism should also be commemorated in metal, mineral, fluid or mediated sculpture in the capital.'[19]

The claim for the erection of other memorials is not focused on the Holocaust, not even on victims of persecution, but on the visibility, safety, monumentality and centrality of commemoration projects which are pursued by and for the memory of different victim groups.[20] We will now see what, if anything, is particular about commemorating the Jewish victims in this framework.

Conclusion: moving from the abstract to the concrete through the Jews

In the workshop 'Art,' the pupils are asked to write a poem or a haiku about the memorial. Most of them neglect this assignment but some do write a poem.

This worksheet gives an example on the right and the children write their own poem next to it or on a separate sheet. The example tries to reflect on the memorial's aesthetics, on the feelings evoked and on Holocaust fragments. The majority of pupils, however, write about the fate of Jews and the Holocaust, and build one narrative as opposed to the fragmented text in the example.

Here I present three of the poems written by pupils, the example they were given appears on the right.

Pupil's poem 1
Jews
In National-socialism
They have suffered
Only for their religion
Grief

example
Big
Gray awry
Uncountable shadows past
Present children laughing future
Memory-space

Pupil's poem 2
Jews
Murdered Jews
They have suffered
Now they are dead
Shame

Pupil's poem 3
Elfchen (elevenish)
Huge
Dark narrowed
Confusingly shadowed earlier
Terrible death memory future
Memorial

In a conversation with Memorial Foundation workers I was told that the form of the short poem was chosen to help pupils express themselves because it corresponds to the prevalence of short, telegraphic text messages or email communications that the pupils use in their everyday lives. The example uses concepts like 'space' and 'memorial'; descriptions of the actions in it: 'children laughing'; and its spatial qualities: 'big grey and awry'. It then alludes to memory work and history through 'past and present.' These are also the only two concepts that connect two lines in the poem. Leaving aside the quality of the assignment and the poems, and thinking of them as cultural product where central symbols of holocaust memory are played with and performed, the Memorial Foundation in its educational programs creates a pendulum of distance and proximity to the Holocaust and Jews, through the very symbolic and ritualized means of using photographs and metaphors. This of course corresponds to prevalent images of Holocaust memory and the induction to feel sorrow that the pupils reproduce in their poems (as well as in their other figurative artistic work).

There is an inherent tension in the role of the Foundation (of which they are of course aware) between increasing and offering knowledge and enhancing an experience. We have discussed this tension between creating and historically grounding knowledge, which is one of the historical goals of museums at large and is connected to another goal of creating a public civil space (Bennett 2006; Kirshenblatt-Gimblett 2006). This is not done through the appreciation of artworks but here, and increasingly in other memorial museums, through creating some atmosphere, or experience, which is moving for the visitor and is supposed to stay with them in the future. An example of this is that teachers often tell guides at the memorial that if the pupils leave the visit having more questions than they came with, the goal of the visit is achieved and the memorial will be connected to their life experience.

On the stairway leaving the Information Center in April 2011, I overheard a middle-aged Dutch-speaking couple talking about the exhibition. The woman said that 'the movies and photos were very emotional, but the letters were the most emotional.' Her husband agreed. Talking about being emotionally moved in the memorial, as we saw in the first chapter, is central to a visit to the memorial, and not only for Germans. The visitor's survey (much like guided tours and workshops) asked the visitors to the Information Center to say which room they liked the most. Most visitors said that the room that moved them the most was the Room of Dimensions, and that the victims' last letters and notes left the strongest impression on them. In this instance, speakability is made possible by the distancing effect of speaking about 'being moved' by artifacts, or by the actual performance of evaluation. It uses very little memory of the exhibition or information about the Holocaust, and instead the memory of rooms and their content are signifiers of the experience as a whole. We will see next how a guide, taking the liberty of actually engaging in conversation about present politics, invites and enables different outcomes from the visit.

In February 2010 at the end of a workshop on families, which took place in the Information Center with 25 pupils from a vocational school, the guide asked what the pupils took from the workshop and a few of them said that 'we should respect each other.' The guide added: 'respect is important, also understanding, and trust is most important. You have to make up your own mind what it means when people say "Jews are our bad luck" or "all Muslims are terrorists" [there were five female pupils wearing headscarves in the room]. One of the pupils then said that respect means for him 'to understand, respect and accept each other, and not to curse.'

The Levi quote is employed in eliciting reactions to the workshop and the memorial, connecting it to contemporary discourse on racism (without naming it, notwithstanding). The experience of the memorial is then easily linked to present-day experience of the pupils as migrants. This is a discursive mode which stems from all forms of speakability: shame and guilt by the reference to 'Jews are our bad luck,' silence by the guide's call for action when one hears racist or anti-Semitic talk, witnessing by the references to hearing such statements, but more importantly, by asking what this means for them as engaged citizens. Knowledge is the least active mechanism in this interaction, although the guide assumes that the pupils have heard such racist utterances. The employment of the four kinds of speakability brings up (a) the act of speech, and (b) various discussion topics which connect to the installation, discussions on memory in Germany, and discussions about social and political problems in Germany past and present. The Jews are referred to either as a symbol of the atrocities against them in the Holocaust or as the symbol of a limit case of racism which should serve as a warning in today's Germany. The texts that the pupils themselves produce present Jews only as dead victims. By offering the concept of speakability, I have alluded only to an acquired and performed ability in a new site of memory, not to its qualities, political promise or depth. In the third chapter, I will discuss the visitors' presented moral career and moral transformation in the memorial and connect it to these learned practices.

3
Memory in Action: New Ethics of Engagement with Holocaust Memory

> Take some time and go through the Field of Stelae in all possible directions. What exactly do you see? What do you hear when you close your eyes? What do you sense when you touch the stelae? Make some notes for yourself about your observations and feelings.[1]

When one comes to or passes by a place of memory, one enters the realm of engaging with public remembrance that is considered ethical, or simply put, good. The role of this place, of visiting and of experiencing it, is usually clear; thus we see in the recent two decades, as Leggewie and Meyer (2005) note, politicians and intellectuals speaking in favor of accidental remembrance, or everyday remembrance that will, willy-nilly, make one engage with oneself and others, and with the past. This centrality of ethical remembrance, however, is rather new (Margalit 2002), and shifts the focus from the unethical and unruly deeds to the good deed of, first, facing and then engaging with the past. There have been shifts in ethical theory which complement the move from rejecting the unethical deeds into enabling 'many ethics' that challenged and transformed the universalistic, subject-centered and exclusionary intellectual bias of traditional ethics. As Zapf summarizes: 'Instead of a unified system of knowledge and belief, plurality, diversity and heterogeneity have been foregrounded as new ethical orientation' (2008: 172). Zapf maintains that de-hierarchization, process and cross-cultural openness and dialogue are the new leading ethical values. That such a shift has already occured in the memorial is clear on two counts. First, in the new focus on ethical engagement with the past and the ability to assess one's dealing with the past in moral terms which are performed and mirrored in the site. Second, with the focus on openness and plurality of standpoints in relation to the past, with the only exclusion being those who are unwilling to engage in this very action of search and discussion.

In the course of engaging with the past in the 'new Berlin', in newly constructed memorials to victims of National Socialism within a memorial quarter (Till 2005), we can see two parallel processes. First, the Holocaust Memorial site is newly constructed and the discussions preceding it long and spiraling (Cullen 1999; Heimrod, Schlusche and Seferens 1999; Quack 2002; Young 2003), leading to a call for a new ethics of engagement, whose main imperative is to mobilize discussion. Second, the imperative of discussion is framed by a polite and inviting engagement between the past and oneself, in the open and in public, having in mind sites of atrocity where this form of engagement is not possible.

In this chapter I focus on the first process, the call for engagement through articulation, advanced by direct and indirect moralizing (Luckmann 2002). I argue that moralizing actions and norms in the memorial create a set of steps towards engagement in discussion. The first step, 'getting in,' consists in the presentation and performance of the visitor's moral career. This is achieved by the invitation to enter the site, and face one's relationship with the past through the rules of conduct written on the ground upon entering the site. The second moralizing phase, 'getting lost,' is the invitation to explore the site individually and reflect on one's thoughts and feelings during this process. Here, the visitor is practically stripped of their knowledge regarding self-presentation in sites of memory and this temporary confusion or embarrassment is met with a void of figurative meaning in the site above ground. The visitor is expected to reflect on that void in comparison to the abundance of meaning and information underground, and in other memorial sites. The third phase, 'getting "it,"' contains the confrontation between what visitors are used to in other sites of memory and what is actually happening in this site. At this stage, the individuals become part of a mature political community engaging with its past openly and freely in motion, and in relation to each one's moral career of dealing with the past.

The moral community, into which the appropriately behaved memorial visitor is inducted, is opposed to a hypothetical community that does not remember, or has the wrong memories and thus does not properly deal with its past. Indeed, such an improper memory, or failure to remember, was one of the main fears leading to the memorial's construction (cf. Rosh 1999), and is discussed as a reason to be proud of oneself, both as a German visitor to the memorial and as a guide in it: being a member of the community who built this central Holocaust Memorial. It is, however, crucial to see that taking pride in the memorial's mission to remember the murdered Jews is not a monolithic action, and that the ground for undergoing change is the pursuit of unshared moral sentiments. In other words, I suggest that German visitors to the memorial, in talking about what they are supposed to feel in the site, reflect on the absence of a shared moral sentiment toward World War II and the murdered Jews. The moral community, then, proves multifaceted, and illegitimate parts of it are performed and discussed.

Before we explore the ways the visitors progress though the moral stages in the memorial, we should consider the narrative structure of undergoing change in the site and talking about it. As we saw in Chapter 2, visitors describe the experience of the *Stelenfeld*, as well as of the Information Center in terms of change, either of their world views ('I did not know that so many Jews were shot in the East') or their emotional standing: as in reflections on the Room of Dimensions being the room where feelings of sadness for the individual victims arise.

§1   Two narratives of moral experience in the memorial

I will first address the narrative of showing and disclosing emotions and then move to ask about the narrative of change. However, before we proceed to delineate the two, it is necessary to answer an earlier question: why do the emotions of the visitors matter in the memorial, to them and to us studying them? According to Illouz, as a category of inquiry in sociology, emotion 'is not action per se, but it is the inner energy that propels us toward an act, what gives a particular "mood" or "coloration" to an act' (2007a: 2). Emotions, for Illouz can thus be defined as the 'energy laden side of action, where that energy is understood to simultaneously implicate cognition, affect, evaluation, motivation and the body' (2007a: 2). Illouz maintains that 'what makes emotions carry this "energy" is the fact that it always concerns the self and the relationship of the self to culturally situated others' (2007a: 3). If we follow Illouz's definition, the emotions performed and discussed in the memorial are compressed cultural expectations from memory work at a given point in time and a given place. The fact that they sometimes appear as unreflexive aspects of action means neither that their affecting actors do not reflect on their feelings and their disclosure, nor that what propels them are psychological mechanisms that pre-date culture and history, but that they put in a nutshell the mechanism and energy of action in the site. What is particular about this in the Holocaust Memorial is the expectation that everyone will perform their emotions according to specific historic roles and that those roles are prescribed historically, in accordance with family relations, national and religious origin, and also with the aesthetic of this site and its newness.

1.1 The narrative of showing and disclosing emotions

According to Illouz, the *narrative of recognition* combines an aspiration for self-realization with a claim to emotional suffering. Understanding this narrative not only helps us to situate the emotional work as part of action in the site, and in other public sites not necessarily related to Holocaust memory, but also to look at the extent to which different groups claim recognition in the site. Showing emotions in the site is not enough. One has to describe them to one's peers or, in many workshops, write about them in one's worksheet. The 'textuality' of emotions helps by not only locking it in time and space and raising recognition in the feeling person and her emotions in that time and place, but it also creates distance between the experience of emotion and the person's awareness of that emotion. It is not only visitors who speak about their emotions in the site. Hosts are expected to be able to handle issues having to do with the coat check, order in the Information Center, but also to answer questions regarding the Information Center's exhibition and to address emotional reactions in the site. Illouz maintains: 'The reflexive act of giving names to emotions in order to manage them gives them an ontology, that is, seems to fixate them in reality and in the deep self of their bearer, a fact, we may claim, which goes against the volatile, transient, and contextual nature of emotions' (2007a: 33).

Presenting and discussing one's emotions in the site fixes those emotions to the context of the visit, the site's aesthetics and one's moral standing in relation to it, but also 'fixes' the site in the visitors' imagination as a place in which such emotions arise. However, those emotions are supposed to arise spontaneously and find their bearer unprepared for their occurrence and intensity. When visitors reflect on the lack of emotions that they and others feel in the site, or show understanding of the process of manipulation in which certain emotions of sadness and grief are expected, guides find it problematic and disturbing to proper experience of the site. An interesting example comes from research toward a dissertation in psychology and education that Dr Marion Klein, a former guide in the site, conducted among school groups visiting the memorial. Klein initiated 24 group discussions with high school pupils from Berlin. They would go unguided in the memorial and Information Center and then, whoever accepted the invitation to join her in the seminar room (usually around five or six pupils out of around 15–20 in a group) would follow her into an open discussion of their experience. The opening question was for the pupils to talk about their experience in the memorial and the Information Center: How did you feel? What did you see? What did you do there?

Klein found that all groups, reflexively or not, took seriously the demand to connect feelings, especially of sadness and partly of guilt, with the theme of the Holocaust. All groups, after presentation of their own experience and feelings, used different modes or 'strategies of authentication,' according to Klein. Following Brumlik (1997), Klein describes sadness as a 'close emotion' in which the victims have to be close to the visitors so that they are able to feel sad. As an example, Klein told of a girl who described her strongest experience in the Information Center: 'standing in front of a photo of a girl who was born on my birthday, I told myself: now you are really sad.' The pupil expresses the authentic, surprising, but expected feeling of sadness as an achievement and as the goal of their visit. Their audience was most concerned about the fact that the pupils knew about the need to feel and express ones' feelings and saw it as a legitimate manipulation they had to undergo at the memorial, and especially in the Information Center, and so engaged in the ritual of expressing feelings.

The expression of one's feelings as the basis for communication about the site's experience, the anchoring of sadness with the site, and then the reflection on this after an act of witnessing, 'standing in front of a photo,' then of reaction through the statement in the second person: 'now you are really sad.' The pupil described an act of declaring a specific emotion as, firstly, an event to be generated and, secondly, because of achieving the popular, temporary, bodily and intrinsic understanding of emotions as the surprise that informs the height of one's expectations at the site. This achievement is a turning point toward talking about change, not only as regards one's knowledge of the Holocaust, but also in one's relations to it through feelings. Both the talk about emotions and the talk about change are situational in the ways they position the individual within a certain context, that of visiting the memorial. This model of communication about feeling, according to Illouz, suspends one's emotional entanglement in social life and creates personal entitlement to legitimately express ones' own feelings and at the same time, neutralizes the emotional dynamic as such of sadness and guilt.

In Freudian tradition, identity is constructed through narrative distortion and inner conflicts which can be overcome through verbalization of one's own psyche and self (Illouz 2007b). The verbalization of experience, or the action of making sense in and of the memorial and other places like it, helps deconstruction of the sense-making activity in regard to memory, because of the narrative conflict involved in how to experience Holocaust memory. This conflict eventually leads to the building of a new sense of both place and memory. The constant search for meaning in the memorial, I suggest, is aimed, by memorial workers and visitors alike, at self-help that is not directly related to illness and only sometimes directed toward recovery (one should not recover from feeling sad about the Holocaust), but instead is aimed at overcoming the inability to feel and express their feelings about it, while at the same time making sure that the search will continue forever. Much like the mechanism involved in psychoanalytic recovery from neurosis, a cyclical work of change and transference, such as letting oneself fall into feeling lost and sad in the memorial over and over again, might lead to social transformation. This is the main mechanism of action that connects the narrative of emotions with the narrative of change. But how are the emotions expressed connected to witnessing the victims' suffering and then to self-help?

According to Illouz (2007b: 47) the therapeutic narrative of suffering puts the narrative of self-help into motion. Illouz analyzes narratives of the self-inflicted suffering of individuals, while here we look at individuals witnessing the suffering of other (murdered) individuals, expecting to feel sad with them and, through that sadness, to self-transform. The structure of witnessing we will see later on in the chapter, while creating a form of speakability, is not necessarily built on identification with the victims. The following example will help elucidate just that. It is part of a conversation I had with a guide at the memorial at the time a group she guided toured the Information Center in April 2011:

GUIDE. I would really like to hear more about the perpetrators in the Information Center. It will help us get closer to the present.

ID.   I think that there is no perpetrators' narrative yet.

GUIDE. Yes.

ID.   The Skopos interviewers [responsible for the visitors' survey at the Information Center] also said that the visitors would like, in the memorial, to hear about the victims, and respect them, not to be shocked.

GUIDE. Yes, because what do people know about the victims? That they were gassed. It does not get any worse, and people got accustomed to it. This is what they expect to hear.

ID.   Do they make any use of the data banks?

GUIDE. Yes, but I cannot say how much. What happens to me very often is, I see standing there a German fellow and he types his own family name into the Yad Vashem victims' names database. Then I ask: 'Do you have Jewish relatives or friends?' And they answer: 'No,' or 'I see!' I once saw a pupil looking for a name I was not sure was Jewish and I asked the teacher: 'Is he Jewish?' And she answered: 'No.' Perhaps this is over-identification with the victims.

ID. Really?

GUIDE. Perhaps not really, but better to be on the victim's side, better to see Anne Frank than Albert Speer. It does not cross their minds at all that it could have anything to do with them.

ID. I do not think that it has so much to do with identification with victims.

GUIDE. If people think about anything at all, they'd rather be on that side. I mean, I grew up Catholic. And I took a summer language course in Israel ten years ago and there were so many Germans, and women, almost everyone converted. And I thought: what is going on with you! But I still don't think it is connected to an actual feeling of guilt.

ID. Like Welzer says: the third generation does not want to hear that the grandparent was a Nazi and prefers to see him as a victim. Besides, the people here don't talk with you about their families.

(The guide changed the topic of the conversation here.)

The guide separates identification of German visitors with the victims from actual feelings of guilt and of the possibility that they actually identify with victims, as they themselves feel victims, primarily of the war (Olick 2007a,b). I would add that German victimhood is engrained in the visitors' perception of victimhood in relation to World War II, which prompts one to search for one's own family name: to find out if perhaps they were victims, not necessarily Jews, in a victim's data bank that, in a way, can contain all victims groups. The guide then extends her observation to German women traveling to Israel for a Hebrew language course, and then converting to Judaism, and still prefers the explanation of identification to that of guilt. We can think of it in different terms to offer a third way to illuminate the binary problem: we can name the category of identification, transformation – be it from Christian to Jewish, or from not moved to sad when visiting the memorial – a transformation enabled by witnessing Jewish suffering, suffering with the Jews not from the position of family members of former perpetrators, and then uniting with one's own authentic suffering. The structure of suffering with the victims does include the precondition of being German without a discussion of family history or even of potential family roles. I heard no German visitor stating that they position themselves on the side of the victims as in 'this could happen to me,' but many migrants to Germany as well as Jews stating this. We did see visitors' book entries in which German visitors stated that their relatives were perpetrators.

Many hosts I spoke with talked about people breaking down in tears at the memorial and say that they are ready to provide tissues for visitors who cry. They told me that people cry at the memorial, not too often, but it happens, and the hosts help them recover after visiting the site. Individuals are expected to disclose certain emotions of grief and sorrow. It is interesting to note, however, that expressing emotions in public during discussion or a demand to discuss or relate to them in public is often seen as problematic by guides and hosts.

Following are two examples of the ambivalence around the expression of emotions and personal memories. The first is taken from an interview held in December 2005 with an Israeli guide who had studied in Berlin. The second is of a guided tour of elderly people from Brandenburg in April 2006, who talked about their experiences as children in Berlin before the war:

GUIDE. My worst group was a mix of two: Israelis and Germans. I walked with the Israelis above ground and everything went well. Then the two groups got together to the seminar room underground. So there was a minute of silence, unplanned. I asked: 'Why are we in silence?' The teacher said to me in a didactic tone: 'Sometimes, guide, it is okay not to talk.' Then they all started crying. I did not know what to do with myself. I would never cry with a German. I have a roommate – we are good friends, but I will never show feelings with him. In the end everybody becomes a victim.

Guides and hosts often talk about occasions in which visitors cry at the place of information. This guide found the occasion of Israelis and Germans crying together problematic, not the act of crying on its own. The visit can be emotionally charged and challenging, but to him each national group should act within its designated role. He certainly did not want to see Israelis expressing feelings with Germans, hinting that the offspring of the victims have reasons to cry, whereas the fact that future generations of victims and perpetrators cry together means that they all become victims, and that this has become legitimate and prevalent today. The point of mixing perpetrators' and victims' roles will now be further discussed through the guided tour with elderly German visitors from Brandenburg (April 2006), and later on with a third example, a group of German adults from Brandenburg expressing emotions through the discussion of their family engagement in the Holocaust, this time in April 2011.

In the first example, the elderly citizens were sitting in the seminar room for a discussion after a guided tour with two guides.

VISITOR 1.	It is important to teach the memory to the younger generations. I come from Brandenburg, I know Sachsenhausen, and I cannot understand how people said they did not know. We knew.
VISITOR 2.	I knew that Jews were something bad. I remember, as a child we were by an ugly house and someone said 'the Jews live here.' We ran away. My mother told me that she was in Berlin near Alexanderplatz, near the Volksbühne, where Jews were taken off. She was horrified. We grew up with the notion of Jews as something bad. We had anti-Jewish feelings, anti-Semitism. So we have to say the National Socialists had their helpers.
GUIDE 1.	Yes, there were cases in which not only Nazis or police killed, but civilians helped and took part. Of course, what you just described are people who were ready to take part.
VISITOR 3 (F).	Also, people who went to church heard that the Jews killed Jesus.
VISITOR 4 (M).	I am simply impressed with the fact that the installation exists here, 60 years after what happened. I remember how Lea Rosh fought for it and I am glad that it is realized and that the genocide (*Volk-mord*) is not blurred, that we made a memorial for all the possible groups that were executed.
GUIDE 1.	I find what you said very interesting, how you said it, since exactly that discussion was the origin of this memorial. Precisely those questions led the discussion on the memorial: whether it should be dedicated the way it is. It is how the civil initiative grounded the singularity of this dedication.

VISITOR 1.   It is good to have this Primo Levi citation at the beginning of the installation: it happened and therefore it can happen again. There is anti-Semitism and racism in Germany today [...] racism comes from fear because of social conditions.

After the discussion the two guides and I stayed in the room and talked about the guided tour. They were both extremely unhappy with it and I was at first surprised, because the conversation was so rich and people were willing to talk about 'what happened,' which I took to be a very unusual and positive discussion.

GUIDE 1.   I know these GDR citizens. How they think that whoever is poor is afraid, and whoever is afraid becomes a Nazi. They do not believe in democracy. What they want to talk about it resistance and anti-Semitism.

GUIDE 2.   They jump with it in your face. The visitor who said that was totally aggressive.

GUIDE 1.   He was first aggressive when he needed to go through the security check.

Posing a threat to German democracy, the two guides imply, the visitor must have felt threatened by the memorial. This guided tour was unusual in the length of discussion and the topics covered. It was also rare to hear elderly people talking about their experience of the war in the memorial, and openly admitting anti-Semitism and racism as part of their culture then, and now. However, both guides' reaction was about the visitors' origin from the former East and their criticism of German democracy before and after 1989. They chose not to acknowledge that this discussion touched important issues which were leading causes of the Holocaust and which Germans in the East and the West shared to a large extent.[2] The conversation was about the outcomes of unification through what the visitors saw as former and current fascist threats, which the guides interpreted as posing a threat to democracy as it is embodied, celebrated and exercised in the memorial. This is what brought up the security check as litmus paper for people who are for or against the memorial and German democracy.

Illouz (2007b: 54) maintains that 'the narrative of self-help and self-realization is intrinsically a narrative of memory and of the memory of suffering.' However, the injunction to exercise one's memory of suffering in order to free oneself of it works differently in our case: one witnesses the suffering of the other, the Jew, in order to free one's speakability. Speakability bears many traits of the therapeutic narrative. It is not surprising given the cultural resonance, and institutional recognition and reliance on the latter. However, what make the affinities interesting are the mutual relations to the cult of victimhood that both the therapeutic and speakability memory work entail, and the way they both position the communication of one's own story in the center of a personal narrative of search and change. Thus, some of the reasons for the cultural resonance of the therapeutic narrative can explain the work of speakability.

Much like the therapeutic narrative, the memorial discussion of emotional change is performative: it recognizes experience as it tells it. The experience is that of touring the memorial (which is the reason for how crucial it is for guides to hear from the visitors about their memorial experience. This corresponds with what Illouz (2007b: 55–6) concludes about emotion, change and (ethical) subjectivity: 'It is in the experience of self-change and in the construction of that experience that modern subjects experience themselves as being most morally and socially competent.'

The therapeutic discourse can address and explain contradictory emotions. Illouz (2007b: 55) offers the examples of loving too much or not loving enough. In the memorial's case, feeling too much or not being able to feel for the victims at all. Both speakability and the therapeutic narrative use the cultural template of religious narrative, which is regressive because it deals with past events and progressive since the goal of the narrative is to produce progressive redemption of either emotional health or freedom from guilt and trauma. However, differently from the therapeutic narrative, guides at the memorial often discuss with adult visitors and among each other the fact that in German homes today, there are no longer stories (or for that matter the necessity of avoiding talking or answering questions) about World War II and the Holocaust, as it simply matters less in the everyday lives of the third generation. Guides think that this is a problematic process and take the role of reviving speech about the Holocaust, but no longer in order to achieve emotional health, or that they think that the public has been 'cured,' but rather they fear that once it is not a burning issue, a slippery slope toward obliviousness and denial will occur.

I would like to briefly return to the discussion held after the presentation of Klein's (2012) study among Memorial Foundation workers. If we recall the three memory models that Klein offers for pupils' engagement with Holocaust memory – (1) 'memory without sadness'; (2) 'sadness through memory'; (3) 'sadness without memory' – we can see, first, that the most important part of the model is sadness, or emotional engagement. Among the discussants, the worrisome process was of 'memory without sadness.' They discussed at length the fact that the pupils reflected on the need to feel that is expected from them, because of the pupils awareness of the manipulation but, more crucially, because it does not come 'naturally'.

We saw in the work of Klein (2012) that authentic feelings can arise in the inauthentic memorial through verbalization of sadness. Likewise, in conversations with memorial guides and hosts many claimed that one can have an authentic, free experience only in a non-authentic memorial like this one. Habermas (1999) argues for the same action in his piece in favor of the memorial construction, that is, it will afford future generations with critical engagement with history and self-reflection. This experience depends, first, on freely sensing place, as we saw in the guided tour examples. In the process of making sense of the place, it is also crucial to witness others doing the same and evaluate their externalized experience.

Illouz writes: 'The therapeutic narrative makes one responsible for one's psychic well-being, yet does that by removing any notion of moral fault' (2007b: 55). According to Illouz, this might enable the constitution of communities of suffering. This trait of cultural resonance of the therapeutic narrative that the discussion of emotion and personal change also bears is an opportunity to examine the latter as standing independently of the weight of historical responsibility for the Holocaust, which is usually discussed as the origin of guilt, then leading Germans to choose the side of the victims. If, rather, we consider the prevalence of the therapeutic discourse and the way it was adopted to suit the discourse on responsibility instead of guilt *vis-à-vis* German Holocaust memory, the structure of performing affect can then become relatively free from the knowledge of history. At the same time, the younger generation's challenging question, 'What does it have to do with me', is in this sense not necessarily connected to the question of fault and wrongdoing (with which they really are not implicated), but with the combination of the need to demonstrate engagement together with the liberating mode of discussing one's actions independently of historic responsibility.

This therapeutic discourse duplicates and spreads to collaterals, such as children and grandchildren. In this sense, Illouz argues, it can activate family lineage and continuity. In a workshop in April 2011 with adults from the former East Germany great resentment was displayed to questions that the guide presented. When she asked about the basis for their reaction a few said that they felt 'judged.' When the guide said that all she talked about was the 'perpetrators' generation,' they repeated that they felt that a wholesale judgment was exercised and only later on – when I followed two of them who stormed out of the workshop before it ended – that they themselves felt judged as individuals. We will return to this example shortly. This is a fascinating case of the lineage of trauma and the condensing of the community of suffering and victimhood (Olick 2007a,b).

The changes in the workshops' names over the years illustrate both the manner in which more work is dedicated to discussing individual suffering and to individual experience and interpretational work on Jewish suffering by the visitors. Workshops have been offered since 2007. The first five workshops were: '"We were always a family, all together I mean": the fates of families,' whose title was changed in 2011 to 'Discovering worlds: Four families and their fates in the Holocaust'. The workshop on 'self-testimony,' whose official title was: 'At least this will be left for us: Diaries, letters and other self-testimonies,' has been changed to 'Searching for remnants: Diaries, letters and other records.' The art workshop's official title was 'Memory thread: Sensing, reflecting and creating one's own memorial design,' is now changed to 'With words, pictures and paper: Create a memorial by yourself.' The subtitle of another workshop, 'Why did it happen: Discrimination, exclusion and annihilation of the European Jews,' was changed to 'Exclusion, disenfranchisement and murder.' For older pupils, there were two more workshop options: on places of killing whose official title was 'Death ways and annihilation places: The organization of the European Jews' mass murder' has its title changed to 'Treblinka, Babij Jar and Auschwitz: Ways to death'; while the title 'Would people in posterity be able to say how we lived and died here: The Grossmann family in Ghetto Lodz,' was changed to 'Mendel Grossmann photographs: (Families') lives in the Lodz ghetto.' There were a further two new workshops on offer in 2011: 'Ever still Gipsy: The persecution of Sinti and Roma' and 'Forbidden love: Homosexuals' persecution under National Socialism.'

There are three main characteristics of the titles change. The first has to do with the fact that each workshop had an unofficial, shorter name used between memorial workers, such as 'art,' 'families' and 'places.' They were general and did not allude to individuals, experience or historical specificities. The official workshop titles before April 2011 were more general, used quotes and did not directly address the participants and their supposed activity. The titles since April 2011 reflect the third characteristic of enhancing personal experience of individuals' and families' fates and affording a laboratory-like visit. We will return to personal experience through the use of media in the memorial in the next chapter.

The experience is important, but how we represent and remember it is even more important. As Halbwachs (1992) argued, remembrance is mediated by cultural agencies, among which are the guides and hosts, the education system and media. Having created a unique experience above ground and breaking a possible narrative underground are means in making the place work. In other words, it is not the *Stelenfeld* alone and it is not the *Stelenfeld with* the Information Center that is responsible for creating the memorial. The moving-moved visitors make the memorial. The visitors, their actions and reflections, or their potential lack, give the place its meaning. Only the right action, which manifests itself in the verbalization of experience, makes the memorial 'work.'

We can also see an explanation of the functioning of the memorial from the perspective of its designer In Eisenman's words:[3]

> The slabs are whole lined up with rows, like Nazis. The whole idea is rationality gone mad, entropy entering rationality.
>
> You go and walk in it and you feel uncertain. These things are tilting, I don't know where I am going, am I going to get lost? I am alone. I can't hold anybody's hand. And that, when it gets done, is what it felt like to be a Jew in Germany in the thirties. That's all. That is the monument.
>
> We want to get over this idea of the Jew as the other. So my monument is both a memory and a hope for the future. It is to bring the Jewish cemetery into the everyday experience of the German in the middle of the city, but also it could be a series [...] if you look at them, they are foundation stones for a new society.

The slabs are in rows 'like Nazis.' The visitors walking between them have to feel lost, which is how it must have felt to be a Jew. The action of feeling like a Jew will eventually make the Jew not an 'other' (while making visitors feel the Jew as an 'other'). This process, as Eisenman sees it, actually offers many ready-made metaphors with which to relate to Holocaust memory in Germany. It will later be interesting to see how this instructive mechanism is used as an entry point to discussing the memorial by visitors, and negated by guides. The interviewer (Marian Marzynski) in Eisenman's interview gets confused. To him is seems that the similarity of the slabs to gravestones suggests that the Jews among the Germans today, however accepted they are, are dead:

MARZYNSKI.   Are you saying that through this monument the Germans would accept Jews as living among them?
EISENMAN.   Yeah, yeah–
MARZYNSKI.   –But there will be dead Jews–
EISENMAN.   –No, no, no, no–
MARZYNSKI.   –They *will* be dead Jews–
EISENMAN.   –Not only dead Jews, but the idea for the potential re... you know what a gravestone is? It is
                     (*The interview is cut here.*)

Eisenman suggests that the memorial is a background, or facilitator, of a certain imaginative activity: to feel lost (like a Jew is the 1930s) and to sense Jewish existence in the heart of Berlin. Having an imaginary cemetery in the center of Berlin serves as 'foundation stones for a new society' built on the acceptance of guilt ('like Nazis') for the death of Jews ('it is like a Jewish cemetery'). A crucial illustration of self-help for individuals as well as on the societal level is the use of the metaphors describing the *Stelenfeld* as a change 'from a graveyard to a playground.' A Memorial to the Murdered Jews of Europe, this alludes to a place where the 'we' and the Jews are buried, or worse, do not have a grave, toward a place where 'we' and others can now play. This self-help is achieved through the transformative, ever-searching activity of sense-making and play, as we saw in Chapter 2. It is also reflective of the judgment of action and moral standing when one faces the difficulty of representing this particular historical past discursively, as we saw in Chapter 1.

In the memorial, the articulation of feelings is entangled with the visitors' 'moral career,' and their moral judgment of each other and the site, while sense-making activities at the site, of its form and aesthetics, are done through verbalization of its experience and culminate in miscommunication. This miscommunication is between guides and visitors, as guides attempt to blur, rather than refine, meaning and understanding of the memorial. Miscommunication around the question of what the memorial means or how one is supposed to engage with it is the basis for most forms of indirect self- and group-moralizing in the site. It frames the likely interpretations of visiting the Memorial.

Luckmann (2002: 21) differentiates between the thematization of morals and moralizing. Clearly, the rules of conduct one encounters upon entering the site are of the first kind, and enable a plethora of direct and indirect moralizing activities. The addressees of moral communication and moralizing can be the objects of moralizing themselves or they may be the recipients of moralizing about others, as in the case of gossip, or witnessing public shaming. To follow Luckmann's understanding of 'morality in use,' or the face-to-face as opposed to institutionally coded, as the basis of moral interaction, we will look into moralizing actions which occur in visiting the site and in articulating one's thoughts and feelings following the visit.

Irwin-Zarecka (1994) suggests separating articulated and privately held views, both relying on the resources people share, when studying collective memory. Using Goffman's notion of framing, Irwin-Zarecka (1994: 4) directs our attention to the 'powers inherent in public articulation of collective memory to influence the private making of sense.' In the memorial, workers and visitors articulate their feelings in regard to the site and what it is meant to move within them, in a way that makes the private shape the public and vice versa, within a framework that endures constant articulation.

The broken story and the excluded elements in it make the place and its advocates vulnerable, just as much as they make the visitors insecure. The guides, the visitors and metaphorically also the memorial itself in its abstractness, are then all partaking in a reassessment of their moral career, where suffering and victimhood as well as liberation from them lead the narrative of experiencing the place. This means that the visitor must first acknowledge a failure to understand the memorial, the Holocaust or both. This failure is always connected to experiences of other Holocaust memorials and stories, and it makes them wanderers in the memorial and its debate. The more they wonder and wander, the more internal their look turns. The visitors' decision to visit the memorial and their experience of it, together with what they can possibly take home from that experience, or what is altered in them following the visit, are all counted toward their moral assessment, which is also future oriented, since so long as the memorial is visited and debated, this is proof that it did not serve as a '*Schlussstreich*,' or a final line drawn on German engagement with their past.

The following is taken from an open-ended interview in July 2006 with a host at the memorial. I asked him about visitors' engagement with the memorial:

Host: The visitors see that the memorial is open to a variety of meaning perspectives: it applies to people with a perpetrators' perspective or a victims' perspective. It could be used as a memory sign for what happened. In coming years it will become clear that the memorial is open to almost any interpretation outside the fascistic. Anything goes, it is so abstract. It can stand for membership in the Waffen SS or a concentration camp. I have to say that when it comes to fascist architecture, I don't think that anything goes. Every stone is individualized. There is no stele that looks like any other.

Peter Eisenman did hold back in giving interpretations for the memorial, although in one of the first interviews he talked about his concept of rationality. He said that what was so bad about National Socialism is not that the Nazis were stupid and rotten; they could use the highest intellectual capacities. Rationality was a fundament of their action. This is why it cannot be open to *any* interpretation, and what the host has to do here is not only to engage in aesthetic discussion, but to encourage people to see the memorial as an imperative and to force the visitor to think. Unlike a visit to a library, or even three dissertations written about the topic, after which a person can lean back and say 'now I understand, I made it': it is crucial not to understand, to leave the disquieting inability to understand aside and not to let one view-point reign like in a lecture hall. So the host's duty is to bring the memorial into discussion so that it does not all remain in the realm of the abstract for the visitor.

The host says that the memorial is abstract, but that it should not stay abstract for the visitor – that is, not as a work of art, but as a facilitator of engagement with the past. He relates to interviews Eisenman gave in the German press before and around the opening of the memorial as a vantage point for the discussion of its aesthetics and interpretations, but also for stressing what the memorial should not be compared to: the rationality of the Nazis (which should nevertheless lurk in the background). This is where the discussion, in the interview quoted earlier, was apparently taking a wrong direction and had to be stopped, I suggest, not so much because of the comparison of Nazi rationality with today's rational interpretations, but rather because of the fear that interpreting the symbolism of the memorial today through fascist art may enable such fascistic thinking and rational acts, which is something memorial workers would not like to provide a platform for. Demanding that the visitor think in a certain direction connects the transformative self with possible transformations in the public sphere that are deemed good but can be dangerous.

Memorial workers often extend their demand from visitors toward the state and the public sphere, asking what the state does for, and how other groups engage with, the memorial. The Memorial Foundation executive director Mr Neumärker told me, and in public, that time and again he has asked state officials to come to the memorial, stating that he would be happy to greet them there.[4] All workers in the memorial talked about the scant financial support they get from the federal government, which hinders their ability to develop the memorial and to maintain it as the charter obliges them. Wolfgang Thierse, the Bundestag president, resigned from heading the board of trustees, as he wanted Dr Norbert Lammert, the incoming president appointed by the CDU, to take responsibility over what should be in his hands. All these demands, actions and complaints made clear the disparity between the enormous success of the memorial in terms of visitor numbers, and the paucity of recognition the workers felt they received from state institutions and civil society. They reflected on how the memorial turned from a hot discussion topic into a fact that does not require further civil work after its opening; and stressed their work with other memorial sites, research institutes and documentation centers.[5]

Visits by groups that have been working on Holocaust commemoration are considered extremely important and sometimes are given special attention by senior Foundation workers. Thus, the demand for engagement is extended from individuals to groups and the state, and links to the transformative experience of society in deciding on the realization of the memorial and the transformative experience of individuals visiting it. This extension of demands from the visitor to the state and civil society thus links to the need for Germany as a society and the German state, and not merely individuals who visit the memorial, to 'make sense' of the memorial in active engagement with the site and in the recurring verbalization of the ever-changing experience it avails groups and individuals.

1.2   The narrative of change

Progressing through the three phases of getting in, getting lost and getting it, the memorial visitor is exposed to a blend of directness and indirectness in the moralizing, from the most direct (such as following the rules of conduct written on the ground in the *Stelenfeld*) to the most indirect (such as accepting, for oneself, the impossibility of comprehending the Holocaust as a visitor to the memorial). This process culminates in the third phase, called *memory in action*, where visitors, having undergone the compulsion to articulate, realize themselves as members of this moral, mature community.

Understanding action in the site, together with the moralizing processes which realize mature and engaged publics, reflects not only the discourse on German memory politics, but also that on European integration past and present and the discussion of identity politics in the enlarged Europe. In this light, the memorial serves as a 'symbolic marker' (Eder 2001: 223) implying a normative definition of inclusion and exclusion. In order for the included person, group or attitude to be loved, the symbolic representation of what is emotionally and normatively shared with that person, group or attitude, should be created. Or, as in the case of the memorial, the void of figurative meaning and norms is represented as a marker of the need to find new norms of engaging with memory (not necessarily with minorities) freely and openly. According to Eder (2001: 226), the processes through which collective experience is remembered shape the collective memory. We will see how through engaging with the past in a pleasant, newly constructed site, not only the experience of the past is changed, but also its symbolic markers as well as the possible publics which can engage in memory action are altered. I suggest that here the memory of the Holocaust serves first as a unifying mechanism for the creation of a reflexive distance from oneself and from the past, and then it mobilizes people to remember remembering ethically, which then leads to 'memory in action,' a perpetual, politically engaging process.

In the quote that opened this chapter, taken from a worksheet given to pupils at the memorial, sensing the site and oneself in it is encouraged while visitors are touring the memorial. We already saw that making sense of the memorial as a project, as an abstract site and in its location in an 'inauthentic' place where Jewish persecution did not take place, is an activity through which one articulates one's knowledge of the past and oneself within it.

Guided tours build on the lack of instructive or figurative meaning and the endless metaphorical interpretational possibilities of the site above ground, in contrast to the clarity offered in the Information Center underground. The sense-making activities in which visitors engage with the memorial, raise questions such as 'What is it' and 'What is it not.' The discussion of feelings and thoughts raise the questions: 'What do I feel here? What am I supposed to feel here? What should I not feel here?' These frames of memory action are studied through the prisms of verbalization, or induction into putting one's feelings about the memorial into words; aesthetic and moral judgments, or assessing the success of the memorial to move its visitors as individuals and as groups reflecting on the past in today's Berlin; and political articulation, or posing questions regarding the necessity of the memorial and its connection to one's engagement with the past.

§2 Three phases in visitors' moral career

2.1 'Getting in': moral career and judgment in the memorial

The tensions between the mediated story of the memorial and the actual personal visit to the site creates a space for what I see as the construction of a moral career for the visitor, the guide and the memorial project at large. The memorial was claimed by Martin Walser in the Walser-Bubis debate (Carrier 2005; Quack 2002) to be moral intimidation of the German public and thus the roots of linking it to moral affirmation or intimidation precede its opening.[6] As Habermas (1987) claims, the political perspective offers a reading of the narrative construction and implosion as a form of deliberative politics: one must engage with the past not through shame but through doing.[7] Reiterating one's relations to the memorial is a vehicle for doing justice to the history of the Holocaust and its victims, as well as to a proper, ceaseless engagement and confrontation with the past that is one of the bases of a healthy, vibrant and responsible German democracy.

In the memorial a visitor's moral career, or the ways he or she presents her former engagement with history, is examined and assessed through five forms of judgment: moral, aesthetic, historical, hermeneutical and political (Dekel 2008). Here I focus on moral and aesthetic judgment. Moral judgment brings forth the moral standing of a visitor or a group of visitors. They ask themselves and others in the site (watching each other's action) what their relations to the Holocaust and its memory are. In guided tours and conversations at the memorial, Memorial Foundation workers set a threshold to measure one's moral position in relation to Holocaust memory, relying on historical knowledge and the willingness to discuss it: political affiliation, education, Eastern or Western origins and nationality. Thus, moral judgment is directed toward and among people visiting the memorial, and toward it as a project and its initiators. Aesthetic judgment is a seemingly simpler form, as it is directed at the memorial solely, though, as we will see, it is imbued with the potency of moral judgment, because of the very possibility of exerting aesthetic judgment of *A Holocaust Memorial* design and then asking whether it *functions* or can stand as a memorial for the Holocaust of the Jews. This is a highly liberating form of judgment, since it is the first time in which visitors (especially German ones) can reflect on the aesthetic value of a Holocaust memorial, after all other values have been secured or have become no longer so pressing to discuss.

This memorial is the first place having to do with Holocaust memorialization about which visitors can say 'I do/don't like it.' So, talking about 'it' (the site) also reflects on the discourse about the other 'it' (the Holocaust), and how it is commemorated. In this regard one has to know what this site stands for in order to have a political relation to it, and the role of the Information Center – as the Memorial Foundation describes it – is to 'ground' this experience in information. The lack of clear figurative meaning, the refusal of its workers to offer interpretations of the site or hint at proper action in it, and the elusive reference to other suggestive meanings in other memorials such as the resemblance to a graveyard or labyrinth, create a low threshold for entering the realm of discussion, and call for constant attempts to interpret the site based on its form. These attempts at interpretation and articulation are at the core of action in visiting the memorial.

Every guided tour starts in the site itself. The guides meet the group by the entrance to the Information Center and walk with them into the *Stelenfeld*, where the first part of the tour is held. The guides present the history of the site as a non-authentic Memorial to the Murdered Jews of Europe and the debates that preceded its building. They invite the group to interpret the impact and experience of being in the site. The visitors are then asked to tour the memorial by themselves for ten minutes and then reassemble back where they were.[8] They talk about their experience of the *Stelenfeld* (what was new to them, what they saw and felt) and are then taken to the underground Information Center where they hear an introduction to the installation which revolves around bits of the history of the Holocaust that add to the sequence of Holocaust stories told above ground. The following excerpts are taken from a guided tour in November 2005 with 12 eleventh grade pupils. We will see how before the pupils return from touring the memorial site, the guide practices and endorses political articulation, moral and aesthetic judgment and, after the tour, when the pupils answer his questions, the conversation culminates in miscommunication.

GUIDE.   This area where the memorial is now built was a no-man's-land. There was nothing here. There is no sign here to the fact that here the murder of the Jews is remembered. In regard to the question of who the memorial should be dedicated to, it was decided that it will be only for the Jews, a decision taken by Wolfgang Thierse, President of the German Bundestag.

As for the question of what should be built, there were two competitions. In 1995 the winning proposal was that of Jakob Marks – to make one stone on which all the names of Holocaust victims known to us would be engraved. There was also a design that would include the names of concentration camps. Do you know the names of concentration camps?

PUPILS.   Ravensbrück, Sachsenhausen, Auschwitz.

GUIDE.   The second proposal that won was for the names, which Kohl rejected and said that what was needed, then, was not a *Denk-mal* (a memorial), but to pause for thinking (*Denk-Pause*). In 1999 Eisenman won with a proposal similar to this one. He wanted 4000 stelae and got 2711. Do you know why?

PUPIL.   There was no money.

GUIDE.   Not only. It was also too bombastic. It could not merge with local architecture. The main reason, however, was the gap between the stelae. The ground here is wavy. And we wanted people to be able to walk around, and also be able to do that with wheelchairs.

Now you can go by yourself around the memorial. We will meet here in 10 minutes.

The pupils laugh and ask: 'How will we find you?' The guide laughs with them and says: 'You will.'

The pupils are back. They said they felt lost and that the place was narrow and sad.

GUIDE.   This place is not authentic. There is nothing concrete you can do with the Holocaust. But around us there are many historical places. Here it is Wilhelmstrasse. In 1871 the Ministry was built here. In 30.1.33 Göbels said here 'now we have Wilhelmstrasse', indicating the importance of this street for German political life. At the same time, Max Liebermann saw the Nazis marching through the Brandenburg Gate from the window of his apartment. Around us we also see symbols of German partition.

In the *Stelenfeld*, everything is anonymous.

What meaning can there be to commemoration without knowledge? We will think about this underground in the Information Center.

The guide constructs a narrative that combines telling the story of the memorial and telling Holocaust stories. This narrative contains 'entry' and 'exit' points into the history of Jewish persecution in World War II: bits and pieces of information, usually information that the guides assume that the audience is not familiar with. One of the crucial entry points to the story of the memorial, setting the low threshold for engaging with it, is that it is a non-authentic place. MacCannel (1973) in his analysis of 'staged authenticity' shows that tourists in modern times are believed to have a non-authentic experience since they are outsiders, consuming a place, having no access to 'back regions' in Goffman's terminology. In the memorial, an inauthentic new touristy place offers an authentic (or real) experience for the wandering and wondering self. This might happen there, according to memorial workers like the guide in this example, because of the newness of the site, its loose relations to the reality of the Holocaust, and to proper Holocaust remembrance elsewhere. Guides create an authentic experience in and of the memorial based on its inauthentic form (Wang 1999). The statement that 'there is nothing concrete to do with the Holocaust' connects all the valid routes in the memorial above ground with the declaration that 'all is possible in the memorial': what Godfrey (2007: 239–78) describes as an inexhaustible space for experience and judgment.

The memorial exists as an authentic work of art only in the set of coordinates of the time and space of its presence. Probing its authenticity is an act of questioning its authority in comparison to the authority of other memorials that are not (solely) works of art and their authority derives from a singular set of historical evidence and traces in the place of their existence. They are very 'concrete' and there are certain thoughts and feelings they induce. This act of questioning the memorial's power to move ends up adding authority to it as a work of art consisting of absence of meaning and iconic meaning that dwell in the same place above ground, and an abundance of information and meaning that the visitor encounters underground. In the guided tour this tension between present and absent meaning, does not stay intact, as the guide said, after a visit underground one can see that memory without knowledge is incomplete, and justifies the necessity of the underground Information Center. Additionally, in order to distinguish the memorial project from other memorials in the GDR and earlier, which were built on remnants of the past believed to be the ultimate tool to bring people to learn about the past, the memorial offers an experience that is not based on authentic artifacts and that is supposed to stem from the individual as they meet themselves and others, and as they experience motion and transformation in it (Dekel 2009a).

Just as it has often been argued, following Adorno (1951), that no narrative of the Holocaust is possible, or as the guide put it in this example 'There is nothing concrete you can do with the Holocaust,' so too guides make sure there is no coherent, redemptive narrative of the memorial. Rather, they provide only hints toward its possible construction and negotiation and watch carefully that the rules of 'no rules' are closely followed. In other words, the structure of the guided tour is that one must 'know' about the Holocaust, but one cannot ever attempt to 'understand' and fully fathom its meaning and scope. As the guide presents it: 'In the *Stelenfeld* everything is anonymous.' 'What meaning can there be to commemoration without knowledge?' He suggests a way of looking at and experiencing the memorial, while saying that there is no one way to understand 'it.' This 'it' alludes to a broken story of the Holocaust that remains unfinished so as to be open for discussion, while parts of it are dictated in the Information Center. This is an example of how verbalization is directed at making sense of the movement and physical sensation of being in the *Stelenfeld*, with reference to being in touch with one's broader engagement with Holocaust memory.

We can see in the guide's call for engagement with the memorial through political articulation around his presentation of the site: The area was also realized by the highest political body – the Bundestag in 1999. Aesthetic and moral judgments are intertwined through the presentation of questions: whether it is a work of art and talking about the competition and the first winning design that was deemed inappropriate.[9] Bringing up concentration camps, the failure to decide on a design after the first competition and the need for a break in action around the memorial all call for active engagement through moral and historical judgment, and reach their peak after the pupils say they felt lost in the memorial. The conversation then culminates in a productive miscommunication when the guide states that the memorial is not authentic and that there is nothing concrete to do with the Holocaust. This miscommunication is directed at enduring puzzlement in regard to the ways to engage with memory, and leads us to the second moralizing stage of getting lost.

2.2 'Getting lost': memorial moves, limitation and liberation

In the quotation that opened this chapter, taken from a worksheet for pupils, individuals are asked to literally make sense of the place; make observations and record feelings. They have to do so in motion. They have, first, to see, then refrain from seeing and use hearing and touch. They are then asked to make notes of that experience. They are not exactly stripped of their knowledge, but nevertheless are encouraged to be reflective after they use their senses. No concluding thought or remark is asked for.

Locating individual experience and individual fate is at the center of both the above ground *Stelenfeld* and underground Information Center, creating a framework for verbalization of experience in two opposite directions: toward the inability to understand and grasp the Holocaust and also toward identification with the victims as victims who were murdered and insufficiently remembered as individuals.[10] This latter component of engagement with the memorial – the evaluation of commemoration places and practices and of one's acquaintance with them, I suggest, connects the individual to public action. As such, the therapeutic practice of verbalizing experience locates the searching self in the center of a potential civic engagement based on accidental encounters with others, who are also in the midst of exploration of, and for, themselves and others.

One is accountable for one's own sense-making through a process of verbalization, as a self-contained experience whose ground is clarified in the Information Center. As we saw, performing the ritual of sense-making and acknowledging one's failure to grasp the place above ground and underground is a condition for engaging with the site, and through it with others. However, this failure is extended to the moral standing of the visitor through the discussion, or its lack, of victims and victimhood. The discussions of Germans as victims in World War II (Niven 2006) and of German national responsibility are individuated in the memory work done in the memorial, not through a sense of guilt and shame, but through the self-limitation which is uttered in reaction to the site.

We have seen the connection between speakability and therapeutic discourse. We will now look at the specific relations between the focus on the self and transformation in public. Observers of popular therapeutic discourse (Foucault 1990; Illouz 2007b), associate the phenomenon with focus on the self. Furedi argues that the 'therapeutic imperative is not so much toward the realization of self-fulfillment as the promotion of self-limitation' (2004: 21). This realization of self-limitation promoted in other sites unrelated to the memory discourse is very much present in the memorial, and is performed there. We can see how self-fulfillment is achieved in memory action, aware of its self-limiting character, while also celebrating the liberating moment occurring in a site that does *not* require former sets of self-limitation, which hitherto were the meeting grounds for looking into one's national identity through engagement with the past. For example, the bewilderment with regard to whether a place of Holocaust memory should also be a place for the performance of leisure was widely discussed in the German press around the opening of the memorial.[11]

Engaging with the past as a collective national story and also as a personal one is part of a therapeutic culture which is derived from individuation, or care for the self. The memorial's focus on individual experience of individuals' fates, I suggest, stems from the therapeutic trend as much as from historical responsibility toward the victims.[12] Within this framework, the boundaries are sometimes blurred between different perpetrators and perpetrators and victims, because the very identification with a victim makes one feel like a victim, as we can see in the following interaction which I heard from the guide, about an experience he had with a pupil after a guided tour. The guide related humorously to this interaction, as he told me about it:

PUPIL.   I did not like the security control in the entrance to the Information Center.
GUIDE.   Why?
PUPIL.   It made me feel like a Jew.
GUIDE.   You say something really problematic. I will have to tell the police about it.
PUPIL.   Bye now.

The pupil took the time to tell the guide that he felt offended by the security control line. It was a ritual confirming his moral inferiority (we saw the same projected moral inferiority in the example of the elderly visitors). The pupils felt suspicious, like victims must have felt.[13] Did he mean to say that he himself became vulnerable? Was he making Jews vulnerable in theory or in reality by declaring that he felt like a Jew? Other visitors and workers? Furedi claims that 'Victim identity is fluid and subjective and can attach itself to virtually any contemporary claim. Since this identity provides one of the most legitimate routes to both recognition and claims-making, there is considerable incentive for people to embrace it' (2004: 177–8). Giesen provides the historical-political context for this argument in his discussion of the failed ritual of the Bitburg Affair in 1985: '[O]n the one hand, the construction of victims is bound to inclusion. On the other hand, this construction of victims cannot dispense with perpetrators; it is ritually staged by public acts of repentance and accepting collective guilt' (2004: 184).

The pupil's choice to feel like a victim who is also a suspect was unacceptable in the memorial. Why did the guide take this as a potentially unlawful offence? If anything, it affirmed the success of the Foundation in making visitors identify with the victims. But it also showed how far the visitors position themselves from the victims, and how crossing the line, even only in declaring one's feeling of insecurity, is dangerous. It marked the moral dimension of victimhood: the fate of the Jews as depicted and protected in the memorial threatens the well-being of a German pupil and if this is the case, the well-being of other fellow citizens. The German security people in the memorial and the structure of the security control makes him feel like a potential perpetrator, a potential victim, be it a killed one or a survivor (morally charged and hence, again, suspicious). Here we encounter the performance of literally getting lost in the discourse about the meaning inferred in the site, which is all encompassing and includes similarly meaningless objects like the security control.

Many visitors, in verbalizing their experience of the memorial, say that perhaps 'this is how the Jews felt' in the Holocaust: lost, scared, disoriented. Eisenman also alluded to it in his interviews. Identifying with the victims is marginal to the main goal of identifying with the necessity of the memorial and its civil functions. However, visitors are not supposed to be transformed into Jews at the end of the visit, but into (German) individuals recognizing the work of the memorial for themselves, in dedication to dead Jews. What the pupil said sounded to the guide like Holocaust denial. There were other instances in which visitors reflected on the site, particularly through the security-check procedure, as a simulation of how the Jews felt in the Holocaust. A host told me that some visitors see the security check; say it is 'too much for them' and leave. A Foundation worker told me that an elderly German woman said, upon standing in line for the security check: 'The security personnel are like Kapos. I don't like it.' The more the security check was an issue among visitors, the more central it became in the preparation the guides provided about it. They presented it as necessary for the visitor's own safety. Guides do not have to stand with their group for the check, and meet with their group after they have been checked.

The security-check structure is also made to seem intentionally mundane: 'like in an airport, or the parliament,' say the guides to groups before they let them in. If the *Stelenfeld* is guarded mostly for the sake of visitors' safety; the Information Center is guarded to find and exclude potential offenders who will hurt others or the center. The police have been invited a few times to remove butterfly knives and their carriers. Both carrying a knife and confessing that one feels like a Jew are made suspicious and are subject to announcement and investigation, which takes place in and outside the memorial, and sometimes involves the police. This is an example of direct moralizing staged in the midst of moral confusion and search for moral direction at the site. However, when male pupils do or say something threatening, the police are invited, or the offender is informed of the fact that his act was of the kind that should involve the police. The elderly lady was just a disgrace.

What makes the utterance, 'This makes me feel like a Jew' dangerous and offensive, and 'This is how the Jews felt,' welcome or harmless in the memorial? I do not think it is merely the potential blurring of boundaries between perpetrators and victims, or false engagement with the memorial. To the contrary: it is the refusal and failure to keep Jews as an intact category of Holocaust victims. This could be the reason why many Foundation workers, when asked by Israelis (or other easy to identity Jews) whether they should go into the Information Center, or take an extended visit to the memorial, answer that this place is not for them. They have no discourse to get lost in. Similarly, in several interviews with the German press, architect Eisenman was cited as saying that whenever he comes to Germany, he comes as an American and leaves feeling a Jew. His transformation seems welcome in light of the mission bestowed on him, the design and erection of the memorial. In all instances, the moral career, identity and their performance are called into question and determine the likely forms of engagement with the site, through the prism of bewilderment and transformation.

A repetitive questioning of categories to be used around remembering the Holocaust is an additional indirect moralizing mechanism of getting lost; the most important one after Jews seems to be anti-Semitism. For many German visitors, it is not clear what counts as anti-Semitism today (adding to the growing number of mores invented in this new memorial). They are embarrassed and frightened by the mere thought that anti-Semitism will occur again in Germany and in Europe. They also do not accept it as a primordial social fact but as one's choice (Giesen 2004), and because not many ever talked with Jews, certainly not lived with them, there are certain utterances, usually evaluating things as 'Jewish' or questioning the necessity of public memory action and its current forms, that sound anti-Semitic and hence alarming to them. The repeated fear of anti-Semitism is a crucial part of the moralizing mechanism of getting lost, because of the history of being perpetrators and also because this history is connected to the memory of totalitarian regimes. An additional security-check metaphor a host shared with me was of Stasi agents. Hence, connecting Germany's 'double past' with local sites of memory brings up all sorts of threats to democracy which often boil down to the fear of anti-Semitism.

In the last example we saw how the call for interpretation of the memorial, sense-making and feelings create an atmosphere for public action that is based on the judgment of the visitor's engagement with it in the present. In this framework and through its performativity, the communication in the memorial should be extended beyond the actual visit, and hence the failures to comprehend its impact are powerful, productive and moral bases for proper engagement with it.

2.3 'Getting it': duty to oneself and the realization of the public

In concluding this chapter, I will, first, connect the phenomenon of self-exploration (Dekel 2009a) to public political action and, second, suggest seeing it as a tool for the realization of the public itself. In the memorial, the fragmentation of informal communication constitutes a potential meeting ground that embodies its own failure: only individuals can figure out for themselves the meaning of the place. Since they are also bound to fail in this pursuit (the place potentially infers numerous meanings for each visitor), they have to search forever, and communicate the search and sense-making endeavors in their actions and reflection about it.

We can so far see a sense of universal moral responsibility which makes crossing the lines between victims and others dangerous. In a similar vein, a senior host told me in an interview in June 2006 that 'it is important for Germans visiting the memorial to make sure that something like the Holocaust will never happen again, nowhere in the world.' He saw the memorial as a proof and reminder (or a warning sign, *Mahnmal*, in German) for moral responsibility which will make it bearable and, later, even positive to think of oneself as a German after the Holocaust. One can recognize two claims here: (1) recognition of a state of victimhood elsewhere and potentially in Germany; (2) a plea for moral recognition, having the credibility of former perpetrators victimized by their own lack of moral authority (which brings them closer to the victims). Here, the duty of the individual to themself collides with their public duty. Thus, perhaps saying, 'This place makes me feel like a Jew' implies a mirrored case: 'This place makes me feel like a German.' This is similar to Butler's reflection on Aretha Franklin's 'You make me feel like a natural woman' (1990: 22). Butler illustrates the point that feeling feminine is fluid and does not necessarily happen at all times, just like with masculinity. Perhaps, following this line, the utterance, 'This makes me feel like a Jew' makes the category 'Jew' fluid, and that is something that memorial workers cannot allow. All options (a collectively victimized or victimizing group or a group that may grow independent of its past) are dangerous to label and explore in the memorial, while at once making the discussion in it so powerful and compelling.

In celebrating the first anniversary of the memorial's opening in May 2006, there was a roundtable discussion with Foundation workers, hosts and guides. The speakers were asked about visitors' reactions to the memorial. A Foundation worker and guide, answered: 'People expect something more monumental. There are people who have issues with the dedication of the site to Jews only.' The guide added: 'There are also nonsense questions: "Why is it built here, why are the stelae corners not round; why did it cost so much?" This shows [something]. It shows if you are for the memory or against it. It is always there. This is a memorial we have built for and from ourselves. It is not an authentic place.'

Being 'for or against the memory', or having issues with the dedication to the Jews or the memorial's cost helps to assess the visitor's personal values and morals in relation to contemporary politics, as we have seen in earlier examples. The questions regarding meaning, as well as 'nonsense questions', illuminate the endless quest for interpretation that should be done individually. The relationship between the visitor's search for meaning (note that the speaker only relates to individuals and not to groups) and her moral assessment leads to verbalization of experience in the site based on metaphorical projection of what the place can tell one about Holocaust memory, and what one can find out there about oneself and others, creating a public engaged in memory politics.

Conclusion

In creating a meeting ground for personal moral and ethical reflection, all sides involved in visiting and introducing the memorial have in mind certain individuals performing in public, whose dramaturgical performance as well as utterances have to do with their engagement with the past and attitude toward 'memory.' Memory, presented as a personal quest for the remembrance of personal stories, which in turn form the story of the memorial together with the Holocaust stories, relates both to the inducement to inquire and the inability to understand. This misfit between needing to know, but being unable to understand leads most communications about the memorial to end in failure: a failure to comprehend the memorial parallel to the inability to comprehend the

Holocaust. Precisely the tensions between knowing and not knowing, with its parallel of feeling and not feeling, produce the inducement to speak and interpret, creating and sustaining an involved and ever-evolving public that should keep asking questions about engagement with the past. A public whose present political stance will reflect this action just so long as there are people in the memorial, there is a memorial, and the inducement to question it all.

4
Mediation at the Holocaust Memorial

We have discussed the creation of virtual communicative memory and the transformative discourse which uses trauma discourse and post-trauma tropes in Holocaust memory as symbolic anchors but departs from them. In this chapter, we will discuss mediation in the memorial, or the interplay of material and symbolic practices that constitute its understanding (Hennion 1997, in Marontate 2005). We will focus on the role and use of various media in the memorial as they facilitate and reflect meaning and knowledge production, consumption, staging and transmission in the site. The prevalent form of media used in the memorial is still-photography and not live media. The unplanned nature of action at the site is elevated in the press through, for example, the discussion about security in and of the site. This discussion, as we saw in Chapters 2 and 3, brings together the alleged moral career of the society that remembers with the individuals belonging to it, and suspense concerning their outcomes in the site. The latter is referred to in the numerous 'emergency calls' regarding the shaky condition of the stones, the stairs and the Information Center, which allude to the shaky condition of 'memory'.

Mediation, according to Radstone is a 'direct and necessary activity between different kinds of activity and consciousness, which has its own specific forms' (2005: 134, following Williams, 1976). In the case of the past which is mediated by memory action, Radstone (2005: 135) points out that this mediation shows the difference between memory and history and memory's specific activities and forms. Taken together, mediation and articulation help disentangle the relations between memory action and the past, and see that 'texts and practices are complexly related to the broader social formation in which their meaning is forged' (2005: 135). Radstone is interested in the *mediation of already mediated* memory discourses, images, texts and representations in the public sphere. I find this task important but would like to probe its premises. If we agree, after Halbwachs, that all memory, even the most personal, is mediated, then we are already dealing with a second and third order of mediation. The question, then, remains of how diverse social institutions articulate certain texts and how individuals within these institutions perform and stage their knowledge and emotional position in relation to those texts and discourses.

With the narrative network analysis of Smith (2007) and Bearman and Stovel (2000), I would first like to show that meaning emerges from the structure of relations between narrative elements which (a) do not relate to an event but to the description of transformation *as* an event. In other words, the sociological understanding of 'event' is that it 'durably transforms structure and relations' (Wagner-Pacifici 2010: 1356). Visiting the memorial is often presented as a transformative experience and, through that, understood as an event. The second argument I would like to advance is that the narrative structure of the visit (b) adheres to the rules of partaking in an *interactive spectacle* (Kelner 2010). By this I mean that people configure their experience through a powerful filter of social media representations, news entertainment, and that of the communicative action theory I discussed in the first chapter. I depart from Kelner (and Debord), who see the spectacle as either a contested terrain or a hegemonic one, and rather see it as the performance of producing a technologically mediated event that is also fleeting and repetitive (Abbott 2001, in Wagner-Pacifici 2010). On its own, it is not at the center of interest for large publics. Additionally, the interactivity actually happens on the ground, in relation to agents and conventions outside the time and space of the visit and not between or within various media. To follow Wagner-Pacifici's method of studying events beyond their narrow historical frame, we can see that the unbounded event of the visit is understood instantly by its actors through its transformative significance and how it is conveyed in photos that will be posted or looked at elsewhere.

Hoskins claims that 'Contemporary memory is not principally constituted through retrieval, nor representation of some content of the past in the present, but, rather, it is distributed through our sociotechnical practices, including our everyday usage of the internet' (2009: 3). The connection between these sociotechnical practices; available media; and prevailing discourses about how the past should be remembered and how memory ought to be performed by institutions, communities and individuals stand at the center of this chapter. In this way I hope to be able to say something about the work of memory in a memorial site and less about the use and functions of media.

I will analyze speech acts about the experience of the visit, then present what kind of event it is and how it is mediated, and, lastly, discuss the actual means of mediation and ask what kind of new practices develop in the site. I will then ask how they are affected by (1) media used in the Information Center and in visiting the site; and (2) institutionalization processes that illuminate the changing landscape of cultural authority that is reflected in the relations between museums and publics. These relations include interactive processes of meaning-making, community involvement and public controversies as forms of constructed and contested recognition (Marontate 2005).

§1 Dislocating narratives: victimhood, suffering and survival

Based on the model of reading life stories through the mechanisms of 'becoming' and 'being' a Nazi developed by Bearman and Stovel (2000), and with no connection between the themes they read and the themes discussed in the memorial, one important structural element of the narrative of change is that it is complex. Complex in the sense that the narrative has core elements that connect parts of the narrative; which, if removed, would break the underlying plot into disjointed stories. The 'being' story has a disjunctive nature. Unlike in the written life stories Bearman and Stovel analyze, here the narrators speak, while writing only rarely in the visitors' book and in response to worksheets that many pupils leave behind. Both visitors and guides relate to macro-level elements like historical events to substantiate their relations to the Holocaust more as the story of change than an emotional one. The visitor's relation to the site is formulated only vaguely in terms of their social and political experience in the present. As much as guides try to make it the case that the memory of the Holocaust will be linked to local, state and international politics, visitors often ignore, and even resist, this attempt.

Do the narrative structures of change and talking about emotions coincide? They do coincide around the issue of group representation, as we will see in the following example, where the performative role played by the guide through her use of the term 'generation' was alluding to a conventional German representation of the remembered past, namely that of the almost-gone generation of perpetrators. Conflict about the use of this concept emerged between the guide and a group, as the groups performed a perlocutionary use of the term (Austin, in

Wagner-Pacifici 2010), insisting on the consequences of such use as it pertained to their own families. This conflict was not resolved, and revealed the different cultural assumptions and repertoires with which visitors and guides construct the narrative of the visit as a narrative of participation, transition and reorientation.

The workshop 'Searching for remnants' took place in April of 2011 and focuses on written notes left by victims before their death and displayed in the Room of Dimensions. The group was an unusual one, of adults (the vast majority of workshop clientele are school groups, and they are particularly designed for them). This group's members, six men and 12 women, aged from their mid-twenties to mid-forties, were participants in a vocational course. They came from a town in East Brandenburg (in the former GDR). Many of them had already visited the site before and showed their discontent and unwillingness to participate in a workshop. Their responses to the guide's questions were scarce, though some showed extensive knowledge about the Holocaust. They spent a long time visiting the Information Center and worked on the tasks of interpreting texts they were given in the beginning of the workshop. I present long parts of the discussion here, following the individual and group work in the workshop.

The group returned from the Information Center and was asked to sort and organize documents taken from the Room of Dimensions and Room of Families, given to them by the guide:

VISITOR 1. That is for school groups?
GUIDE.   Yes (*laughing*). They are much faster than you, if I may say this. Maybe it is simply because you think too much.
VISITOR 3. Yeah. Maybe also because we are hungry.

Guide and visitors convene and read the texts. The guide directs the visitors' question: 'Who wrote the text? If it were a postcard it would have been different.' Most visitors engage in reading the texts and discussing it in light of the questions:

GUIDE.   You read a text and see a picture that is of Shlumo Feiner. I don't know who worked on this.
VISITOR 1. We have, right. Shlomo (Guide: Shlumo, Shlumo) Feiner? From Poland. He is a slave laborer. He was in a death camp, earlier he fled from the Warsaw Ghetto but was caught and taken to Kulmhof and then to the death camp of Belzec and there, at age 42 he was murdered [...].

GUIDE.   Now the question is why people wrote in such situations. He was a slave laborer. What is a slave laborer? In the Warsaw Ghetto there were people who collected paper and hid it. Why? It is so people do not forget.

VISITOR 4.   To use it in trials.

GUIDE.   Exactly. It is about naming perpetrators. They collected information about what happened in the ghetto for the time after Hitler [...]. And so someone like Shlumo Feiner who came from the outside and gave this testimony: that was uncannily valuable and uncannily dreadful. If you are forced to move into the ghetto, into the Warsaw Ghetto, and there are terrible problems with food and hygiene, but then someone from the outside comes and tells you about gas wagons, you understand that this is about murder. And this is the year 42. Those texts show what people simply knew, in a closed place where people could not get in or out. This organization was also responsible for smuggling information to London, where the Polish exile government was. And those calls were based on the hope, so early, that the world would do something once they know what the Germans were doing to the Jews, and that this would also steer the Allies' war targets toward preventing the extinction of the Jews. This did not happen.

              Ok. I would like to hear perhaps the Etti group.

VISITOR 3.   The Etti group. Ahh.

              (*Two more groups present their findings.*)

GUIDE.   OK. Would anyone like to say now how this morning was for you? Was it too much, too long?

VISITOR 1.   I found it good, interesting. Learned many things I did not know on different levels.

VISITOR 2.   It was somehow too close (*laughing, sigh*), so that you realize that it was simply just brutal, and that something like that, which happened, must be remembered.

GUIDE.   I spoke about it with Irit, who is dealing with the memorial scientifically, and this is the aim of the memorial. You see it in the citation of Primo Levi [...] and the question is what you, visiting here, think that it has to do with you. Do you take anything with you for the present?

VISITOR 3.   But for us, now, here in the circle, perhaps it can be comprehensible. For one or the other there was a family who was engaged in this [...]. Perhaps for the guilty generations, but for the following generations, how guilt is being dealt with is getting harder and harder to comprehend. I do not know what I will tell my daughter in three years, how she will get it from me. As knowledge, well OK.

GUIDE.   But what does it have to do with you? You mean, you have relatives, I mean, in what relation?

VISITOR 4.   No, not I personally, but people in the family who took part.

GUIDE.   But it is relatively many generations. I mean, my parents also did not take part. It is an interesting question. That there is a proposal that the grandparents, ehm, somehow were still part of the perpetrators' generation. Is this what was meant here?

             (*Many visitors talk at the same time.*)

VISITOR 3.   My father was a soldier. That is the title.

GUIDE.   Yes, but he was part of the perpetrators' generation. These are people who were adults then.

VISITOR 4.   My parents were German but could not stay home [...].

VISITOR 3.   What kind of a title is it?

VISITOR 5.   There was also the victims' generation

VISITOR 3.   A generation.

GUIDE.   For the victims, the age does not matter. Children were murdered. It is about the fact that my grandparents were in an everyday situation in which they could be perpetrators.

The group talks about how today people are less emotionally moved by the topic and in 50 years they will be even less moved:

VISITOR 4.   You do not know how you would act if you were in those situations.

VISITOR 5.   I get emotional about relatives who you say are the perpetrators' generation and I call the victims' generation.

GUIDE.   But what I am still conflicted about is that I am 35 years old and I am emotional about a story today. Why would people in 20 years not be moved? The reaction should stay the same. When we read in 200 years about someone who was persecuted are we then moved? It is exactly the question. What is it that we take with us? In what situation do we develop a stronger sensitivity to unlawfulness?

VISITOR 4.   But I can also say that it is right or wrong the way people were then dealt with. Yes, sometimes there were people who murdered and we can say that they were not at all perpetrators, but victims, because they were forced to do it.

GUIDE. The people, eh, the people who killed others are victims?

VISITORS 4. Yes, they did not stand there and say, 'Yes, I'd like to kill someone now,' they were equally forced.

GUIDE. So, I mean, it is a very difficult field when one deals with perpetrators. The Topography of Terror has an exhibition about the perpetrators and their organization, and they show that those who did not want to shoot others simply did not do it. But it is a very bold thesis to say that all the perpetrators were victims. So go once to the Topography of Terror.

(Visitors talk at the same time.)

VISITOR 3. People would shoot. With a refusal no one would get shot...

GUIDE. Mass shootings actually did not come from above, from some generals. It is exactly the discussion about the *Wehrmacht* or the *SS*. Who was in the *SS*? The people were not forced to join. The *Wehrmacht* were soldiers who accidentally got there?

VISITOR 3. The *Wehrmacht* also shot [were involved in mass shooting, ID]

GUIDE. Yes, exactly, and there are cases where people who were accidentally there and did not want to, were not tried.

VISITOR 3. But when it is argued this way, you must start with causes of how the National Socialists could get to power. Then you have to put about 98 percent of the German, I mean it generally now, on trial. And then we are all perpetrators. I am naturally critical.

GUIDE. But we cannot then say that the perpetrators were victims. I also do not say that all the Germans were perpetrators and murderers.

(Visitors talk at the same time: But this is how it comes out.)

GUIDE. So this is the question what do we mean by the 'perpetrators' generation.' It is time-bound.

VISITOR 4. I find it problematic that you say, for example to your school classes, which ages had kids and who are part of the perpetrators' generation. Then those kids say, 'oh, grandma and grandpa were perpetrators.' I found it hard.

GUIDE. We do not often get to this theme of the perpetrators generation. There are also not many children whose

	grandparents were part of it. This is a hard question. But I find it nevertheless interesting what you, in the last two-and-a-half hours were so quiet and then flipped out about this theme.
VISITOR 3.	It is about my parents who were of that generation, and my grandparents too, aunts too.
GUIDE.	And you'd happily say that they did not commit any crime?
VISITOR 3.	No, that I did not say. I do not know that. That has to do with what they told or did not tell me. But I reject the wholesale sentencing [condemnation] of people that takes place today. I am only against that.
GUIDE.	But why did you not ask?
VISITOR 3.	Of course one asks. The question is what one is told. Yes, what one does not want to forget. What one wants to forget, that would not be told.
GUIDE.	This is a different theme that I personally find very interesting, I don't know if it was clear enough to you to detect what your grandparents had done. There is information about the *Wehrmacht* available and you could find out. I mean, my grandparents are dead. They died so early that I could not ask them what I would ask if I were older. Na...
VISITOR 3.	One has a totally different relation to it when it is one's relatives.
GUIDE.	You want to protect them.
VISITOR 3.	I do not want to protect them, I want only... I start trembling because I simply don't want people to be sentenced wholesale. I stand against this only.
GUIDE.	By the concept of perpetrators' generation I only meant people that were old enough to be perpetrators at that time. My mother was born in 1943 and she is not a part of that.
VISITOR 3.	My father was born in 1926. All are of the perpetrators' generation.
VISITOR 6.	My mother in 1940.
GUIDE.	Would anyone like to say anything for conclusion?
VISITOR 3.	I go now. I am shaking.
GUIDE.	I thank you for the discussion and also that you all cooperated.
VISITOR 4.	I also go now. This is also very impolite.
VISITOR 6.	I mean, one second. You are the one being impolite.

VISITOR 4.	No, I am not being impolite.
GUIDE.	As always, many thanks that you were here and a nice day.

(The group left.)

GUIDE.	(*to me*) What do you say? What happened there?
ID.	I don't know. It was bad. I ask myself too because they wanted to talk about their families.
GUIDE.	Somehow yes.
ID.	I am thankful that you asked that question. I will go out and ask them actually.

I went out and found Visitor 3 and Visitor 4 by the exit stair of the Information Center, smoking.

ID.	May I ask what was so upsetting for you?
VISITOR 3.	I don't know how anyone can judge a whole generation. I spoke about it a lot with my relatives.
ID.	Let's forget 'generations.' How can *we* talk about it?
VISITOR 3.	No clue.
ID.	For us, for our 'generation' if you will.
VISITOR 4.	She does not know what it is like to sit with your grandmother and she cries and cries and tells things. One puts all the Germans in and I, as one person, am guilty. When I travel and people are speaking other languages, English, Spanish, I am guilty because I am German. This is sickening.
VISITOR 3.	I would like to be judged for what I do, not for what my father did. It is not about asking for forgiveness. Just that we all are judged. [...]

I told the couple that I have researched in the site for a few years and that most visitors, including Israelis like me, do not think of the people living in Germany today as perpetrators.

VISITOR 3.	You see, I have very short hair and people think that I am a right-radicalist. I am simply losing my hair and I find it nicer this way.
ID.	My brother also cuts his hair short for the same reason.
VISITOR 4.	It is hard.
ID.	I understand, thank you.

VISITOR 4.	It is hard when there is someone who sat with us who was affected.
VISITOR 3.	Sat among us. She has Jewish relatives.
ID.	The one who said that she has relatives who were victims? But she is on the other side.
VISITOR 4.	Yes. And then you listen to your grandmother and you don't know what you'd have done in such a situation. It was all so cold, there was nothing to eat and there was war. It is important to say. There is a Jewish memorial but there were also German victims [...].
VISITOR 3.	I collect documents from that time. It is hard. It is totally different when you have these documents from your family, not in an exhibition.
ID.	Thank you.
VISITORS 3 and 4.	Good luck with your research.

This example sought the connections between parts of the narrative on change and those on emotions and asked how they proceed and whether they coincide.

The argument about emotions that the guide made was based on the educational program of the Memorial Foundation which aims at creating an empathetic relationship between the German pupils and the Jewish victims. Instead, what created an emotionally charged discussion was not that of the victims, but that of the perpetrators. The visitors in this example see their culture as that of perpetrators' descendants who are being represented or reproached in the site (in ways that offend them and their families). The guide, as a representative of the institution, positions herself as coming from the same perpetrators side ('my mother,' 'my grandparents', but aimed at discussing: (1) victims (whose culture is only partially represented as sufferers of persecution and murder); (2) the acts of perpetrators; and (3) how to remember it, in a more detached fashion, by using the illocutionary concept of 'perpetrator generation.' She talks about 'getting emotional' when she deals with victims (and reproachfully when telling the group that they 'flipped out'). The visitors 'get emotional' when talking about their own families. With her every attempt to locate this concept of the perpetrators' generation as a framing device for distant time and distant actors, the visitors insisted that the perpetrators were actually victims. They thus used the reverse of that concept and framed it with the 'generation,' so that the perpetrators' generation was equaled to the victims' generation, which are one and the same.

What is the narrative structure of talking about emotions? Do the narrative structures of change and emotions coincide? What creates these events is reflection through metaphors, on the transformation of emotions in facing the memorial, not actions or clusters of actions. Specifically, and as we saw in earlier chapters of this book, Radstone (2005) reminds us that memory politics linked to narratives of victimhood, trauma and survival shifts the attention from collective forces, obligation and accountability toward narratives of individual suffering and individual blame. In this example, with no sequence of action which bears relations to another we will see sequences of feelings which bear relations and fortify each other, to create an emotions-laden zone in which actions are in the hands of perpetrators and the guide and communicated in the verbs 'kill,' 'cry,' 'shoot,' 'tell,' 'judge' and 'leave.' These invite further reflection – in the same perpetual manner. These verbs are connected to feelings expressed by the visitors, and those feeling always produce more feelings. In our example, once the discussion shifted to perpetrators as victims, the guide was detached and analytic while the visitors expressed how moved they were by announcing 'I am shaking,' 'I am leaving now,' and in the later conversation mentioned the crying grandmother, being affected and feeling sick.

We additionally saw which narrative elements are more vulnerable to shifts and become dead ends and that the sequence actually builds on its own breaks, or inner failures: whenever one person tries to talk about action, the other narrators, usually the guide, changes the subject or the point of view. Thus, in this narrative structure we see three unpredicted elements: (1) the drive to hold the narrative together as one whole sequence is actually the result of the breaks around the perlocutionary elements of statements such as 'perpetrators' generation,' which are inherent to the conversation. In our case, (2) when a unit does not support the overall narrative structure (Smith 2007) such as the concept the visitors offer of the victims' generation, it creates breaks which in turn are responsible for the narrative sequence proceeding by returning to the perpetrators. While (3) in other guided tours that discuss the emotional experience in the *Stelenfeld*, the narrative proceeds through abstractions (in our case 'someone persecuted'), which create metaphorical events happening to universal individuals if they are the victims. If they are visitors, then those metaphorical events of being moved or transformed frame a singular experience that cannot be repeated or fully explained.

What are the elements that all groups have in common? Talking about others' experience (either in the memorial or during the time of the Holocaust) in emotional terms and talking about victims. As we saw in earlier examples throughout the book, those elements are organized in different sequences and create different meaning in each group, but in each of them there is some mention of victims, and in each the site is seen as a site for learning and transformation. (In this unusual example, however, this was debated, as Visitor 3 claimed that the experience of collecting family documents is much stronger than that of seeing other documents from that time in a museum.) Lastly, the shifts between the speaking bodies of 'me,' 'I' and 'you' happened whenever the guide tried to make a personal statement about the visitors, which would then generalize the perspective or the protagonist to 'one' or 'people'.

In earlier chapters we saw how performing the right emotional memory work entails and facilitates belonging to the German people. Rothberg and Yildiz argue in regards to migrants living in Germany: 'Clearly, full citizenship requires more than legal structures: it requires, as Senocak and Tulay imply, both memory work and affective labor across society' (2011: 36). Here I will focus on the parts of the performance that hold it together. We will now look into the ways the Holocaust Memorial experience is mediated by media and technology, and ask whether the various media create new forms of engagement with the past. I show how, when looking at the ways memory of the Holocaust is presented in new archives, one can see the shift from the discourse on memory transmission to mediation of the experience of memory.

The unique self-understanding of the memorial, as both transcending space and time and being a non-immediate ('inauthentic') place of memory, is crystallized here. Here I am interested in the form of presentation and usage of interactive media in the Information Center, and focus on the work of new archives. The various strategies of presentation include the projection of text and photos using the last letters or notes of victims in the first room, the 'Room of Dimensions.' In the 'Room of Families,' documents, photos, short films and maps present the fates of 15 families. In the 'Room of Places,' short films, photos, text and audio stations present the 'places'of killing.

There are five archival presentations, which are new in the ways they utilize documents and photos that are presented elsewhere and newly researched for their presentation in the Information Center: (1) Yad Vashem's victims' names database; (2) the European Holocaust Memorials database; (3) a database to the specific Holocaust Memorial debate. The last two have been created by the Memorial Foundation. Finally, there is (4) a database of survivors' testimonies, which opened to the public on site in fall 2008, and (5) the memorial book of the Federal

Archive has been open to the public since 2008 and presents the fates of Jews in Germany between 1933 and 1945, with the name, date of birth, city of residence, date of deportation and death. All archives can be searched by interested individuals visiting the Information Center. In the case of Yad Vashem and the Fortunoff Archive of Holocaust testimonies, the Memorial Foundation added information to the archives that was already available in the memorial in the Room of Names or, as in the case of the Fortunoff Archive, 850 testimonies were adopted for presentation in the memorial, digitized, transliterated and codified, so that visitors can look up relevant information directly from the testimonies texts and fast-forward to those topics and events in which they are most interested.

The new archives are analyzed here as interactive media used in the memorial to create a certain kind of involvement in memory action that is inherently in flux and is directed toward discussion of the Holocaust and ways to deal with it. Information taken from other sites in the form of photos, texts, recorded testimonies and archival materials adheres to the wish of visitors to be alone and in a meditative mode. This happens in what Hall (2006) calls an 'experiential complex' of themed exhibitions that engage the senses and circle around the story memorial museums create in a manner that makes the authentic and the simulation meet. In the Information Center – with the effects of light and darkness, voice, texts located on the ground, up near the ceiling and in front of the visitors' eyes, as well as audiovisual engagement and the archives – information about the Holocaust works to raise both knowledge and emotions, other known images of the Holocaust and their meaning are alluded to in the context of the place and time of their display (Zelizer 1998), creating a precarious proximity to the time of the Holocaust, to victims and survivors, while keeping a distance from authentic places of memory precisely through new modes of presentation.

§2   From knowledge toward experience

Crane (2000) maintains that, like memories, museums exist on several levels: in the spaces of their building and spaces of exhibitions, shops and cafes, and in their portable versions – the catalogues – and we should add YouTube, Facebook and their own web-pages. In the Information Center, one can see that certain media are used to offer information and raise questions (such as about the relations between the numbers of Jews killed from each country available in the Room of Dimensions along with the last letters of victims displayed on the floor there), but avoids the so-called 'shocking' affects by offering a more soothing version of Holocaust representation in addition to a meditative mood inspired, for example, by the six large portraits of Jewish victims in the entrance and the Room of Names. What is of interest for us here is the reference to the possibility of being moved in the memorial, as a starting point of experience.

The Holocaust Memorial is not a museum. However, it corresponds with museum presentations as it presents documents taken from other archives and memorials. Some become 'memorial objects' (Lustiger-Thaler 2008) with the aura of an authentic museum exhibit. Such as the letters and notes written as a last testimony by Jews that are displayed in the Room of Dimensions; some are endowed with the aura of museum objects, although their presentation form in an installation or an archive that also exists elsewhere makes them 'once removed' from representing the experience of the Holocaust, while connecting the Holocaust Memorial to those archives and memorials and to their tasks.

The Holocaust Memorial separates the two main functions of the museum: collection and presentation (Williams 2008). The goal of the Information Center, as formed by guides and memorial foundation workers, is to clarify what the vast abstract site is all about: the Holocaust. The other goal is to move people to engage with the memory of the Holocaust either in the subversive form desired by Chancellor Schröder: 'as a place to which people will happily go' (Leggewie and Mayer 2005), or conversely, as a place by which they will be moved, altered and transformed. Both options help us shift the theoretical framework away from trauma theory, as they focus on a different experience that does not assume affective engagement as the means of transmission, but mediation, or a 'third party' that stands between the survivor-victim and the visitor: the archive.

Literature discussing the characteristics and limitations of representation of the Holocaust to generations who did not experience it often think of this task through the means and possibility of transmission (Hartman 2004; Hirsch and Kacandes 2004; Landsberg 1997). 'Post-memory' assumes this transmission between those who experienced the Holocaust to those who are related to them and, most importantly, to their stories (Hirsch 2008). In the post-memory age, video testimonies and archives can be catalysts for individualized, affective engagement with the Holocaust among generations to come (Heckner 2008).

In Chapter 1, I suggested that trauma theory is insufficient for the framework needed to probe the means of transmission, which is no longer between generations 'inheriting' the experience and affect of trauma, but among actors for whom we cannot readily assume knowledge or affect in relation to the Holocaust. As we saw in the most recent example above, the only possibility of emotional engagement other than through siding with the victims is claiming one's own status to be that of a victim. Visitors usually display a mix of perplexity and questions regarding the right way to deal with the Holocaust. For instance, after visiting the Information Center, many visitors admit to guides: 'I did not know that so many people were shot or that there were so few German Jews,' and in the same breath reflect on the ways visitors behave in the memorial above ground. The new archives in the memorial show how the 'medium,' is no longer pure transmission and affects the 'message' (here, knowledge and dealing with memory of the Holocaust) and vice versa. As in 'authentic' memorials, this one mediates, above all, absence (Lustiger-Thaler 2008). Unlike memorials where atrocities took place, though, the reflection of absence of people, evidence and means to fathom and represent what had taken place on their ground, the Holocaust Memorial adds to the

Figure 4.1   Holocaust Memorial 2006, view from the entrance to the Information Center toward the line of visitors waiting to enter the site
Photo: Irit Dekel.

referential absence of those sites from the point of the presence of visitors in a new site. Those 'present' visitors above ground then go underground to the Information Center to supplement experience with knowledge.

2.1 The work of archives in the Information Center

I use an extended meaning of the term 'archive,' which describes not only institutional collections of records, but libraries, museums, internet sites such as You-Tube and semi-, sub- or counter-institutional stores of knowledge. The archives in the memorial present information on individuals in a way that grants both presenters and visitors' authority and legitimacy by the very act of research, compilation, presentation and again, search, of personal information. The media of archivization and its forms, together with what is being archived and how it is presented, produce knowledge rather than merely storing it, while also creating new forms of engagement. The memorial develops a technique of supplementing and connecting with knowledge at any point of the visitors' interest and at any stage of their willingness to engage with such information. This a technique and not a strategy, not merely because the mediated form of representation in the Information Center deploys technology, but because this deployment provides a mediating tool for engagement, and because using this technology in this manner creates the possibility of mediation through research.

Memorial Foundation workers told me that visitors enter the Information Center and come out different both in regard to knowledge about the Holocaust and in regard to justifying the building of the memorial. According to Uhl (2008), the Information Center offers a synthesis of making the visitor emotionally overwhelmed, contemplative and empathetic. This is not the most expected mix of categories to describe the work of a memorial experience, and Uhl clarifies that it is precisely these content and spatial limitations of the Information Center that have originated a new type of institution, which amalgamates the reception of 'historical information' with 'emotional remembrance.'

Landsberg (1997) discusses the politics of empathy as a mode of transmitting memory after the survivors, or the 'living memory' passes away; one manifestation of this phenomenon in the attempt to extend the life span of living memory is the assembly of video archives of survivor testimonies. The Fortunoff Archive, which is used in the Information Center, is the largest. Landsberg argues that 'Mass cultural technologies […] are making available […] strategies and arenas within which an alternative living memory gets produced in those who did not live through the event' (1997, 66). In order to produce living memories in those who did not experience events, one has to assume some kind of physical and emotional proximity to the act and will of remembering. I suggest that the Holocaust Memorial relies instead on accidental engagement with memory through curiosity about the Field of Stelae, its history and experience. As much as it was conveyed to me in conversations about the site and in the press discussing it that it 'works' best when people visit with some background knowledge about the Holocaust and of the memorial itself, they do not take for granted that visitors know about the Holocaust or are willing to engage with its memory.

In the same vein, Landsberg suggests: 'It might be the case that contemporary mass-cultural forms enable a version of experience, which relies less on categories like the real, the authentic, and sympathy, than on categories like knowledge, responsibility, and empathy' (1997, 75). We can look into this claim through examination of the modes of knowledge production used in the memorial's archives and the distance between the mediated knowledge on offer and its experience not in terms of intensity, but as a mode of political engagement. When the visitors either refuse emotional engagement or are emotionally engaged with the wrong group (namely the perpetrators as victims), this engagement is assumed to be wrong and is not welcomed. In an interview in May 2011 with Dr Daniel Baranowski, who is in charge of research and the operation of the testimonies' archive at the Information Center, he said that he and the Foundation see two goals in the visit to the archive: the first is that the visitors understand the reasons for giving a testimony as a personal, present-related task of the survivor and that they will potentially revisit the memorial. The second goal is tied to a form of cultural tourism that will afford the visitor the experience of research and of piety, and of its regularity in the performance of both. Baranowski spoke of the importance of not cutting and editing the interviews, which gives the visitors a chance to also think about the advantages and disadvantages of such a medium in telling one's life story. It is also clearly related to the attempt to keep the original and authentic in its own form, although the codification of text makes it possible to go back and forth and self-edit the interviews.

The Europeanization and personalization dimension of the exhibitions materialize here in a number of ways: 70 percent of the visitors who use the computerized video archive use it in English, and then they usually find a testimony in their own language, or from their own country, to listen to. The chosen testimonies are of survivors from all over Europe, so that even a quick look at the archive options reveals an all-European telling of history, connected to present-day Europe both in the background of the survivors during the war and during the interview, and her or his references to current political events at the time of the interview. The information added to the interviews by the Foundation makes the historical background to the testimonies clear. Just as with Yad Vashem's victims' names database, the Foundation reworked the testimonies, added information on them, and is conducting new interviews on the memorial's premises, in the archives' room. This decision has to do with the limited rights given to it by the Yale Fortunoff Archive, but also with the attempt to contribute to post-war endeavors to tell the stories of the victims and survivors. The Foundation Memorial also contributed to an exhibition focusing on the Eichmann trial from the dimension of the survivors with the Foundation 'Topography of Terror.' Here we can see how the perpetrators' perspective meets the victims'. However, it is important to remember the fine balance that the Foundation is trying to strike, a balance between the need to represent all victims' groups and actually standing for the Jews. For instance, Baranowski told me that visitors call the hotline and ask about testimonies by Homosexuals, Sinti and Roma, and other minority groups. Sinti and Roma are well represented in the video archive, but other groups are less represented, and Baranowski attested that he found himself telling visitors: 'Essentially, we are here to commemorate the Jews.'

To consider the relations between sources, people and stories in the archives, one has to recognize that the first two of these (different sources, Jews and other groups of Holocaust Victims) are sometimes unknown to many visitors. According to Baranowski, many visitors are therefore cautious and hesitate before they even enter the room. Here we can see how, in the archive, the memorial experience is metaphorically extended to seeing survivors and hearing their voices, with the added intensity of watching victims and survivors in films made between the 1970s and the 1990s. It thus comes as no surprise that visitors ask whether there are also interviews form the Spielberg Archive (Shoah Foundation), and that they reflect on *Schindler's List* and other films in their assessment of the memorial experience.

The interpretative framework developed in the memorial draws a parallel between the originality of the memorial's structure, in its 'inauthentic' place, and the inauthentic qualities of the materials presented in its archives. It allows for an encounter that in itself is supposed to afford the visitor an authentic experience (Wang 1999) of memory work, disconnected and reconnected to the work of memory done in authentic sites, but at the same time, by mediating, indexing and choosing certain materials from the archive, now liberated from the political engagement with history they entail. In a workshop presenting the Fortunoff Archive to memorial guides in February 2010, one guide reflected on the search tools of the testimonies: 'The narration and indexing is great. I looked at the testimony of Mr [...] and was wondering when he was going to talk about the Displaced Persons Camps already there. Then I could go to that part of the testimony.' As an expert, the guide thought of the technical tool as helping in research, but this technical ability also enabled her to 'skip' parts of the survivor's history in which she was less interested or knows a lot about. This technical ability can reflect a different 'will to memory' (Eyal 2004) that is based on the practice of distancing oneself through exploration, which can be based on acquiring knowledge, as in the case of the guide skipping to the Displaced Persons Camps part of the story, or the visitor wondering about information they were not aware of in the 'story' of the Holocaust.

As we have seen, archival knowledge in the memorial is used more for pedagogical purposes than as proof against deniers. The tension between the real and the unbelievable, the authentic and the reworked adds a new form of authority to the Memorial Foundation: not to carry authentic materials and knowledge, but rather to store and make available and accessible, well-esteemed, and already exposed and presented artifacts. Here again, we can see the movement from reflection on what is available and what is unattainable, the small space of the Information Center and what can be presented and made moving differently from other sites, and its re-presentation in the Information Center.

This new experience of memory not in a place of atrocities, through newly researched and coded materials that are presented in the original in other places of memory, enable new forms of authority in relation to the past, which do not rely on the singularity of the artifacts but rather on the order and form of their display and the unique experience they afford the visitors. It is a second-order presentation that restudies the factuality of the artifacts and exists simultaneously in several places, including online, as in the case of Yad Vashem's names database and the memorial book for German Jews held in the Federal Archives. The memorial thus brings together visitors who would not otherwise visit places of atrocity, but encounter their second- and third-order representations, on site and in browsing the archives, that are themselves fluid and selective, alluding to the old, fixed archives. The Memorial Foundation becomes a mediator between the first presentation in place and time of the information that its archives present, and short-term research during the period of the visit.

2.2   From documentation to transformation to mediation

The visitor becomes engaged in investigating the archives for information, while this self-search happens in a setting that raises one's apprehensions, alluding to the feeling and experience in authentic memorials: the rooms are dark and there is very little noise except for the reading of names in the Room of Names. Stoler (2002) directs our attention to the archive as a site of knowledge production, and not merely of its storage and retrieval. The five archives in the memorial reproduce knowledge in its re-presentation on site in reference to its original sites of preservation and presentation.

According to Derrida, 'the archive takes place at the place of originary and structural breakdown of the said memory. There is no archive without a place of consignation, without a technique of repetition, and without a certain exteriority' (1996: 11). At first glance, the multiplication of consignation places strengthens archival authority. But we should ask whether the fragmented archive that is presented in two, three or more locations is still an archive, since it is brought back to the realm of memory through the mimetic. According to Derrida, 'the archivization produces as much as it records the events' (1996: 17), as 'the archival technology [...] no longer determines [...] merely the moment of the conservational recording, but rather the very institution of the archivable event' (1996: 18).

The medium of archivization and its form, together with the actual content that is being archived and its manner of presentation, produces and transmits certain knowledge, ways of reaching it, and the institutional storing of it and making it accessible to the public. The two archives that are of interest here, the Yad Vashem names database and the Fortunoff Archive, address other archives as well as the visitors. Voices of survivors tell their stories, leaving the interviewer anonymous in the Fortunoff Archive and speaking either from a computer stand that mimics both the ones in Yad Vashem and at home, or from the wall, by a voice reading a name and a short biography. In the seminar room where the Fortunoff Archive's computers are located, parts of testimonies in a variety of European languages, and German and English translations are written on the surrounding walls, together with a photo of the survivor from the testimony. The dead are brought back to life for a glimpse, in their relocation in time and the space in the memorial and the archive. The Fortunoff's archive project at the memorial is called 'living with memory': one is made aware of the fact that the survivors and those who heard them had to live with memory and so do the visitors hearing them today.

Moreover, in 'returning the archives to the visitors' in the format of the museum database, they also change the form of their possible researches and produce them as museum objects in relation to other objects in the Information Center and in other museums. For example, a host told me that a young Israeli visitor once took a picture of the Yad Vashem database computer, with the screen showing his grandfather's handwritten page of testimony. When the host approached him and offered a print out of the page, the visitor said that he entered this page many times, and could do it at home too, but the very fact that it is in the memorial is important and moving. I heard this same story from other hosts and Foundation workers, who related to the significance of the very existence of the Yad Vashem database in Berlin. The materiality of the computer inside the memorial thus blends with the performance of searching and finding something, in this way connecting to an 'authentic' experience of revelation.

Stoler and Strassler (2000) separate colonial archival production from the politics of its consumption. The initial storage of this information and its openness to research in original archives such as Yad Vashem is separated from the display of this information in other places such as the Holocaust Memorial in Berlin, and not just because the location produces a different experience of the archive, and a different context to browsing it. One can browse it from any computer connected to the internet. It is – and the other three archives at the Berlin memorial help us see this clearly – an act of saving from oblivion in a new site, achieved through the multiplication of archives or their fragments that (a) speak to the visitor, and (b) produce a database. The memorial's database and the Memorial Debate archive exist only in the Berlin Memorial and act as original archives with the innovation of their virtual materiality: they dwell only in the Information Center, only in a computer.

2.3   Types of representation and the creation of others

According to Alexander, Otto Frank, Anne Frank's father who published her diary, was well aware of the fact that his daughter's personal focus in describing her own world in hiding was part of the diary's potential universalizing appeal (Alexander et al. 2004: 232). Many visitors to the Berlin memorial look for Anne Frank in Yad Vashem's names database. If they do not do an advanced search they do not find her; her father's wife filled a page of testimony for her in 1988. The interesting point for us is the actual search for Anne Frank. I heard German pupils who were deeply disappointed when they did not find her and so were their guides who feared that this would serve them in potential Holocaust denial. We can see Frank as a universal victim (being a child, Western and a good writer helps of course). But we can also see the tension between the Berlin/German presentation of 'universal individuals' and Yad Vashem's insistence that the database is a Jewish project presented in Germany and potentially in other memorials in Europe, thus creating 'particular individuals' in their attempt to reconstruct personal history from oblivion.

The 'particular individuals' in Yad Vashem's project turn into universal ones in other venues where they are presented and re-searched. The 'Room of Names project' to raise donations for the research and display of more names is an attempt, according to Lea Rosh and the board of trustees, to 'give victims back their identities in the Berlin Holocaust Memorial Room of Names,'[1] as a substitution for graves. This is a reverberation of Yad Vashem's 'pages of testimony' project that mixes research, presentation and 'relocation' attributes together with the traditional legacies of perpetrators and victims in a way that sounds pompous at best. This movement from particular individual subjects of memory (these individual victims whose names are to be researched and displayed) to universal ones occurs through their presentation and research in memorial archives. These archives are used to commemorate and demonstrate historical factuality, and they deploy the media of oral history as the tool for transmitting knowledge and emotions. This is achieved through the reading of names and personal information or testimonies of selected individuals whose stories will be retold in the archives long after they are gone.

The Information Center does not offer a biographical exhibition, instead displaying fragments of biographical stories, much like in other museums, in order to make identification, sympathy and understanding of a historical era easier, while keeping the stories broad enough to contain other unknown lost lives. We see this phenomenon best through the six portraits in the entrance foyer of the Information Center, which are reproduced as posters, postcards and are central to workshops held in the site. The exhibition, however, tries to create a biographical narrative that uses fragmented personal stories of both the people exhibited and the visitors. They do so in workshops offered by Memorial Foundation guides, trying to bridge the gap between the dead Jews and the living visitors, then and now. But they add a layer of engagement with the biographical objects on display. They tell visitors that these objects (like the notes before death, or photos of individuals) have not been recognized in the past for various reasons, most of them having to do with the sheer magnitude of annihilation. They were forgotten, and the memorial, alongside other institutes, saved them from oblivion.

This enlarges the evocative power of these objects, since they are not 'authentic' and stand for the 'saving power' of other potential stories and individuals. These objects could exist simultaneously in the past and in the present (Albano 2007: 18), but we are told that in the past they did not exist, but long awaited discovery, and could have remained unknown but for the fact that they were researched and are displayed here, open for personal research, forming a stronger relationship with the absent subject that is created and documented in them. They thus connect the new experience of the archive with the new burden to research, and know documents and traces, that in their second- and third-order representations reconnect visitors, guides, scholars and other memory activists to a new experience of memory that is always already located in the present, and always potentially changing in a way that does not only diversify the people who come across this knowledge but also the form and time of their pursuit.

Conclusion

During the World Cup games there were very peculiar
questions from visitors. An old German man asked me:
'How do I get to Auschwitz today?' It was late morning
and I told him he might have to wait for tomorrow,
since it is close to Krakow, in Poland. But he was
determined to make it that day. So I told him he could
take a train to Krakow then a bus to the camp, but
then I thought: 'Hey, Easyjet also goes to Auschwitz.'
So I told him he can take a flight to Krakow and even
be there tonight.

(taken from a personal interview with a host
in the memorial in summer 2006)

The excitement and immediacy in and around the new Berlin memorial, connecting it to the mythical site of Holocaust memory, was very
much part of the urgency of experience, motion and transformation
that the memorial's opening created. By 2010, I no longer encountered
such intensity. Instead, the mix of metaphors pertaining to feelings and
reflection on the memorial's aesthetics were common in guided tours
and in interviews with visitors and guides. One could in good faith say
that I, myself a medium for the transmission of this site to you the reader,
did not look for this, or that the site found new ways to communicate
about the past which I did not recognize. Closing this ethnography as
a sociological study of a social institution and its visitors, one can also
say that this is simply due to processes of institutionalization and the
inevitable rigidity instilled in the self-understanding of both the site
and its visitors that accompanies this process.

Both assumptions are valid. However, I suggest that it would be more interesting to think about the relations in the discourse surrounding Holocaust memory in Germany as a means to affirm different positions about the past that make the discussion of the past and sites of atrocity redundant. We have to recognize, however, that this happens at a time of the unprecedented popularity of memorial institutions, such as the newly built Topography of Terror, which, together with the Brandenburg Gate, the Holocaust Memorial and the Jewish Museum are among the most popular tourist attractions in Berlin. One has to accept the fact that such popularity is connected to an interest in learning about the past as much as it is tied to the attractiveness of the signature architecture in which they are hosted, and how conveniently packed they are together in this new topography of memory (Blumer 2011).

In concluding this book I wish to argue that the energy originally generated by and in this new site of memory has been transformed into a cultural inventory of metaphorical communication though which discussions of topics other than the Holocaust or the role of Holocaust memory in Germany are aired, alongside often emotional, and often family-centered comments and revelations about visitor's own relationship to the past.

This was demonstrated in the first chapter through the introduction of the 'rule of experience' and the ways it is performed in reflection on the tension between abstract and concrete in the memorial aesthetic, alluding to visitors' comprehension of the inability to represent and comprehend the Holocaust. In the invented, emptied and accidental space of this new memorial, we analyzed the movement from abundance of meaning to absence of meaning in relation to Holocaust memory. The first chapter closed with the suggestion that the analysis of action in the site should focus on the architecture of feeling and reactions to it.

The second chapter introduced the concept of speakability. It is the condition and outcome of interaction in the site and the mirror through which I proposed that we view the framework of relations to the past as a container for the history of former relations, prolonging them through this self-conscious reference to history. In this sense, the record of this memorial experience, as much as it is easily transferrable, and arguably transformative, is bound to its own place and time. In an earlier article (Dekel 2009a), I argued that the memorial commemorates its own rememberers, an analysis discussed by Crownshaw (2010) as an unintended truth stemming from my idealizing view of action in the site. To be sure, I saw the new forms of engagement with memory in

2005–6 in their potentiality, but argued then, as I do now, that without alliance with memory of one's relations to learning about specific events, this memorial is directed at self-proclamation.

Moral career and self-transformation were analyzed in the third chapter through therapeutic self-help discourse (Illouz 2007a,b) and the three phases of the memorial visit: 'getting in,' 'getting lost' and 'getting it.' I suggested that through the motion between those phases 'memory in action' occurs. Without evaluating its achievements, I suggested that the phases ultimately culminate in the realization of a certain public that sees itself as Germans engaging in memory work, facing inevitable difficulties to comprehend what exactly such work can mean in relation to the specific past of the Holocaust, but maintaining that it is necessary both for the realization of a certain civic sphere which is more cosmopolitan and open to others, and that what holds it together in this specific act is the memory of the Jews. Jews were thus understood as a category of memory since they were persecuted, and referring to their persecution can be used as a warning against racism in Germany today. Mostly, though, we saw that it is used to facilitate public acts of performed sorrow.

Analyzing action in the memorial availed me a fascinating case of memory work which utilized all the anchors of the work of memory that Assmann (2010) lists: affect, symbol and trauma, with the last one serving as a liberating mechanism in its absence both in reference to actual experience and in its coding of the inability to narrate. Assmann argues that the three can be 'triangularly arranged from a pathological external orientation to free self-determination' (2010: 30). The affect does magnify fragments of the micro-narrative within memory, always in relation to the site: feeling lost, being powerless, and grief. The symbolic codification according to what I termed in the book the 'symbolic index' ties the embodied experience of the site, other Holocaust memorial sites and other experiences one has had with Holocaust memory in school, in watching films and among one's own family.

Assmann reminds us that these symbols are tied with strong affect and get 'integrated into a meaningful narrative structure. When the affect exceeds a certain affective limit, it loses the power to anchor memories, shattering them instead' (2010, ibid.). This, Assmann argues, happens in trauma. I would suggest, it also happens if an affect cannot be any more tied to a certain meaningful narrative structure in its non-relations to the past and in its reliance on sporadic references to its representations.

In the fourth chapter, I focused on narrative of emotion and change, and looked at the ways the Holocaust Memorial experience is mediated by media and technology. I asked whether the various media create new forms of engagement with the past. It was then argued that the new archives in the memorial afford a form of memory action that is inherently in flux and is directed toward perpetual discussion of the Holocaust and the ways of dealing with it, while also redirecting affect and knowledge in ways that do not get discussed because they stay on the individual level, are very short term and spoken about by visitors only when asked specifically. Through observation of the work and experience of the new archives in the memorial we learned that the 'medium,' which is no longer pure transmission, affects the 'message' (here, knowledge and dealing with the memory of the Holocaust) and vice versa. The outcome of mediation in the memorial is absence, and it adds to the referential absence of victims and authentic sites, pointing to the presence of visitors in a new site. The fourth chapter ended with a discussion of the institutional need of the Memorial Foundation to stand for the memory of the Jews alongside other victim groups, closing with a discussion of the effects of 'the European dimension' of remembrance in the Information Center and whether it alludes to a European, more cosmopolitan memory.

Notes

Introduction

1. As I was told in interviews with various Memorial Foundation workers and as stated in workshops and educational materials developed in and used at the memorial.
2. The brochure is in 14 languages including Arabic and Turkish, alongside European languages, Hebrew and Chinese.
3. Within the first five years of its opening, a sign was positioned by the entrance to the Information Center, in which the Foundation's address and the memorial's name are written.

1 Navigating Experience

1. The term *wiedergutmachung* was coined in the immediate post-war years to describe the reparations paid to victims of the National Socialist occupation. It literally means 'making things right again' and marked post-war German identity discussions.
2. Lothar Heinke, 'Das Jahr der Steine' [The Year of Stones] 7.5.2006, http://www.tagesspiegel.de/berlin/das-jahr-der-steine/708694.html (accessed 25 February 2011).
3. The standardized survey was designed and delivered by Skopus.de (an institute for market and communication research).
4. See source in German at http://www.stiftung-denkmal.de/var/files/pdf-dateien/pressefactsheet_de.pdf (accessed 3 June 2011).
5. See photos and more information about the site at http://www.holocaust-mahnmal.de/var/files/pdf-dateien/pressemappe_2009_en_web.pdf (accessed 23 July 2009).
6. With the exception of Israeli tour groups and politicians, who sometimes lay wreaths of flowers at the site.
7. As seen in the 2009 visitors' survey in the Information Center.
8. Translations from German are mine, unless otherwise stated.
9. Levy and Sznaider's (2002) concept of cosmopolitan memory captures the ways in which the Holocaust becomes a reference point to present discussions of individual and public dealing with the past in local, national and cosmopolitan frameworks, and that the latter shapes the ways the past is remembered and acted upon, striking comparisons between the Holocaust and other genocides. I think that Germany, like Israel, still very much has a national narrative of the ways to relate to the Holocaust, and that those national specificities are indicative of complex relations between the effects of transnational trends and local discourses.
10. I thank Tamar Katriel for illuminating this.
11. Jackie Feldman and Anja Peleikis's study of the Jewish Museum in Berlin in comparison with Yad Vashem analyzes this.

12. Claudia Keller, *der Tagesspiegel*, 9.5.2006: 'das Denkmal ist Ernst und macht trotzdem spass' (although the memorial is serious, it is also fun), an interview with Eisenman on the occasion marking a year from the opening of the memorial.
13. Parts of this section were published in Dekel 2009. 'Pan-topia: Exposing the Palimpsest of Meanings at the Holocaust Memorial, Berlin,' *History and Theory: The Protocols Bezalel Academy of Design* 14.
14. Hanno Rauterberg, 'Building Site of Remembrance,' in Lars Müller, *Holocaust Memorial Berlin*. Lars Müller Publishers, 2005.
15. After the opening of the memorial the Foundation insisted that it is a 'Denkmal.' Nevertheless, many still call it 'Mahnmal.' The foundation's website can be reached from www.holocaust-mahnmal.de or www.holocaust-denkmal.de (accessed 6 March 2008).
16. Architect Peter Eisenman, in *Zeit* interview, 'über jüdische Identität und Demonstrationsfreiheit für Neonazis am Holocaust Mahnmal,' 25.01.01 (a conversation with Thomas Assheür, Hanno Rauterberg and Ulrich Schwatz).
17. Ibid.
18. Claudia Keller, 'Eisenman ist ein Genie' (Eisenman is a Genious), *Der Taggespiegel*, 10.05.06, p. 10, http://archiv.tagesspiegel.de/archiv/10.05.2006/2520751.asp.
19. Jan Feddersen, *Die Erinnerungslücken bleiben* (The Memory Gaps Stay), 10.5.2006, p. 6, http://www.taz.de/pt/2006/05/10/a0136.1/text.
20. Erik Meyer, political scientist and a co-author (with Claus Leggewie, 2005) of a book about the memorial, in an interview on 05.08.05, 'Kein steinerner Schlussstrich' (No Closing line), on ZDF national TV; my translation.
21. I look at the trauma discourse in explaining relations to social memory as a phenomenon, thus suspending questions regarding its metaphorical deployment and truth claims (Kansteiner and Wilnböck 2010).
22. Eisenman is not alone in building memorials that offer a visceral transformation. Libeskind's Jewish Museum in Berlin affords a visceral experience through voids and the 'lightning' structure of the museum (see Young 2000).
23. I would argue that neither present events from a perpetrator's perspective, since, although documents and photos produced by them are presented and discussed, there is no attempt to understand their views, thoughts and motives.
24. Norbert Frei, 'Gefühlte Opfer,' *Zeit* (21.10.2004), http://pdf.zeit.de/2004/44/kriegsende.pdf (acessed 9 September 2011).
25. http://www.youtube.com/watch?v=Qm80Xc4Mouk&feature=fvsr (accessed 25 February 2011).
26. The same term is used to describe feelings of being moved and sad by visitors to the site.
27. http://www.berliner-woche.de/Erinnern-als-Erfolgsgeschichte.433.0.html (accessed 30 July 2012).
28. http://www.bild.de/regional/berlin/holocaust/ist-gedenkstaette-holocaust-mahnmal-nicht-mehr-zu-retten-11679260.bild.html (accessed 30 July 2012).
29. http://www.sueddeutsche.de/panorama/holocaust-mahnmal-muss-saniert-werden-denkmal-mit-rissen-1.662554 (accessed 31 July 2012).

2 Spheres of Speakability: Old and New Discursive Modes

1. The term *stelae*, which describes the stones in the memorial, is taken from Greek. However, it resonates with the German verb *stellen*, which means to place, to put.
2. Historians working for the Memorial Foundation told me that they re-check the accuracy of records given to them by other memorial museums and that they found inaccuracies or missing information about individuals and events in them.
3. According to Iser (1974), the *implied reader* is a model that enables describing the effects of a literary text without assuming a particular reader or reality, but instead considering the aesthetic response generated within the space between the reader and the text. Iser regards the reader as an active agent in the construction and synthesis of the text's meaning. However, whereas literature can take the reader's imagination beyond the constraints of experience, the text discussed here, namely the memorial, focuses on experience that is bound to place and is likely to linger over time, ever returning to the praxis of the visit and other visits to other places of memory.
4. The discussion around Günter Grass's poem 'What Must be Said', published in April 2012, is a good example of such media-driven controversies, which allude to the rules of how Germans are to remember the Holocaust and hence to relate to Israel and the Jews, bounded to convention. Grass laments that a German should not criticize Israel ('what cannot be said'). This allusion to what cannot be spoken reverberates typical age-old claims in the GDR about the imposed silencing of certain topics, thus tying together the memory of the 'two dictatorships' and how it affects society and politics today.
5. Emphasis in the original.
6. The information available is: place of birth, age, place and date of death, if known.
7. On personal passports in the US Holocaust Memorial Museum, see Weissberg (1999).
8. Taken from a conversation with a German-Jewish host, about his work at the memorial.
9. *Auseinandersetzung* means dealing, engagement, discussing, arguing and contesting, and is used to convey present German engagement with the past which is inexhaustible and endless. It is a legal term that conveys dispute and conflict and can describe collective as well as personal acts.
10. Sometimes it is in the writer's handwriting and sometimes in a typed manuscript of those who found, archived, and translated it to their local language. The items are thus shown in the authentic-like form of an old-looking photo of the most original item (in Yiddish, Russian, Hebrew, Polish, or German, among other languages), and in translation to German and English.
11. Note that he mixes mountains of bodies with graves, perhaps alluding to the *Stelenfeld*'s most conspicuous metaphor of gravestones.
12. On framing experience in memory through the experience of place, see Bajc (2006); Casey (1987).
13. For more on references to other places of atrocity in guided tours, see Dekel (2008), 100–56.

14. The Room of Places shows terrible scenes before, during and after mass shootings, alongside drawings and photos of concentration and death camps around Europe. It is thus interesting to note that the visitors probably point not to a question of scale, but to types of photos depicting bodies, nudity and physical humiliation which are displayed in the Room of Places, but among other, softer, photos showing 'just' devastated families and individuals awaiting their death.

15. The Memorial Foundation visitors' service asks teachers, when booking a tour, about the former knowledge and level of preparation with which the pupils are coming to the memorial. This information often appears in the guides' schedules.

16. See more on museum's contemporary politics, visitors reactions, mass entertainment and education in Hooper-Greenhill 2007; Kirshenblatt-Gimblett 2006; Kratz and Karp 2006; Macdonald and Fyfe 1996.

17. 'It happened, and therefore it can happen again. This is the core of what we have to say.'

18. This is the most popular song played on Holocaust Memorial Day on Israeli radio, recited in memorial ceremonies and cited very often in this context. See Neiger et. al. 2011.

19. Peter von Becker, 'Das neue deutsche Einheits-Mal Schale ohne Kern' (The new German Unification Memorial: Shell without a core,' *Tagesspiegel*, 14.4.2011 (accessed 15 May 2011).

20. Blumer 2011.

3 Memory in Action: New Ethics of Engagement with Holocaust Memory

1. The excerpt is taken from a worksheet given to high school groups visiting the memorial. The worksheet contains instructions and questions about every room in the Information Center. Workshops supported the worksheets and made them focus more on the history presented in the Information Center since 2009.

2. On the topic of images of the past that East and West Germany shared, see Robert G. Möller (2006).

3. In a Frontline documentary called 'A Jew Among the Germans': http://www.pbs.org/wgbh/pages/frontline/shows/germans/memorial/ (accessed on 10 March 2008).

4. Visits of officials: politicians; celebrities; cultural figures and diplomats have been documented in the memorial's website: http://www.stiftung-denkmal.de/en/press/press-releases.html (accessed 31 August 2012).

5. See a list of connected memorials, partners, traveling exhibitions and events at: http://www.stiftung-denkmal.de/en/exhibitions.html (accessed on 31August 2012).

6. Remembering Jewish persecution and annihilation in the Holocaust had been linked to moral standing in Germany before the memorial initiative (see, for instance, Mitscherlich and Mitscherlich 1967), and thus the memorial's link to public moral standing is an enactment of this question, linked to questions of victimhood (Olick 2006), responsibility and atonement.

7. See also reflections on the historians' debate in Alexander (2004: 244).
8. The quote from the worksheet related to these 10 minutes.
9. See more about the debate over the Jakob Marks design in Cullen (1999: 13–19). Newspaper articles reflecting the debate are compiled in Heimrod, Schlusche and Seferens (1999).
10. The focus on individual stories, remembering them (the individuals and through them the stories) as individuals, is a phenomenon that one can see in other memorials and memorial museums (see Dekel 2008: 143–4).
11. See Uhl 2008.
12. See on the centrality of victimhood and victims in German memory politics reflected in novels, movies, memorials and museums since the German reunification and the blurring of boundaries between perpetrators and victims (Niven 2006; Olick 1998, 2006; Schmitz 2007).
13. We have to recognize that both sides were also somewhat joking, or at least relaxed enough as to not create a security-personnel involved event of this incident. The minor role of such an interaction, its joking manner both on the ground and as a story, and the fact that it was nevertheless remembered, make it all the more relevant for our discussion.

4   Mediation at the Holocaust Memorial

1. https://www.holocaust-denkmal-berlin.de/ (accessed 1 January 2013).

References

Adorno, T. W. (1995 [1951]) 'Kulturkritik und Gesellschaft', in *Lyrik nach Auschwitz? Adorno und die Dichter*, ed. P. Kiedaisch. Stuttgart: Reclam, pp. 27–49.

Albano, C. (2007) 'Displaying lives: The narrative of objects in biographical exhibitions,' *Museum and Society* 5(1): 15–28.

Alexander, J. (2006) 'Real Civil Societies: Dilemmas of Institutionalization,' in *The Civil Sphere*. Oxford: Oxford University Press, pp. 23–36.

Alexander, J. (2011) 'Iconic power and performativity: The role of the critic,' in *Performance and Power*. Cambridge: Polity, pp. 204–16.

Alexander, J. C., Eyerman, R., Giesen, B., Smelser, N. J. and Sztompka, P., eds (2004) *Cultural Trauma and Collective Identity*. Berkeley, CA: University of California Press.

Assmann, A. (2006) *Der Lange Schatten der Vergangenheit: Erinnerungskultur und Geschichtspolitik*. München: C. H. Beck.

Assmann, A. (2007) *Geschichte im Gedächtnis. Von der individuellen Erfahrung zur öffentlichen Inszenierung*. München: C. H. Beck.

Assmann, A. (2010) 'Three Memory Anchors: Affect, Symbol, Trauma,' in J. Straub and J. Rüsen, eds, *Dark Traces of the Past: Psychoanalysis and Historical Thinking*. New York and Oxford: Berghahn Books, pp. 19–32.

Assmann, J. (1995) 'Collective Memory and Cultural Identity,' *New German Critique* 65: 125–33.

Bajc, V. (2006) 'Introduction to Collective Memory and Tourism: Globalizing Transmission Through Localized Experience,' *Journeys* 7(2): 1–14.

Ball, K. (2008) *Disciplining the Holocaust*. New York: SUNY Press.

Bartov, O. (2003) *Germany's War and the Holocaust: Disputed Histories*. Ithaca, NY: Cornell University Press.

Bateson, G. (1955) 'A Theory of Play and Fantasy,' *AP: Psychiatric Research Reports* 2: 39–51.

Bauman, Z. (1996) 'From Pilgrim to Tourist – or a Short History of Identity,' in S. Hall and P. du Gay, eds, *Questions of Cultural Identity*. London: Sage, pp. 18–36.

Bearman, P. and Stovel, K. (2000) 'Becoming a Nazi: A model for narrative networks,' *Poetics* 27: 69–90.

Benjamin, W. (1968) 'The Work of Art in the Age of Mechanical Reproduction,' in *Illuminations*, ed. H. Arendt. New York: Schocken, pp. 217–52.

Bennett, T. (1995) *The Birth of the Museum*. London: Routledge.

Bennett, T. (2006) 'Exhibition, Difference and the Logic of Culture,' in I. Karp et al., eds, *Museum Frictions*. Durham, NC, and London: Duke University Press, pp. 45–69.

Bishop-Kendzia, V. (2013) *The Jewish Museum Berlin: Visitor Experience in the Context of Political Education*. Forthcoming PhD Dissertation, Humboldt University, Berlin.

Blumer, N. (2011) *From Victim Hierarchies to Memorial Networks: Berlin's Memorial to the Sinti and Roma Persecuted under the National Socialist Regime*. PhD Dissertation. University of Toronto.

Bodemann, Y. M. (1996) 'Reconstructions of history: From Jewish memory to nationalized commemoration of Kristallnacht in Germany,' in Y. M. Bodemann, ed., *Jews, Germans, Memory: Reconstruction of Jewish life in Germany*. Ann Arbor, MI: University Press of Michigan, pp. 179–226.

Bodemann, Y. M. (2002) *In den Wogen der Erinnerung. Jüdisches Leben in Deutschland*. München, DTV.

Boltanski, L. (1999) *Distant Suffering: Morality, Media and Politics*. Cambridge: Cambridge University Press.

Boltanski, L. and L. Thévenot (1999) 'The Sociology of Critical Capacity,' *European Journal of Social Theory* 2(3), August: 359–78.

Borneman J. (1992) 'State, Territory, and Identity Formation in the Postwar Berlins, 1945–1989,' *Cultural Anthropology* 7(1): 45–62.

Boym, S. (2001). *The Future of Nostalgia*. New York: Basic Books.

Brumlik, M. (1997) 'Generationen und Geschichtsvermittlung der NS-Erfahrung: Einleitende Überlegungen zu einer künftigen Didaktik der Menschenrechte am Beispiel ihrer Verletzung,' in D. Kiesel, G. Kößler, W. Nickolai and M. Wittmeier, eds, *Pädagogik der Erinnerung: Didaktische Aspekte der Gedenkstättenarbeit*. Frankfurt/M: Haag and Herchen, pp. 19–38.

Butler, J. P. (1990) *Gender Trouble*. London: Routledge.

Carrier, P. (2005) *Holocaust Monuments and National Memory Cultures in France and Germany since 1989: The Origins and Political Function of the Vél' d'Hiv' in Paris and the Holocaust Monument in Berlin*. New York: Berghahn Books.

Caruth, C. (1993) *Unclaimed Experience: Trauma, Narrative and History*. Baltimore, MD, and London: Johns Hopkins University Press.

Casey, E. S. (1987) *Remembering: A Phenomenological Study*. Bloomington, IN: Indiana University Press.

Cohen, E. (1979) 'A Phenomenology of Tourism Experience,' *Sociology* 13(2): 179–201.

Confino, A. (1997) *The Nation as a Local Metaphor: Württemberg, Imperial Germany, and National Memory, 1871–1918*. Chapel Hill, NC: University of North Carolina Press.

Confino, A. (2006) *Germany as a Culture of Remembrance: Promises and Limits of Writing History*. Chapel Hill, NC: University of North Carolina Press.

Crane, S. A. (2000) 'Of Museums and Memory,' in S. A. Crane, ed., *Museums and Memory*. Stanford, CA: Stanford University Press, pp. 1–16.

Crownshaw, R. (2010) *The Afterlife of Holocaust Memory in Contemporary Literature and Culture*. Basingstoke: Palgrave Macmillan.

Crownshaw, R. (2011) 'Perpetrator's fictions and Transcultural Memory,' *Parallax* 17(4): 75–89.

Cullen, M. S., ed. (1999) *Das Holocaust- Mahnmal Dokumentation einer Debatte*. Zürich: Pendo Pocket.

De Certeau, M. (1984a) 'Theories of the Art of Practice,' in M. de Certeau, *The Practice of Everyday Life*, trans. S. F. Rendall. Berkeley, CA: University of California Press, pp. 43–90.

De Certeau, M. (1984b) 'Walking in the City,' in M. de Certeau, *The Practice of Everyday Life*, trans. S. F. Rendall. Berkeley, CA: University of California Press, pp. 91–110.

De Certeau, M. (1984c) 'Reading as Poaching', in M. de Certeau, *The Practice of Everyday Life*, trans. S. F. Rendall. Berkeley, CA: University of California Press, pp. 165–76.

De Certeau, M. (1984d) *The Practice of Everyday Life*, trans. S. F. Rendall. Berkeley, CA: University of California Press.

Dekel, I. (2008) *Public Passages: Political Action in and around the Holocaust Memorial, Berlin*. Dissertation submitted at the New School for Social Research.

Dekel, I. (2009a) 'Ways of Looking: Observation and Transformation at the Holocaust Memorial, Berlin,' *Memory Studies* 2(1): 71–86.

Dekel, I. (2009b) 'Pan-topia: Exposing the Palimpsest of Meanings at the Holocaust Memorial, Berlin,' *History and Theory: The Protocols Bezalel Academy of Design* 14.

Dekel, I. (2011) 'Mediated Space, Mediated Memory: New Archives at the Holocaust Memorial, Berlin,' in M. Neiger, O. Meyers and E. Zandberg, eds, *On Media Memory*. New York: Palgrave Macmillan.

DeKoven Ezrahi, S. (2004) 'Questions of Authenticity,' in M. Hirsch and I. Kacandes, eds, *Teaching the Representation of the Holocaust*. New York: MLA, pp. 52–67.

Derrida, J. (1996) *Archive Fever: A Freudian Impression*, trans. Eric Prenowitz. Chicago, IL: University of Chicago Press.

Eder, K. (2001) 'Integration through culture: The paradox of the search for a European identity', in K. Eder and B. Giesen, eds, *European Citizenship: National Legacies and Postnational Projects*. Oxford: Oxford University Press, pp. 222–44.

Eder, K. (2005) 'Remembering National Memories Together: The Formation of a Transnational Identity in Europe,' in K. Eder and W. Spohn, eds, *Collective Memory in the Enlarged Europe*. Aldershot: Ashgate pp. 197–219.

Eder, K. (2009) 'The making of a European civil society: "Imagined," "practised" and "staged,"' *Policy and Society* 28: 23–33.

Eder, K. and Giesen, B., eds (2001) *European Citizenship. National Legacies and Postnational Projects*. Oxford: Oxford University Press.

Eder, K. and Spohn, W. eds (2005) *Collective Memory in the Enlarged Europe*. Aldershot: Ashgate.

Eisenman, P. (2005) 'The Silence of Excess,' in *Holocaust Memorial Berlin*. Baden: Lars Müller Publishers.

Eisenman, P. (2007) *Written into the Void Selected Writings 1990–2004*. New Haven: CT: Yale University Press.

Erll, A. (2008) 'Ethics in Stone: The Architecture of the Raj,' in A. Erll, H. Grabes and A. Nuenning, eds, *Ethics in Culture: The Dissemination of Values through Literature and Other Media*. Berlin and New York: Walter de Gruyter, pp. 231–54.

Erll, A. (2011) *Memory in Culture*, trans. S. B. Young. Basingstoke: Palgrave Macmillan.

Erll, A. and Nuenning, A., eds (2010) *A Companion to Cultural Memory Studies*. Berlin and New York: De Gruyter.

Erll, A. and Rigney, A., (2009) 'Introduction: Cultural Memory and Its Dynamics,' in A. Erll and A. Rigney, eds, *Mediation, Remediation and the Dynamics of Cultural Memory*. New York: De Gruyter, pp. 1–14.

Erll, A. and Rigney, A., eds (2009) *Mediation, Remediation and the Dynamics of Cultural Memory*. New York: De Gruyter.

Eyal G. (2004) 'Identity and Trauma: Two Forms of the Will to Memory,' *History and Memory* 16(1).

Feldman, J. (2008) *Above the Death Pits, Beneath the Flag: Youth Voyages to Poland and the Performance of Israeli National Identity*. London: Berghahn.

Feldman, J., Peleikis, A. and Schnepel, B. (2009). 'Die Zeit nach den Zeitzeugen: Holocaustforschung in Halle und Beersheba,' *Scientia Halensis* 17(1): 28–9.

Felman, S. (1992) 'Education and Crisis or the Vicissitudes of Teaching,' in S. Felman and D. Laub (1992) *Testimony: Crises of Witnessing in Literature, Psychoanalysis and History*. London and New York: Routledge, pp. 1–56.

Felman, S. and Laub, D. (1992) *Testimony: Crises of Witnessing in Literature, Psychoanalysis and History*. London and New York: Routledge.

Foucault, M. (1990 [1978]) *The History of Sexuality*, Vol. 1. New York: Random House.

Frei, N. (2002) *Adenauer's Germany and the Nazi Past: The Politics of Amnesty and Integration*. New York: Columbia University Press.

Furedi, F. (2004) *Therapy Culture: Cultivating Vulnerability in an Uncertain Age*. New York: Routledge.

Fyfe G., and Ross, M. (1996) 'Decoding the Visitor's Gaze: Rethinking Museums' Visiting,' in S. Macdonald and G. Fyfe, eds, *Theorizing Museums: Sociological Review Monographs*. Oxford: Blackwell, pp. 1–8.

Gerson, J. M. and Wolf, D. L., eds (2007) *Sociology Confronts the Holocaust: Memories and Identities in Jewish Diasporas*. Durham, NC: Duke University Press.

Geyer, M. and Hansen, M. (1994) 'Jewish Memory and National Consciousness,' in G. H. Hartman, ed., *Holocaust Remembrance*, Oxford and Cambridge, MA: Blackwell, pp. 176–90.

Giesen, B. (2004). 'The Trauma of Perpetrators: The Holocaust as the Traumatic Reference of German National Identity,' in J. C. Alexander et al., *Cultural Trauma and Collective Identity*. Berkeley, CA: University of California Press, pp. 112–54.

Gillis, J. R. (1994a) 'Introduction: Memory and Identity: The History of a Relationship,' in J. R. Gillis, ed., *Commemorations: The Politics of National Identity*. Princeton, NJ: Princeton University Press, pp. 3–26.

Gillis, J. R., ed. (1994b) *Commemorations: The Politics of National Identity*. Princeton, NJ: Princeton University Press.

Godfrey, M. (2007) *Abstraction and the Holocaust*. New Haven, CT: Yale University Press.

Goffman, E. (1961) *Encounters: Two Studies in the Sociology of Interaction*. Indianapolis, IN: Bobbs-Merrill.

Goffman, E. (1963) *Behavior in Public Places: Notes on the Social Organization of Gatherings*. New York: The Free Press.

Goffman, E. (1974) *Frame Analysis: Essays on the Organization of Experience*. New York: Harper & Row.

Goldfarb, J. C. (2006) *The Politics of Small Things: The Power of the Powerless in Dark Times*. Chicago, IL: University of Chicago Press.

Habermas, J. (1987 [1984]) *The Theory of Communicative Action*, 2 vols, trans. Thomas McCarthy. Boston, MA: Beacon Press.

Habermas, J. (1997) *A Berlin Republic: Writings on Germany*, trans. Steven Rendall. Lincoln, NE: University of Nebraska Press.

Habermas, J. (1999) 'Der Zeigefinger. Die Deutschen und ihr Denkmal,' *die Zeit* 14, 31 March.

Halbwachs, M. (1992 [1925]) *On Collective Memory*, ed. and trans. Lewis A. Coser. Chicago, IL: University of Chicago Press.

Hall, S. (2006) 'The Reappearance of the Authentic,' in I. Karp, C. Kratz, L. Szwaja and T. Ybarra-Frausto, eds, *Museum Frictions: Public Cultures/Global Transformations*. Durham, NC: Duke University Press, pp. 70–101.

Hartman, G. (1986) *Bitburg in Moral and Political Perspective*. Bloomington, IN: Indiana University Press.

Hartman, G. (2004) 'Audio and Video Testimony and Holocaust Studies,' in M. Hirsch and I. Kacades, eds, *Teaching the Representation of the Holocaust*. New York: MLA, pp. 205–19.

Heckner, E. (2008) 'Whose Trauma Is It? Identification and Secondary Witnessing in the Age of Postmemory,' in D. Bathrick, B. Prager and M. D. Richardson, eds, *Visualizing the Holocaust: Documents, Aesthetics, Memory*. New York: Camden House, pp. 62–85.

Heimrod, U., Schlusche, G. and Seferens, H. (1999) *Der Denkmalsstreit – Das Denkmal? Die Debatte um das 'Denkmal für die ermordeten Juden Europas.'* Eine Dokumentation, Berlin.

Hirsch, M. (2008) 'The Generation of Postmemory,' *Poetics Today* 29(1): 103–28.

Hirsch, M. and Kacandes, I., eds (2004) *Teaching the Representation of the Holocaust*. New York: MLA.

Hirsch, M. and Spitzer, L. (2009) 'The Witness in the Archive: Holocaust Studies/ Memory Studies,' *Memory Studies* 2: 151–70.

Hohendahl, P. U. (1997) Introduction, in *Modern German Culture and Literature Series*. Lincoln, NE: University of Nebraska Press.

Hooper-Greenhill, E. (2007) *Museums and Education: Purpose, Pedagogy, Performance*. London and New York: Routledge.

Hoskins, A. (2009) 'The Digital Distribution of Memory,' in interdisciplinary. net, http://www.inter-disciplinary.net/wp-content/uploads/2009/03/hoskins-paper.pdf (accessed 18 August 12012).

Huyssen, A. (2003) *Present Pasts: Urban Palimpsests and the Politics of Memory*. Stanford, CA: Stanford University Press.

Illouz, E. (2007a) *Cold Intimacies: The Making of Emotional Capitalism*. London: Polity Press.

Illouz, E. (2007b) *Saving the Modern Soul: Therapy, Emotions and the Culture of Self-Help*. Berkeley, CA: University of California Press.

Irwin-Zarecka, I. (1994) *Frames of Remembrance: The Dynamics of Collective Memory*. New Brunswick and London: Transaction.

Iser, W. (1974) *The Implied Reader: Patterns of Communication in Prose Fiction from Bunyan to Beckett*. Baltimore, MD: Johns Hopkins University Press.

James, J. (2006) 'Undoing Trauma: Reconstructing the Church of Our Lady in Dresden,' *Ethos* 34(2), pp. 244–72.

Jarausch, K. H. (1995) 'Normalisierung oder Re-Nationalisierung?, Zur Umdeutung der deutschen Vergangenheit,' *Geschichte und Gesellschaft* 21: 571–84.

Jarausch, K. H. and Geyer, M. (2002) *Shattered Past: Reconstructing German Histories*. Princeton, NJ: Princeton University Press.

Jeismann, M. (1999) *Mahnmal Mitte. Eine Kontroverse*. Köln: DuMont.

Jordan, J. (2006) *Structures of Memory: Understanding Urban Change in Berlin and Beyond*. Stanford, CA: Stanford University Press.

Judt, T. (2005) 'From the House of the Dear: An Essay on Modern European Memory,' in *Postwar: A History of Europe since 1945*. London: Penguin, pp. 803–31.

Jureit, U. and Schneider, C. (2010) 'Erinnerung Wir zum Gesselschaftszustand: eine Beobachtungt,' in *Gefühlte Opfer – Illusionen der Vergangenheitsbewältigung*. Stuttgart: Klett-Cotta Verlag, pp. 19–37.

Kansteiner, W. and Wilnböck, H. (2010) 'Against the Concept of Cultural Trauma,' in A. Erll and A. Nuenning, eds, *A Companion to Cultural Memory Studies*. Berlin and New York: De Gruyter, pp. 229–40.

Kaplan, M. and Meyer, B., eds (2005) *Jüdische Welten: Juden in Deutschland vom 18. Jahrhundert bis in die Gegenwart*. Hamburg: Wallstein.

Karp, I., Kratz, C. A., Szwaja, L. and Ybarra-Frausto, T., eds (2006), with G. Buntinx and B. Kirschenblatt-Gimblett, *Museum Frictions: Public Culture/ Global Transformations*. Durham, NC: Duke University Press.

Kaschuba, W. (2001) 'Geschichtspolitik und Identitätspolitik. Nationale und ethnische Diskurse im Vergleich,' in B. Binder, W. Kaschuba and P. Niedermüller, eds, *Alltag & Kultur*, Band 7. Köln, S. 19–42.

Katriel, T. (1997) *Performing the Past: A Study of Israeli Settlement Museums*. Mahwah, NJ: Lawrence Erlbaum Associates.

Kelner, S. (2010) *Tours that Bind: Diaspora, Pilgrimage and Israeli Birthright Tourism*. New York: New York University Press.

Kiedasch, P., ed. (2001) *Lyrik Nach Auschwitz? Adorno und die Dichter*. Stuttgart: Reclam.

Kirsch, J.-H. (2003) *Nationaler Mythos Oder Historische Trauer: Der Streit Um Ein Zentrales Holocaust-Mahnmal Fur Die Berliner Republik*. Köln: Böhlau.

Kirshenblatt-Gimblett, B. (2006) 'Exhibitionary Complexes,' in I. *Karp*, C. A. *Kratz* et al., eds, *Museum Frictions: Public Culture/ Global Transformations*. Durham, NC: Duke University Press, pp. 35–45.

Klein, M. (2012) *Schülerinnen und Schüler am Denkmal für die ermordeten Juden Europas: Eine empirischßrekunstruktive*. Studie VS Verlag für Sozialwissenschaften, Germany.

Koshar, R. (2000) *From Monuments to Traces: The Artifacts of German Memory, 1870–1990*. Berkeley, CA: University of California Press.

LaCapra, D. (1998) 'History and Memory: In the Shadow of the Holocaust,' in *History and Memory after Auschwitz*. Ithaca, NY: Cornell University Press, pp. 8–42.

LaCapra, D. (2001) *Writing History, Writing Trauma*. Baltimore, MD: Johns Hopkins University Press.

LaCapra, D. (2003) 'Holocaust Testimonies: Attending to the Victim's Voice,' in *Catastrophe and Memory: The Holocaust and the Twentieth Century*. Chicago, IL: The University of Chicago Press, pp. 209–31.

Ladd, B. (1997) *The Ghosts of Berlin*. Chicago, IL: The University of Chicago Press.

Landsberg, A. (1997) 'America, the Holocaust, and the Mass Culture of Memory: Toward a Radical Politics of Empathy,' *New German Critique* 71, Special Issue: *Memories of Germany* (Spring – Summer): 63–86.

Leggewie, C. and Meyer, E. (2005) *'Ein Ort, an den man gerne geht'. Das Holocaust-Mahnmal und die deutsche Geschichtspolitik nach 1989*. Berlin: Hanser.

Levy, D. and Sznaider, N. (2002) 'Memory Unbound: The Holocaust and the Formation of Cosmopolitan Memory,' *European Journal of Social Theory* 5(1): 87–106.

Levy, D. and Sznaider, N. (2006) *The Holocaust And Memory In The Global Age*. Philadelphia, PA: Temple University Press.

Lowenthal, D. (1994) 'Identity, Heritage and History,' in J. R. Gillis, ed., *Commemorations: The Politics of National Identity*. Princeton, NJ: Princeton University Press, pp. 41–60.

Luckmann, T. (2002) 'Moral communication in Modern Societies,' *Human Studies* 25(1): 19–32.

Lustiger-Thaler, H. (2008) 'Holocaust Lists and the Memorial Museum,' *Museum and Society* 6(3), November: 196–215.

MacCannell, D. (1973) 'Staged Authenticity: Arrangements of Social Space in Tourist Settings,' *The American Journal of Sociology* 79(3): 589–603.

MacCannell, D. (1976) *The Tourist: A New Theory of the Leisure Class*. New York: Schocken.

Macdonald, S. (2005) 'Accessing audiences: Visiting visitor books,' *Museum and Society* 3(3): 119–36.

Macdonald, S. (2006) *Companion to Museum Studies*, Companions in Cultural Studies Series. Oxford: Willey Blackwell.

Macdonald, S. (2009) *Difficult Heritage: Negotiating the Nazi Past in Nuremberg and Beyond*. Oxford and New York: Routledge.

Macdonald, S. and Fyfe, G., eds (1996) *Theorizing Museums: Sociological Review Monographs*. Oxford: Blackwell.

Maier, C. S. (1997 [1988]) *The Unmasterable Past: History, Holocaust, and German National Identity*. Cambridge, MA: Harvard University Press.

Margalit, A. (2002) *The Ethics of Memory*. Cambridge, MA: Harvard University Press.

Marontate J. (2005) 'Museums and the Constitution of Culture,' in M. D. Jacobs and N. W. Hanrahan, eds, *The Blackwell Companion to the Sociology of Culture*. Malden MA: Blackwell Publishers, pp. 286–301.

Massey, D. (2005) *For Space*. London: Sage.

McIsaac, P. (2007) *Museums of the Mind: German Modernity and the Dynamics of Collecting*. Philadelphia, PA: Penn State Press.

Mitscherlich, A. and Mitscherlich, M. (1978 [1967]) *The Inability to Mourn: Principles of Collective Behavior*. New York: Grove Press.

Möller, R. G. (2006) 'The Politics of the Past in the 1950s: Rhetoric of Victimhood in East and West Germany,' in B. Niven, ed., *Commemorations: The Politics of National Identity*. Princeton, NJ: Princeton University Press, pp. 26–42.

Moses, A. D. (2007) 'Stigma and Sacrifice in the Federal Republic of Germany,' *History and Memory* 19(2): 139–80.

Müller, L., ed. (2005) *Holocaust Memorial Berlin*. Lars Müller Publishers.

Myers F. R. (2006) 'The Complicity of Cultural Production: The Contingencies of Performance in Globalizing Museum Practices,' in I. Karp and C. Kratz, eds, *Museum Frictions*. Durham, NC: Duke University Press, pp. 505–36.

Neiger, M., Meyers, O. and Zandberg, E. (2011) 'Tuned to the Nation's Mood: Popular music as a mnemonic cultural object,' *Media, Culture & Society* 33(7): 971–87.

Niven, B. (ed.) (2006) *Commemorations: The Politics of National Identity*. Princeton, NJ: Princeton University Press.

Nora, P. (1998 [1990]) *Realms of Memory: Rethinking the French Past*, ed. L. D. Kritzman, trans. A. Goldhammer. New York: Columbia University Press.

Noy, C. (2008) 'Mediation Materialized: The Semiotics of a Visitor Book at an Israeli Commemoration Site,' *Critical Studies in Media Communication* 25(2): 175–95.

Olick, J. K. (1998) 'What Does it Mean to Normalize the Past? Official Memory in German Politics since 1989,' *Social Science History* 22(4): 547–71.

Olick, J. K. (1999) 'Collective Memory: The Two Cultures,' *Sociological Theory* 17(3), November: 333–48.

Olick, J. K. (2007a) *The Politics of Regret: On Collective Memory and Historical Responsibility*. New York: Routledge.

Olick, J. K. (2007b) 'The Agonies of Defeat: "Other Germanies" and the Problem of Collective Guilt,' in J. M. Gerson and D. L. Wolf, eds, *Sociology Confronts the Holocaust: Memories and Identities in Jewish Diasporas*. Durham, NC: Duke University Press, pp. 291–312.

Olick, J. K. (2008) 'Turning Points and Myths of German Memory,' *Zeithistorische Forschungen/Studies in Contemporary History* 5(3): 372–86.

Olick, J. K. and Levy, D. (1997) 'Collective Memory and Cultural Constraint,' *The American Sociological Review* 62(6): 921–36.

Ostrow, J. M. (1996) 'Spontaneous Involvement and Social Life,' *Sociological Perspectives* 39(3): 341–51.

Quack, S., ed. (2002) *Auf dem Weg Zur Realizierung: Das Denkmal fuer die Ermordeten Juden Europas und der Ort der Information Architektur unf Historisches Konzept Schriftenreihe der Stiftung Denkmal fuer die Ermordeted Juden Europas Band 1*. Stuttgart and Muenchen: Deutsche Verlags-Anstalt.

Quack, S. (2005) 'Drei Strassen in Berlin: Cora Berliner, Gertrud Kolmar und Hannah Arendt als Namengeberinnen,' in Kaplan and Meyer, eds, *Jüdische Welten: Juden in Deutschland vom 18. Jahrhundert bis in die Gegenwart*. Hamburg: Wallstein, pp. 413–39.

Radstone, S. (2005) 'Receiving Binaries: The Limits of Memory,' *History Workshop Journal* 59: 134–50.

Rauterberg, H. (2005) 'Building Site of Remembrance,' in L. Müller, ed., *Holocaust Memorial Berlin*. Lars Müller Publishers.

Rommelspacher, B. (1994) *Schuldlos-Schuldig? Wie sich junge Frauen mit Antisemitismus Auseinandersetzen*. Hamburg: Konkret Literatur Verlag.

Rosh, L. (1999) *'Die Juden, das sind doch die anderen': Der Streit um ein deutsches*. Denkmal: Philo.

Rothberg, M. (2004) 'The Work of Testimony in the Age of Decolonization: Chronicle of a Summer, Cinema Verité, and the Emergence of the Holocaust Survivor,' *PMLA*, 119(5): 1231–46.

Rothberg, M. (2009) *Multidirectional Memory: Remembering the Holocaust in the Age of Decolonization*. Stanford, CA: Stanford University Press.

Rothberg, M. and Yildiz, Y. (2011) 'Memory Citizenship: Migrant Archives of Holocaust Remembrance in Contemporary Germany,' *Parallax* 17(4): 32–48.

Savelsberg, J. J. and King, R. D. (2005) 'Institutionalizing Collective Memories of Hate: Law and Law Enforcement in Germany and the United States,' *The American Journal of Sociology* 111(2): 579–616.

Schmitz, H., ed. (2007) *A Nation of Victims? Representations of German Wartime Suffering from 1945 to the Present*. Amsterdam and New York: Rodopi.

Smith, T. (2007) 'Narrative boundaries and the dynamics of ethnic conflict and conciliation', *Poetics* 35: 22–46.

Stavginsky, H.-G. (2002) *Das Holocaust-Denkmal – Der Streit um das 'Denkmal für die ermordeten Juden Europas' in Berlin (1988–1999)*. Paderborn u.a.

Stier, O. (2005) 'Different Trains: Holocaust Artifacts and the Ideologies of Remembrance,' *Holocaust and Genocide Studies* 19(1): 81–106.

Stock, M. (2007) 'European Cities: Towards a "Recreational Turn"?', *Hagar: Studies in Culture, Polity and Identities* 7: 115–33.

Stoler, A. L. (2002) 'Colonial Archives and the art of Governance,' *Archival Science* 2: 87–109.

Stoler, A. L. and Strassler, K. (2000) 'Casting for the Colonial: Memory Work and the New Order in Java,' *Comparative Studies in Society and History* 42(1): 4–48.

Tabener, S. (2005) 'Philosemitism in recent German film: *Aimee and Jaguar, Rosenstrasse* and *das Wunder von Bern*,' *German Life and Letters* 58(3): 357–73.

Till, K. E. (2005) *The New Berlin Memory, Politics, Place*. Minneapolis, MN, and London: University of Minnesota Press, pp. 161–88.

Tilly, C. (2000) 'How do relations store histories?' *Annual Review of Sociology* 26: 721–3.

Uhl, H. (2008) 'Going Underground Der "Ort der Infirmation" des Berliner Holocaust-Denkmals,' *Zeithistorische Forschung* 5.

Urry, J. (2002) *The Tourist Gaze: Leisure and Travel in Contemporary Societies*. London: Sage.

Urry, J. and Macnaghten, P. (1998) *Contested Nature*. London: Sage.

Varvantakis, C. (2009) 'A Monument to Dismantlement,' *Memory Studies* 2(1): 27–38.

Wagner-Pacifici, R. (2005) 'Dilemmas of the Witness,' in M. D. Jacobs and N. W. Hanrahan, eds, *The Blackwell Companion to the Sociology of Culture*. Malden, MA: Blackwell, pp. 303–13.

Wagner-Pacifici, R. (2010) 'Theorizing the Restlessness of Events, *The American Journal of Sociology* 115(5): 1351–86.

Wagner-Pacifici, R. and Schwartz, B. (1991) 'The Vietnam Veterans Memorial: Commemorating a Difficult Past,' *American Journal of Sociology* 97(2): 376–421.

Wang, N. (1999) 'Rethinking Authenticity in Tourism Experience,' *Annals of Tourism Research* 26(2): 349–70.

Warfield-Rawls, A. (1987) 'The Interaction Order *Sui Generis*: Goffman's Contribution to Social Theory,' *Sociological Theory* 5(2): 136–49.

Weissberg, L. and Ben-Amos, D., eds (1999) *Cultural Memory and the Construction of Identity Memory Confined*. Detroit, MI: Wayne State University Press, pp. 45–98.

Weizsäcker, R. von (1985) Speech quoted in G. Harrtman (1986) *Bitburg in Moral and Political Perspective*. Bloomington, IN: Indiana University Press, pp. 263–73.

Welzer, H. (2010) 'Erinnerungskultur und Zukunftsgedächtnis,' in *Zukunft der Erinnerung in Aus Politik und Zeitgeschichte* (ApuZ 25–26), Bundeszentrale fuer Politische Bildung, 10 June.

Welzer, H., Moller, S., Tschuggnall, K., Jensen, O. and Koch, T. (2002) *Opa war kein Nazi. Nationalsozialismus und Holocaust im Familiengedächtnis*. Frankfurt/Main: Fischer Verlag.

Williams, R. (1976) 'Mediation,' *Keywords: A Vocabulary of Culture and Society*. London: Fontana Paperbacks, pp. 204–7.

Williams, P. (2008) *Memorial Museums: The Global Rush to Commemorate Atrocities*. London: Berg.

Young, J. E. (2000) 'Daniel Libeskind's Jewish Museum in Berlin: The Uncanny Arts of Memorial Architecture,' *Jewish Social Studies* 6: 1–23.

Young, J. E. (2003) 'Germany's Holocaust Memorial Problem and Mine,' *Religion and Public Life* 33: 55–70.

Young, J. E. (2004) 'German Memory and Countermemory: The End of the Holocaust Monument in Germany,' in M. Hirsch and I. Kacandes, eds, *Teaching the Representation of the Holocaust*. New York: MLA, pp. 274–85.

Zapf, H. (2008) 'Narrative, Ethics and Postmodern Art in Siri Hustvedt's *What I Loved*,' in A. Erll, H. Grabes and A. Nuenning, eds, *Ethics in Culture: The Dissemination of Values through Literature and Other Media*. Berlin and New York: Walter de Gruyter, pp. 171–94.

Zelizer, B. (1998) *Remembering to Forget: Holocaust Memory through the Camera Eye*. Chicago, IL, and London: University of Chicago Press.

Zolberg, V. L. (1998) 'Contested Remembrance: The Hiroshima Exhibit Controversy,' *Theory and Society* 27: 565–90.

Index

191

Libeskind, Daniel, 57, 177n.22
Luckmann Thomas, 132–3

MacCannell, Dean, 73
Macdonald, Sharon, 8, 104–5, 112,
    179n.16
  see also museums
Mahnmal , 49, 105, 146, 176n.5
  see also Holocaust Memorial
media, 71, 75, 131
  reality television, 6–7
  social media, 2, 14, 70, 105, 161, 164
  see also mediation
mediation, 2, 6–9, 13–14, 22, 25,
    54–5, 113, 150–71 *passim*
  see also Jeffrey Alexander; Luc
    Boltanski; Astrid Erll; Susannah
    Radstone
Memorial Foundation (*Stiftung
    Denkmal*), 3–5, 46, 48, 69, 170, 175
  educational programs of, 12–13, 40,
    59–60, 78, 100, 116, 128, 158–63,
    167
  financing for, 84, 99–100, 135
  publications by, 15, 31–2, 42–3, 106
  survey commissioned by, 4, 33, 38,
    95, 101
  see also Information Center;
    pedagogy; tour guides
memorials, 10, 16–19, 46, 49–51, 77,
    84, 94, 162–3, 168–70, 179n.5,
    180n.10
  aesthetics of, 2–5, 32–3, 56, 98–101,
    133, 138–40
  as architecture, 6, 37, 54, 113–14
  vandalism in and of, 9, 50, 61, 105
  see also Homosexuals Memorial;
    Sinti and Roma Memorial; T4
    Euthanasia Memorial
memory:
  collective, 6, 14, 18, 28, 55, 84, 106,
    133, 136
  encoding of, 9, 174
  of individuals, 77–8, 98–9, 135–6,
    142, 147–50
  of institutions, 6, 24, 26, 56, 67, 75,
    81–2, 99, 101, 135, 150, 173
  landscapes of, 18, 23, 46, 49–54
    passim, 73
  as multi-directional, 6, 28, 103–6

post-memory, 1, 39, 54–7, 63, 72, 162
  production of, 18, 22, 24, 68
  reflection of, 36, 54, 122, 131, 146,
    173
  see also mediation; memorials;
    museums; Michael Rothberg;
    victims
memory studies, 56, 76
metaphors, 6, 9, 12–13, 16–17, 24, 30,
    39–40, 61, 66, 73–7, 97, 131–6,
    145–7, 159, 172–3
  see also performance; Holocaust
    knowledge: performance of, and
    emotions
migrants, 117, 125
  Jewish migrants in Germany, 15–16,
    82, 91, 103, 161
  Muslim migrants in Germany, 10,
    82, 117, 160
  see also identity; Jews
monuments, 11, 12, 15, 42, 47,
    115, 131
moral career, 2, 12–13, 24, 28, 50–4,
    61–3, 117–19, 131–2, 137–49, 174
  see also visitors
moral judgment, 2, 23, 71–2, 130,
    132, 136–8, 140–1, 146
museums, 6, 9, 14–15, 34–5, 105
  collecting, 99–100, 164–9
  controversies about, 33, 60
  presentation, 40, 59, 62, 116
  remnants, 56, 161, 170
  see also Tony Bennett; Susan Crane;
    Sharon Macdonald; Barbara
    Kirshenblatt-Gimblett

narrative, 54, 62, 74–5, 101–3, 112,
    115, 120–41 *passim*, 174–5
  analysis of, 57–8, 68–9
  structure of, 46, 120, 150–1, 159, 174
  see also Luc Boltanski
National Socialists, 11, 46, 71, 131–4,
    155, 187
  Nazi architecture in Berlin, 11–12
  Nuremberg rally ground, 8–9, 112
  as perpetrators, 5, 12, 16, 22, 46–54
    passim, 102, 124
  and the persecution of Jews, 3,
    83–4, 126; *see also* Holocaust;
    identity; representation

Printed and bound in the United States of America